Secrets of the

Millionaire Mind

This book includes:
Dropshipping,
Amazon FBA Guide,
Make Money with Blogging.
Get multiple Six Figure Passive
Income streams and take your
Financial Freedom from home

Table of Contents

Dropshipping

Discover How to Create a
Standard e-Commerce on Shopify
Amazon and Ebay.
This ultimate guide explains the
new e-Commerce business model
to Make Money from Home with
Marketing Strategies.

Table of Contents

Description

Drop shipping has been around for nearly two decades, yet it still proves to be a highly effective business model for turning a profit online. These days, if you want to be a drop shipper there is plenty of information out there about how you can get started and what you need to do in order to turn your business into a success. The key for you is to ensure that the information you are reading is relevant and high-quality so that you can find yourself amongst the top earners in this industry.

By giving you some insight as to what this industry is and a clear strategy for how you can get started and grow your business, I hope that you now feel confident in generating your own success. If you really want to make the most out of this information, you need to be ready to apply it with consistency and confidence every step of the way so that you can generate a huge income through your business.

Make sure that you start small and grow out, as this is the best way to ensure that you test your niche first so that you can validate its profitability. If your results are promising, you can use this information to help you increase your sales and grow your business out even further. As well, don't forget to check out my other titles like Amazon FBA so that you can further grow your knowledge in this industry! Knowing exactly what you can do to grow your business through strong sales channels is going to help you get your name out there and maximize your success in this industry.

You also need to make sure that you pay close attention to the tips and advice that I have given you, as this information can help you succeed even faster. The information I have provided you with here is intended to help you quickly grow beyond many beginners' mistakes and challenges, whereby you can step into mastering your Drop shipping business right from day one. Avoid underestimating this advice, as it truly can help set you apart and guarantee your success in the industry!

This guide will focus on the following:

- Understanding Drop Shipping
- The Basics of Getting Started
- Sample Products and Test Marketing
- Getting Started with Product Sourcing
- How to Identify and Work with Suppliers
- Starting Your Own Store
- Marketing Your Business
- The Supply Chain & Order Fulfillment Process
- Analyzing Sales Outlets
- The Main Players
- Different Methods of Drop shipping Business... AND MORE!!!

Introduction

The entrepreneur who wants to use the technique of drop shipping has as a main objective to get rid of one of the most important efforts that are required to those who sell on the web: fulfillment, or the processing of the order.

This process would force us to have to pack, package, create a list with the recipient's data and finally send every single order. Without considering the stock of these support materials: packaging bags, printing paper and much more.

In a short time, we would be doing a warehouse job, which will get us to steal precious time that we could devote to the growth of our business.

Of course, if our business is going to be important enough, we can hire someone to help us. But we would be faced with problems of scalability and flexibility: how many parcels can this person handle every day? And if it was not enough? Or if the quantity of orders were to prove non-continuous over time?

The answer to this problem, for a small company that needs to optimize all resources, is simple: rely on an external company to process orders.

At this point, it is clear what should be the road to our business: to sell, but to send to another company, directly to the final customer.

Standard Drop shipping

The manufacturer ships

Then the Drop shipping model comes into play. With this system, the company must have an agreement with a supplier, who has stock of the asset that he wants to sell. When this item is sold, we will forward the purchase order to the supplier, who will, in turn, send it to the final customer.

The advantages of this system are many and simple to understand: in addition to the important advantage of not having to send orders that are received, we have the very interesting opportunity to create an online sales activity without the need for an initial investment for the warehouse.

Normally, in fact, the entrepreneur who decides to start a business of resale is forced to make an important initial investment, due to the simple necessity of having the products that he will then sell.

Usually, in fact, the steps are more linear: the supplier sells to the entrepreneur, and the entrepreneur sells to the customer.

Drop shipping without inventory allows us to avoid this initial investment, as it will be possible to purchase the items when they are sold.

This is an incredibly important advantage for those who are beginners and is now starting to create a job for themselves: you can create a website with a few dozen euros a month and a few hours of work, but one stock easily comes to cost some thousand euros at best.

We also got rid of a second non-negligible problem: the risk of obsolete inventories. Imagine buying a thousand charging cables for iPhone, and that at the following Apple presentation, you will discover that the cables of the next version of the phone will be completely different from the previous ones.

We will find ourselves having a stock with a quantity of unsold pieces, which will be increasingly difficult to sell with the passing of time — also because the same producers and suppliers will face the same problem, but will have the power to sell at prices decidedly lower.

This risk, very important for those who carry out a traditional business, for us who work with Drop shipping does not exist. This allows us to be agile, to bet on new products that for others would be risky, and therefore to seize the best opportunities.

Drop shipping with FBA
Another partner is shipping

The second mode of Drop shipping is more complex than the first, and loses some advantages but buys others. We will call it FBA, taking its name from the most used service for order management: Fulfillment By Amazon.

The Drop shipping FBA then makes use of the Amazon warehouse management service; Amazon's warehouses are able to receive our goods, keep them in stock and then send them, individually, to our customers.

The scheme for Drop shipping FBA is therefore as follows.

We should therefore start by contacting a manufacturer of the item we want to sell. This is also the moment to think about any customization or modifications of the object, which can lead to the creation of a real brand.

Once the product we wish to sell is manufactured, the manufacturer will send it to the warehouse, or to the warehouse that will take care of the execution of purchase orders.

This step can be direct or it can go on again for our company, or for a third company. The passage can be useful to inspect the elements and for a possible preparation of the products to the warehouse, for example, with boxes, labels or other.

The warehouse — in our case, the Amazon warehouses — will take care to pack and ship the product to the final customer.

Using this method, therefore, it will be necessary for us to own a stock of products. This can be seen as a defect, because it forces us to an initial investment, but also brings with it several advantages, such as the possibility of selling a unique or personalized product, and being able to take advantage of cheaper rates for the purchase of large quantity of objects, which will lead us to have a higher margin on each product sold.

We obviously lose from the point of view of flexibility, because if a product does not sell as much as we would have expected, we risk having inventory inventories for a very long time. We will see later how to handle this problem.

An additional advantage in the use of Drop shipping FBA is the incredible performance: in particular with the Fulfillment By Amazon service, our product has access to the Amazon logistics network, which guarantees deliveries in 1-2 days and, if we decide to sell our product on the Amazon portal, it gives us access to the Prime program, which is recognized and appreciated by our customers.

After briefly describing the two methods, we have a smattering of what will be the topics discussed below in this book.

It is useless to specify that infinite variations can be applied to these systems: for example, it is possible to contact a stockiest, who sends the goods to the warehouse, without going through a supplier, in order to sell products of known brands. Or again, the manufacturer himself can work from stock and then ship directly to customers.

Which one to choose?

Our time is precious and it is important to dedicate as much as possible to the growth of the activity, rather than to prepare the shipments, above all if there are those who can do it for us at incredibly convenient prices.

Let us now summarize the advantages and disadvantages of both options, with some guidelines for choosing one of two ways of working.

Drop shipping allows you to start selling without investing anything in the warehouse, but only by making arrangements with a supplier. The products are, therefore, limited to those already existing, which a supplier can therefore already have in stock.

It is also important to consider the origin of these suppliers: since many producers live in China or in any case in Eastern countries. Advantages and disadvantages of choosing a foreign supplier are many and important, so we will find a dedicated chapter.

FBA instead allows us to make our own product, customized with one of our brands. This involves a further effort, but it will soon be compensated: we will be the only ones able to sell our product!

Let's be clear, the FBA system also allows us, like dropshipping, to work with existing products. However, there is this possibility in more that instead with Drop shipping we would not have.

The cons of all this? The price. Obviously, to be able to send our products to a warehouse that will handle orders, we will first have to buy them.

I invite the reader to think carefully about these two paths. Both are valid and working systems to make money without managing the warehouse, but the differences are substantial.

We want to create a company with a fixed and constant business, which once set up can go on with the minimum work? So let's go on FBA.

Instead, do we always want to sell the latest gadget, working on creativity and without worrying about the technical details? Dropshipping.

Are we going to create a unique product or a brand? It is necessary to use FBA.

Are we going to sell existing products, taking advantage of an already known brand? We can do it with both Drop shipping and FBA.

The standard Drop shipping method (i.e. the one in which the goods are purchased only when they have already been sold) is an excellent way to enter the world of online sales with a minimum investment.

What do we need to start working this way?

It's simple: a supplier and a sales channel.

We will see in detail how to find a product to sell, then how to look for suppliers for that product and then how to create a sales channel, whether a website or a store on eBay, Amazon etc.

If instead we wanted to start our own brand, we move directly to the chapter, aware of the risks but also of the opportunities that this choice would offer us, we must also identify a warehouse that will manage the orders. This may be the same manufacturer, but very often they have no interest in managing logistics as well. Let's see some alternatives in the next chapters.

What to sell?

The first question is certainly this. Ok, we want to sell; we want to do it with dropshipping. But what do we sell?

The answer to this question is personal, but there are guidelines that we can use to choose a product with more probabilities of success, or at least to skim products that would surely be a failure.

It is important to work within a niche sector — whether they are smartwatch straps, scuba diving accessories or vegan foods for children.

Moving within a restricted sector allows us to sell more correlated products, increasing the probability of multiple purchases by the same customer. It also gives us a brand identity, very important especially if we want to create a website, and different operational advantages from the advertising point of view.

Since it is important to have a thorough knowledge of the sector in which you work, I advise you, at this stage, to stop and reflect on what subjects will be passionate about, with which products we would not have problems working for a long period of time. What do you like doing in your free time? What would you never get tired of investigating or trying? On what topic, hobby or passion would you be able to speak for hours, perhaps involving other people?

Do you practice a particular sport? Sell sportswear.

Do you work with watches? Sell work tools.

Are you passionate about electronics? Sell components for the circuits.

Let us not be limited by the fear of not having a target: questions like, "Who will ever care?" or, "Few people will use it" should not stop us, but rather indicate that we are evaluating a very small sector, in which we can expect less competition and loyalty highest.

We always remember that it is easier to be the first if the sector is restricted, we just need to think step by step. If we think of opening a generic store, we would be fighting against Amazon and eBay. Let's go a little more specifically. For example, in consumer electronics, we could find ePrice. We still tighten the field: surveillance cameras.

I'm not aware of a store specializing in surveillance cameras, so I do not have a point of reference.

We always remember that it is easier to be the first if the sector is restricted, we just need to think step by step. Let's imagine we want to open a surveillance camera store. I'm not aware of any benchmarks in the industry, so we can be the first or, in any case, have competition at our level.

Going up a step, we assume we want to expand to be able to deal with all consumer electronics: we would compete with websites like ePrice and Monclick, which are already known to the public, and we would be automatically disadvantaged.

Going further, we would find bigger and bigger websites until we got to generic stores like eBay and Amazon, with which we absolutely do not want to compete at the moment.

A second fundamental point is that of added value. Since we want to work with existing products, created by other companies and sold, certainly, in many other places, why should a customer buy from us?

The answer to this question is anything but immediate, but I can provide some ideas.

The price has always been a very important factor. If we can get a good price on part of our inventory, the advantage for the buyer will be obvious: savings.

Another important role is that of perceived value. The product will be the same, but between a site that presents it with grainy photos, a dated and difficult to navigate graphics, and a second site that has well-defined photos, an accurate description of the product and excellent reviews, from whom you would buy? Our website will also need to be found. Having the right product at the right time is a huge added value, and many users will buy on impulse, if the price is not exaggerated, without even making comparisons with other stores.

The last added value can be the community that is around our website, or the additional services we can provide. For example, an ecommerce that sells materials for sewing, and, at the same time, has articles, tutorials and videos on how to use them, has an important competitive advantage and at the same time has a second channel of purchase, since readers of the articles will in turn be driven to become customers.

The key to finding what to sell is therefore very simple. Let's clear the competition by creating a niche in which we can offer an advantage and be winners.

Finally, a paragraph is dedicated to single-product ecommerce sites, those dedicated to the sale of a single product, perhaps unique or advertised in a particular way.

For a company that is based on dropshipping, I would advise against the creation of a website that sells a single product, because it would automatically exclude us from some dynamics that can allow us to have multiple or repeated purchases. If the intention of the reader is instead to sell, at least to start with, a single product, the FBA option could be a simpler and more convenient way to continue.

Since we ourselves decide which field to play, which game and with which rules, there is no reason to leave disadvantaged. We spend all the time necessary for this phase, then proceed to find the supplier in the next chapter.

Understanding Drop Shipping

Before you start a drop shipping business, the most basic thing you'll need to know is what the business is all about and who the major players involved are. So, without further ado, let's begin.

What is Drop Shipping?

Well, the first thing to note here is that it is not dropping off supplies and/or cargo on a ship somewhere in the middle of the ocean. Now that we've got that straight let's get some basic terminology right too. You may have heard people saying that they want to do drop shipping or start a drop shipping business. While, in common parlance, we may understand what they mean, you need to be very clear that if you venture into this field, you are not the drop shipper. When someone says that they want to start drop shipping, what they're really saying is that they want to become retailers who use drop shipping suppliers.

Drop shipping is a way of retail fulfillment in which the store involved doesn't stock products that it sells. Wholesalers (well, some of them) offer a drop shipping service. When you, as a retailer, have an agreement with a wholesaler who offers such a service, you don't have to take on the shipping or stocking the inventory. When you sell the product to the customer, you buy the product from the wholesaler who ships the product to the customer directly. You never see or stock the product. This means that you don't have to worry about storage, shipping costs or any of the overheads that come with a regular retail business.

Drop Shipping: Role or Service?

Although you may have heard the term 'drop shipper' bandied about quite freely, the truth is that no such term actually exists in this field. There is no one person or entity who can be a drop shipper. Anyone in the supply chain – the wholesaler, the retailer or even the manufacturer – can be the drop shipper.

If the manufacturer you are working with ships the goods directly to the customer, once you've placed an order with them, the manufacturer 'drop ships' on your behalf. In the same way, another retailer also has the capability to drop ship for you: although, in this case, your profit margin may not be as high. A retailer's pricing is going to be higher than a wholesaler's or a manufacturer's.

This brings us to the fact that merely because an entity says that it is a 'drop shipper' doesn't mean that they will offer you wholesale pricing. All it means is that the business is willing to ship the products to you. Therefore, if you want to get the best possible pricing, you need to ensure that you work directly with a manufacturer or wholesaler. I will discuss this in more detail in a later chapter.

The Players

To understand the major players involved in drop shipping, you need first to understand what is meant by the term 'supply chain'. The term basically means the course followed by a product from inception to manufacturing to the customer. Those who look at the supply chain in detail state that the supply chain of a product actually begins from the basic materials such as rubber and oil that are mined to create it. For the purposes of this book, we need only look at the players involved in the drop shipping supply chain.

Manufacturers – The ones who create the product are the manufacturers. They don't generally sell to the public directly but do sell their product to retailers and wholesalers in bulk quantities.

The most inexpensive way to buy products to sell them to the public is to go to the manufacturers. However, many of them have minimum requirements for purchase that you'll need to satisfy. Also, you will need to do the stocking and shipping when you sell the products to your customers. That is why it is generally easier and more cost-effective to buy the products from wholesalers.

Wholesalers – The ones who buy the products from the manufacturers, increase the price by a small margin and then sell the products to the retailers are known as wholesalers. Not all of them have minimum requirements when it comes to purchases, and even if they do, those requirements are fairly easy for you to meet.

A wholesaler will not generally limit itself to one manufacturer, but instead, they buy and stock products from many different manufacturers. However, it does limit itself to a specific niche. For example, a clothing wholesaler will not purchase and sell cellular phones. Most of these companies only deal in wholesale and don't sell to the public.

Retailers – One who sells the products to the public after marking up the price is known as a retailer. Therefore, if you have a drop shipping agreement with a wholesaler or manufacturer and you sell the products to the customers, you are a retailer.

How Drop Shipping Works

Now that we've taken a look at the players in this chain let's see how the whole process works. To make this easy for you to understand, I'll create an example using a hypothetical store called Electronics Showroom which is an online entity that sells electronics such as laptops and cell phones to the public. Electronics Showroom has a drop shipping agreement for its products with a wholesaler that I'll call Wholesale Electronics. Below is an example of how the process will work.

1. Electronics Showroom receives an order from the customer.

   Mr. Smith places an online order for a laptop via Electronics Showroom's online store. The order is approved. This is what happens next. Both Mr. Smith and Electronics Showroom receive emails confirming the order. The store's software usually generates the email confirmation automatically. When Mr. Smith checks out, his payment is captured by the store's payment software, which then deposits the payment into Electronics Showroom's bank account.

2. Electronics Showroom places the order with Wholesale Electronics

   Generally, this is done by Electronics Showroom forwarding the email confirmation to Wholesale Electronics. Since Wholesale Electronics will have Electronics Showroom's credit card information, it will bill the card for the wholesale price of the laptop and include any other fees such as the shipping fee. While email is the usual way of placing an order, there are wholesalers who allow for the order to be placed online manually or use XML order uploading.

3. The order is shipped out by Wholesale Electronics

If the laptop is in stock and the credit card belonging to Electronics Showroom is successfully billed, the order is packed up and shipped directly to the customer by Wholesale Electronics. Now, the important thing to note here is that, although it is Wholesale Electronics doing the shipping, the name and address on the return address label will be that of Electronics Showroom. The same will also be seen on the packing slip and invoice. When the shipment has been sent out, an invoice and tracking number is sent to Electronics Showroom by Wholesale Electronics. While, in the past, there have been some concerns about the turnaround time for the shipping when it comes to dropping shipped orders, in actuality, this is much faster than you may believe. Suppliers who have a good reputation normally ship out the product within a few hours of receiving the order. This means that even if you use a drop ship supplier, you can still promise next day delivery.

4. The customer is notified of the shipment by Electronics Showroom

   Once it receives the tracking number, Electronics Showroom sends that information to Mr. Smith. Mostly this is done through an email interface which is built into the interface of the online store.

Now that the payment has been collected, the order shipped and the customer is informed thus the process is now complete. The difference between the price that Electronics Showroom paid to Wholesale Electronics and charged Mr. Smith would be its profit or loss.

Customers Don't See Drop Shippers

In effect, drop shippers don't exist for the customer. Although the role that the drop shipper plays is crucial in the entire process, it is Electronics Showroom's logo, name, and address that the customer sees on the label of the shipment. If Mr. Smith gets a faulty laptop, he will get in touch with Electronics Showroom. It would then get in touch with Wholesale Electronics to get a different laptop shipped out.

The only responsibility that the drop shipping wholesaler has is to ship and stock products. The customer has no awareness of the wholesaler. The retailer has to take responsibility for the rest of it – from marketing to website development to customer service.

Reasons Why People Consider Drop Shipping

Drop Shipping is considered to be one of the businesses that people choose because of some of the advantages which include the following:

1. Wider Array of Products Ready to be sold - A drop
   Since the drop shipping company does not have to purchase all of the items before the items are going

to get shipped, it does not have to search for a place where the different items are going to be placed. This will help offer a lot of different products to customers.

2. Reduction of Risk

No matter what type of business is going to be opened, it always comes with a certain risk, but when it comes to drop shipping, all of the risks that may come hand in hand with starting an online company becomes reduced significantly. For example, a drop shipping business owner docs not have to worry about the items that are left unsold somewhere. There would not be any problem with storing unsold items as well.

3. No Large Capital Needed

One of the reasons why people decide not to push through with any business is because of the large capital that they have to release. Some people do not have it while others do not want to take any risk. When it comes to dropping shipping, a large capital is not needed in order to start the business. The "drop shipper" only has to purchase an item when an order has been sent by a customer.

4. Ability to Run the Business Anywhere

One of the problems with having any business is that the business owner may have to rent office space and spend a lot of money on renting the different items. Through a drop shipping business, the business owner may start and operate a business from anywhere as long as the person has a PC/laptop and fast internet connection.

5. No Need to Manually Do Each Order
   All of the orders that will be done through the drop shipping company's website will be easy to fulfil because the orders do not have to be written manually.

Of course, if all of the things that are mentioned above will be considered by people, then everyone may want to start a drop shipping business, but there are some disadvantages too that makes people stop for a while and rethink if they would like to start a drop shipping business or not.

1. Low Margins - One of the biggest problems that may be experienced by anyone who would like to start a drop shipping business is that there are a lot of people who may do this as well. For example, if you would start your own company, people may check out your website, but they will always compare it with another drop shipping company. If you would not have low prices, you will not be noticed. At the same time, if you would lower your prices too much, you will not make any profit.

2. Some Issues with Shipping - Since drop shipping companies usually get their items from different

suppliers, the price of shipping tend to be different depending on the supplier where the item will come from. This can be complicated at times because there is a need to create a uniform shipping fee for all of the items. Of course, you may have the option not to have a uniform shipping fee if you would please. It will be discussed further later on.

3. Errors - Whenever the supplier sends a wrong item, it will be the drop shipping company's fault. Even if it is not the drop shipping company that fulfilled the order, they have to take responsibility for the error. Of course, it can be even harder if the suppliers are not good in fulfilling orders at all. A drop shipping company may fail if the owner does not know how to handle everything.

The Basics of Getting Started

You've learned all about this promising business model and how it can earn you large money, and you are ready to get started. By now, you are likely convinced that the Drop shipping business is an incredible business model for you to get into if you are seeking to tap into the online market and earn a large profit. So, we are going to explore the steps you need to take in order to successfully start your own Drop shipping business!

Pick Your Niche

Before you even get into the process of building your business, you need to decide what you are going to sell. While some websites like Amazon.com can get away with selling virtually everything, people who are just starting out are better off if they stick to a single niche. Picking a niche gives you the opportunity to identify exactly who your target audience is, and then successfully market towards that audience. While you can expand in the future, you want to start with something smaller and manageable.

There are a few things that go into making a niche that is going to be a success for your business. First, you want to pick a niche that is performing well. It should not be saturated, but it should be big enough that you actually have the potential to earn a profit from it. Just because a niche is a niche doesn't mean it is a good one. In addition to a niche that performs well, you also want to pick one that you are actually interested in. If you are interested in the niche you are getting involved with, you will have significantly higher success with your business than if you are not interested in it at all. Being interested in the niche you are going to sell in gives you the advantage of having the opportunity to understand what your target audience wants and how you can meet their needs.

To start the process of picking your niche, start by writing down about 5-10 categories for things that you are actually interested in and would enjoy selling. From those categories, you can start conducting your research. Find out which ones perform well and which ones don't. Take the ones that do and use these as the basis for further research. Start by going to places like Shopify and Amazon and looking at how these categories perform. Furthermore, take note of who is in the industry already selling products. To be successful in a niche, regardless of how many people are currently selling in it, you need to be able to have a competitive edge. Identifying whether or not you will have a competitive edge will come from doing some research about suppliers. While you certainly don't need to pick one yet, you will want to discover what type of pricing you are going to be offering for various items in each niche. Find one where you can offer comparable and competitive pricing.

Once you have conducted your research, you will likely have one or two niches left that are qualified for a successful business. If you have one, then your choice is clear. However, if you end up with two or three, then you are going to have to decide which one you want to do. If the choice isn't obvious based on niche performance, then you can simply choose which one you would enjoy most. The final answer will be the niche that you are going to build your entire business around.

Identify Your Ideal Market

Assuming you have chosen a niche that you are actually interested in, you should have a simple time identifying who your target audience is. Knowing who your target audience is will set you up for the future of your business. Every decision you make will be based on the intention of serving this audience and creating a brand and business that will meet their needs and attract their interest. If you cannot effectively communicate with your target audience, then you are not going to be able to make any sales.

It may seem easier to create a broader audience so that you have more potential reach, but the reality is that this will actually dampen your efforts. In the beginning, you want to be very specific about who your target audience is. Once you have successfully served them, it is likely that others will develop an interest in your business and you will be able to broaden your audience. However, keep that as an opportunity for future growth and remain clear and focused on one specific ideal consumer for the time being.

When you are preparing to outline your ideal market, start by researching similar companies and who they are targeting. Take notice of exactly who they are focusing on in their ads. Is it families? Single females? Single males? Pre-marital couples? Individuals with specific interests? Get as clear on the exact person that is being targeted as you possibly can. You can also conduct some research by looking into the products themselves. See if you can find the products being discussed on forums anywhere and take note of the type of people who are engaging in the conversation the most. These are the exact people you are going to want to identify as your ideal audience. The following list consists of things you should consider when you are targeting customers in your business. If you can answer these questions, then you should be clear on who you are targeting which will make establishing your business significantly easier:

1. What is the age range of your targeted audience?
2. Is there a primary gender that appears to be interested in your niche?
3. What hobbies do these people have?
4. Are there any specific phrases or slang that they use when speaking about this niche?

5. How does this particular product category serve their needs?

6. Why are they interested in these products?

7. Do they have anything else in common, regardless of whether or not it pertains directly to the niche?

8. Is there any particular icon, color, logo, or "style" that they tend to be drawn towards?

9. What are their current favorite brands? Who are they purchasing products like yours from the most?

10. What "feeling" do you get from these people?

When you answer these questions, you make it significantly easier for you to develop your brand. You also make the process of choosing products and marketing easier as well. It is vital that you establish the answers to these questions now as opposed to later. Answering them now can be the defining factor that sets you up for total success in your business overall. It is absolutely vital that you take the time to answer these questions in as much detail as possible. While it can take a bit longer than you may have anticipated, it can add a tremendous amount of value to your ability to create a sustainable and successful business out of the gate.

Outline a Brand That Serves Your Ideal Market

Now is the first time that you are going to put your market research to good use. When you are building your website and marketing your new business, you are going to want to have a specific brand image that you operate under. The market research you have conducted is going to assist you in deciding exactly how you are going to create your brand, what image you are going to portray, and how you should portray it in order to speak to your ideal client. If you are already knowledgeable in your niche and have some level of passion in it, then this should be fairly easy for you. The market research you have conducted should make it even easier.

There is a great deal of detail that goes into creating a brand. You want to make sure that your image is consistent, your vocabulary and language should be consistent, and the "personality" your company gives off should be consistent. Should you ever hire anyone to help you, they should be able to create content for your brand that is consistent with the image that you have created. This way, people will be able to identify your brand and establish a relationship with your business as they will feel a sense of recognition and trust for the brand you have created.

The first step you should take when creating your brand is considering your image. Your image is created using actual images, colors, and specific designs. Your primary opportunity to create your image is on your website, though you can use social media profiles to emphasize your image as well. In fact, if you have any social media profiles they should all utilize your brand image to create the consistency that is required to have a strong brand. All of your marketing and ad campaigns should maintain this image as well. Before you start structuring your website and other major projects, start by sitting down and identifying what you want your brand to be. Websites like Pinterest are excellent for choosing brand designs as they offer a series of color palettes and fonts that flow well together. In addition to colors and fonts, you will want to consider actual images. Most brands have a specific symbol that goes along with their brand, such as Nike's check mark or apple's computer. You should choose a symbol that will be used across your brand as well. Then, you should also choose specific images. If you are selling yoga products, for example, you may wish to use only images that reflect the outdoors, freedom, and holistic wellness primarily through yoga poses and other similar activities.

Once you have created your brand image, you should carry on to create your brand's vocabulary and "personality". Using the catch phrases and vocabulary you identified during your market research process, you should develop a slogan. You should also practice creating content and copy that uses this slang and phrasing in order to effectively communicate with your targeted audience. Whenever you are posting about your business, you should use this vocabulary and personality-type in order to communicate with your audience.

Creating a solid brand is vital to the success of your business. In order to have a business that thrives, you need to be able to create a brand that is identifiable and strong. Believe it or not, your brand is a large part of your marketing. If you are able to create a brand that is identifiable, people are going to think about you a lot more frequently. Consider the Apple logo, for example. Whenever someone sees the Apple logo, even if there are no identifiable phrases surrounding the logo, they are well aware of what the logo stands for. The brand has identified itself so successfully that in many cases people even say "Apple" or when they look at an apple they may subconsciously think of the brand itself. This type of branding provides you with the opportunity to stay relevant and fresh in people's minds. While you will not have this immediately, you should aim for this right from the beginning. Thinking about your future success now is what will set you up to earn a six-figure income through your Drop shipping business.

Choose Your Platform

Since you are planning on establishing an online retail business, you want to make sure that you have an effective platform to run off of. Think of your platform as your store front: you want one that will successfully reflect your business and your brand. It should be clean, crisp, easy for users to interact with, and easy for you to interact with as well. Everything should be streamlined so that the shopping experience is simple and effective. If it becomes too difficult, the layout is too sloppy, or the website is confusing, people will be less likely to purchase from your website.

The primary areas you want to focus on with your website include clean and crisp product pages, easy ability to submit and collect payments, easy ability for customer to access support, and an effective backend management system that enables you to operate the website easily. Your website is the driving force for your entire business, so it is important that both you and your customer have an easy time using it as this is what will increase the success of your business.

It may seem like a big task to have to build your website, but it truly is not that difficult. If you absolutely do not want to do it, there are many professional website builders you can hire to complete the task for you. Remember, however, hiring one of these website designers will cost you a fair amount of money, especially since you want to hire one who will be able to create a highly professional website which will positively reflect your business.

If you do not want to host an independent website for your Drop shipping business, you can always choose a platform to run your business from. Shopify, Amazon, WooCommerce, and BigCommerce are all websites you can use to host your Drop shipping business. It is recommended that you go with a host that has high traffic if you are going to choose a third party platform for your business as this will increase your amount of potential traffic which will increase the number of sales you gain.

In Conclusion

The earliest stages of establishing your business are the most sensitive. You want to make sure that you launch a business that will be as successful as possible from the start. The more effort you put into establishing a successful business now, the more success you will experience later. It also leads to having less work to do later as you have laid a strong foundation now for your business.

Market research is vital in the early stages as this is what will give you the best opportunity to leverage your business and establish one that can adequately serve the needs and desires of your targeted market. If you fail to conduct market research in the early stages, you may end up designing an entire business that fails to effectively communicate with your targeted audience. Then, regardless of the quality of your products, website, or service, you will likely never gain customers. It is absolutely critical that you develop a strong brand with an effective ability to communicate with your target audience early on. This will give you the highest opportunity to succeed in your business on a long-term basis.

The Advantages of Starting A Drop Shipping Business

Drop shipping brings in a lot of positives making it a very lucrative industry to get into. For newcomers, this is very encouraging and it helps your business even from the start. If you are not able to invest a lot of money now, you can still go ahead and run a successful Drop shipping business. It is necessary for you to understand that the advantages will give you a leg up in the process but it will depend on you how you work around your niche and know what works best for your business. This is the basis upon which your Drop shipping business can reach its full potential; you just have to keep at it.

Minimizes risk

Starting anything new requires time, effort and most importantly from a business perspective, money - the investment of capital. Drop shipping provides a safe platform where although it cannot eliminate all the risks, it certainly can give you the assurance to keep the risks at a minimum. First and foremost, to purchase any inventory, money does not need to be paid upfront. The investment is in the website which will provide the exposure. In the long run, if the business is unable to make profits, the amount of money spent on designing and running the website is all that you would lose.

Once you get acquainted with the taste and trends of your target customers, you would be able to make predictions about demand. This acts as a great motivator for your Drop shipping business as you will be less prone to loss of revenue due to these very changes in trendsetting products. In addition to the previously pointed out aspects, your expertise would grow and allow you to design better strategies. Among these, the most attractive one would be to offer lower volume niche products with popular best sellers. Your customers would return for the popular ones on a regular basis and if you are able to grab their attention during those traffic hours with the lower volume niche products, it would allow them to consider purchasing and have a positive impact on sales.

Reduces initial investment

The concept of Drop shipping has revolutionized how businesses are run. One of the biggest reasons for its popularity is that the merchants do not have to keep products in the inventory when they are adopting a Drop shipping strategy. In its fundamental arrangement, Drop shipping does not require any investment or payment upfront, allowing retailers to reduce their expenditure on products. This is extremely helpful for those who are newcomers and can afford to take small risks. The experienced can allocate their resources based on current trends and not face a huge loss in comparison to other alternatives to dropshipping. For certain businesses or e-commerce startups, the initial capital required to establish everything in order to start selling may not be as much. You do not have to wholesale purchases nor do you need to pay to manufacture your own products. This encourages more and more newcomers to enter the market.

Offers convenience

The Drop shipping business model makes it a very lucrative choice for many people these days. With the advent of technology, you can complete all your tasks within a much smaller time frame. These automated applications help you keep track of and pay attention to whatever is required, be it customer relationships or finding suppliers. For busy people, this business model does not require all of their time or energy to manage the store. Without being directly involved, you can seek out online tools and make life easier for you! You can filter out your requirements and import these products directly onto your website. Moreover, to promote your store and to maintain a good relationship with your consumers, you can provide them with tracking numbers of their orders, have additional plugins and add-ons, and much more. There are tools available for you to even calculate your markup cost and organize products accordingly. On your part, you can also track your own performance to understand the aspects your store could improve on. You can divide your tasks by week, month, or day with the help of these technological resources. These can help you to make things more organized and allow you to pay attention to the smaller details and make better decisions to avert any issues. On another note, you do not have to worry about packaging and you can add new product lines very quickly since the initial investment required is very low. Overall, the entire system of Drop shipping encourages ease and convenience.

Provides practicality

A common assurance any customer may want when making a purchase is that it will be delivered on time and will be processed through a reliable medium. When you are dealing with large or perishable products, Drop shipping makes it much easier to sell. The biggest advantage is when you do not have to buy and store all the products you want to sell. Your business can have a much wider range of products and can help you keep up with the current trends. Last but not least, there is no need for a physical store or location as everything is on your website. Through your platform, you can obtain orders and proceed through dropshipping. On the other hand, many dropshippers will allow you to have your own labels, making the customers believe that the merchandise was sent to them personally and not through a dropshipper. This huge rise in the number of dropshippers has made these transactions simpler than ever before.

Scalability

As mentioned previously, the initial cost to bring in new products to your store does not require you to make any payments upfront, hence your business can function without having to bear any financial burden. This certainly provides more assurance when you want to test new products. You do not have to deal with the consequences of making bulk orders and not being successful. Thus, your valuable time and capital expenditure are both safe; adopting the model of Drop shipping gives you access to make bigger decisions in terms of dealing with the product line.

Increases lifetime value of customers

By getting into a system of dropshipping, you have the power to add or remove products constantly. You have the ease to either promote a line or take it off the site to make your customers more engaged. They will be more curious to follow what are you offering since you update your inventory on a daily basis. Many physical stores already have dropship programs and your store could be a platform that provides these facilities online.

Expansion into new markets in the long run

When you start your business, you would want to initially survive, but as the days go by, you would plan to expand to achieve higher profit margins. In the long run, Drop shipping helps you to transition into new markets. One of the main obstacles here encompasses foreign countries and their operations when you want to expand. In those circumstances, local suppliers across international borders are the key factors in creating success for you. You can gain better and faster access to similar products when you work through these local suppliers, given that you should strategize beforehand. This also aids you in keeping your costs lower than expected when expanding into new markets. Not only this, this gives a perfect chance to do trial runs on that specific market and whether it is logical and profitable to import them in the long run.

Virtually unlimited inventory

In order to counter a lot of issues faced by the industry as a whole, the concept of Drop shipping came into play. Its main purpose is to provide a helpful platform for the suppliers and retailers to reduce disproportion of inventory, which specifically deals with overstock clearances and out of stock shelves. Today, around the world, the amount lost to overstocking totals to around 800 billion dollars. Hence, to design an effective plan, Drop shipping helps you gain access to unlimited inventory if we are thinking solely in terms of theory. The supply chain needs to be further tapped into in order to apply this theory in real life.

Provides flexibility

Drop shipping reduces dependence on physical communication and is reliant on a strong internet connection. This allows timing to be flexible among all the stakeholders when purchases are being made, be it the customers, the manufacturers, or the wholesale buyers. Orders can be taken and placed from any time and from any location, making it more lucrative for all parties. The communication done among these parties is online and can be tracked during any sudden crisis. This certainly provides more ease and flexibility to coordinate. Customers have the opportunity to directly communicate with the store owners and the manufacturers and answer any queries they may have before and after buying anything. This has the most benefit for the wholesale merchants as this platform allows them to partner up with multiple partners at the same time and in turn, sell more products to the customers. These merchants can acknowledge their own capacity and choose the number of partners they can maintain effective and good relationships with. Based on that, they can then evaluate their practice and expand accordingly to achieve their target sales. On the other hand, the manufacturers have a larger floor to experience flexibility as they can send out more products to be sold.

Leverage

In order to sustain in the long run, you need to try to create balance among all the stakeholders in your Drop shipping business. The wholesalers, who are going to do your dropshipping, need to have enough acknowledgments from your side to feel encouraged to have a long-term business relationship. The strain between the merchant and the supplier can be mostly balanced by having a dependable and reliable arrangement with the dropship wholesalers. On the other hand, in the world of business, a form of leverage is to be able to multiply your time, money, and effort. You need to smart when dealing with all the stakeholders, your customers, your suppliers, your wholesalers, and be able to create an efficient system.

The Disadvantages of Starting A Drop Shipping Business

Like any model, drop shipping also has its share of drawbacks. There are a lot of aspects of shipping and packaging which are not within your reach, making it more difficult to approach an effective solution, if any issues arise. Drop shipping is an open platform and this is its biggest challenge because anyone and everyone can enter the market anytime and anywhere. There are a fair share of positives too but understanding the drawbacks are crucial to upscale your business. You need to learn to work around these uncertainties because you are the middle man who has to look over the execution plan but does not control any of the contributing factors. You have to be ready to avert a crisis if the order is not completely fulfilled and at times even bear losses just to maintain your customer base. The entire purpose of understanding the negatives is to be able to design your store's policies and vision around them and improve the customer experience as much as possible.

Low barrier to entry leads to more competition

As Drop shipping is convenient and very flexible, anyone can enter the market. This does increase the competition but a bigger problem arises when your competitors have the same suppliers and are selling the same products are you are. Pricing is crucial in this case and you need to work on standing out in various other ways. You can start with customer service and learn to rebrand and reinvent your store if you are unable to survive against the competition.

Lower profit margins

You have to remember that there are hundreds of other stores running a similar Drop shipping business like yours and it may not run smoothly all the time. You need to accept that and then make decisions in terms of changes in the market, especially when quoting prices for your products. You are buying the product at a certain price for your customer; the amount that you charge your customer should be higher if you want to make a profit. Usually, you cannot go more than twenty percent higher than the actual price that was set by the suppliers. You will pay the price set by the suppliers but charge a higher price to your customers in order to make a profit. Initially, a lot of newcomers find it difficult to breakeven and yes, it may take much longer than you expect. You may think of charging ridiculously high prices for your products but keep in mind that there are many others who have the same suppliers and niche. Your competitors get an advantage when you increase your prices too much. You will be able to make a profit but the amount would be low, much lower than you would expect. If you spent around 10 dollars for a scarf and are selling it for 15 dollars, your profit is five dollars. Before quoting prices, you should do research online to compare prices and check how your price compares to that of the market price. After all this, there are additional fees, such as SEO and PPC, which further decrease the share of your profit. When you look around, you will have to take into account the non-dropshippers and how they create an impact on your business. It becomes more challenging to stay ahead of the competition when there are non-dropshippers offering the same products at lower prices. In spite of wanting to attract potential customers, you may be unable to lower your prices considering all the extra costs, extra time, labor, and logistics that you have to take care of to fulfill the shipment. It gets very difficult to stay motivated when you see such thin profit margins.

Combatting these challenges occurring due to lower profit margins can be done strategically. The simplest plan would be to increase the number of sales as they will equalize the low profit margin when your revenue increases. However, that requires other promotional strategies that will have a significant impact on the number of customers you can sell to.

Whether these are new customers make purchases or returning customers buy more, will totally depend on what items you are selling. On the other hand, you can focus on making a deal with your supplier. This is feasible and convenient and most importantly, cost-effective. You can negotiate where they will have to prioritize the needs of business whenever an order is placed. In return you can give them your word officially to make them your supply partners for a specific amount of time; annually, monthly, or quarterly. If you are ready to make a commitment, go ahead. In most cases, the suppliers will offer you a reduction in prices and you should be able to save around five to ten percent of your total costs. This would be a great positive since you are able to have a reliable supplier and also do not have to charge a ridiculous amount to make a profit. Additionally, you can look into more high budget items to sell on your store as a cut in your cost price will ensure you a higher share in monetary terms.

Quality of products

You are expected to trust your suppliers and believe that what they showcase will be genuine along with the quality of the product. Unfortunately, since the products are usually in the cheapest range, the quality is mainly what gets compromised in the process. If your customers are served with items that look nothing like the product picture, it is you and your store that have to incur the losses. This generates negative publicity and you will have to get started on a supplier hunt once again. It is extremely difficult to understand how authentic they are, hence you need to have regular checks to stay updated.

In this case, you can only understand the quality of the product only if you receive it yourself. Since Drop shipping does not allow you to pass the products through yourself, you need to act as a customer and order something. You can track down the products that the customers have had problems with and start there. This will take time and slow down the process for your genuine customers who want to order the product but it is much better to test it first and then allowing them to move forward instead of letting them have a bad experience. You should do more research when you are dealing with suppliers. Reviews will help you to understand the authenticity of their advertisements and help you decide whether their quality is at a good standard for your store or not.

Pay per click increases expenditure

Pay per click (PPC) is the fastest way to attract more customers. If you increase the number of visits to your store, the number of sales you are expected to make increases automatically. PPC allows you to gain more traffic as it acts fast. You will be able to notice that your revenue is increasing significantly and you may feel confident that you will be able to overcome the low profit margin. However, it is important to remember that PPC is not free and it will cost you money. The keywords are expensive and using PPC does not let you make a profit that easily. It certainly is the fastest solution but there are other substitutes that you should look into before making a decision. Campaigns on email and social media are other valid options, along with SEO (Search Engine Optimization) for the Drop shipping industry.

What Factors To Look At When Analyzing The Target Market

Demographics

Demographics is a term that relies to certain data about people, such as where they are located, i.e. their geographic location, as well as what income bracket they belong to, and other such information. Being able to gather this data and use it to define a particular market is crucial to understanding just how large your target market really is and where they are centered around, and will be extremely useful in catering the product catalog to their demand.

Gender

One of the undeniable and statistically observed differences between genders is the general shopping and spending patterns between men and women, as men and women have varying shopping patterns when purchasing things, whether online or in a physical store. Gender is not the most controlling factor when deciding on a target market, but it still offers insight that may be useful when targeting a particular market segment. Some things that can be influenced by gender is the type of content that motivates them to buy, what language to use in write – ups to make products more attractive, or even what times of day they tend to shop, all these are factors that may be influenced by gender.

Age

Age is a major factor in deciding a person's spending and purchasing pattern, especially due to the change in tastes over generations, as well as the general difference in spending capacity depending on age. For example, millennials, the nickname given to the demographic group born in the last 2 decades of the 1900's, tend to do a lot of shopping online, but due to the relative youth of this group, have a lower spending capacity and thus rarely spend on big – ticket items online. Another example would be those in the ages of sixty and above, who are generally more unfamiliar with ecommerce and are not as comfortable shopping online, and thus are less likely to buy things through the internet.

Institution

One thing to keep in mind is what type of sales you will be making, if these products will be sold directly to consumers, to other businesses, or even to government institutions. Whether these goods are being sold Business – to – Consumers (B 2 C), business – to – business (B 2 B), or Business – to – government (B 2 G) are all factors in deciding many aspects of the business, such as what types of product should be offered, how many products they will be purchasing, and how these products and services will be marketed. However, most drop shipping businesses sell directly to consumers, using the B2C relation, but in the case that the retailer's drop shipping business will also cater to other institutions, these factors should be taken into account.

Know the Competition

Earlier we discussed how checking up on competitors is a part of market research. This aspect cannot be emphasized enough, as in order to beat the competition, one needs to know them well. For example, if the product that the retailer or merchant wishes to sell is already being sold at a high volume by established and well – known online retailers, then this is a positive sign for the retailer. However, if the retailer notices that that very same product has become ubiquitous on online markets, then it may be too difficult to distinguish the business from everyone else's, and it may no longer be a good idea to focus on selling that type of product.

Here are some tactics and tips when it comes to scoping out the competition:

Use Online Tools

While there is nothing wrong with simply looking over and exploring their website, and that is in fact the first step, in order to get a more in – depth understanding of how your competitors are doing, some online tools may be made use of. There are some site explorers such as SEMrush that allow the gathering of data such as the ranking and domain authority of a website while needing only the URL. This tool would help the retailer get a better idea of where their traffic is coming from, and how people are getting access to their website. These online tools, in conjunction with examining the website manually would give a more holistic view of how they are doing, as opposed to simply eyeballing their business.

Order their products

While this may initially seem counter – intuitive, as ordering from the competition means giving them business, ordering from competitors is a way to get valuable insights. While the general flow of ordering online tends to remain the same, there are always quirks, little things and details that distinguish one company from another, which can give an idea of what things should be avoided, or what things can be improved upon in the ordering process. Remember that in a drop shipping business, the only real interaction that a customer will have with something controlled by the retailer is the product platform and ordering process, so it's to the benefit of the retailer to make the ordering process as smooth as they can. Note that the order process should not simply be copied, but rather used as inspiration for ideas of how to make a well – oiled and smooth order process.

Analyze their social media

In the current day and age, social media is king. Perhaps not literally, but if social media can make or break a long – term established brand, what more a fledgling e – commerce drop shipping business carried out entirely in cyberspace, the same region where social media is located. Social media is one of the best ways to get feedback and to observe how people perceive the business. Watching the social media channels of competitors gives you an idea of the problems that they have, and the things that they are doing right. Picking up tips from how they engage with customers online is a way to improve one's own social media marketing methods. In addition, looking at their content is a good way to be able to find out how to compete and design a marketing strategy that would be able to overtake theirs.

How to Find the Right Drop Shipping Supplier for You

The drop shipping business model is highly reliant on the supplier; after all, it is the supplier that will be fulfilling orders, since they will provide the product and deliver it, and without the supplier there will be no business. Of course this means that the supplier is one of the most, if not the most important part of the puzzle when it comes to establishing a successful drop shipping business. If the supplier messes up a delivery, sends defective goods, or is constantly out of stock, your drop shipping business is the one that customers will blame, so it is of paramount importance that the merchant will be able to find a reliable drop shipping supplier that is capable of communicating well and fulfilling their obligations. The following are a few tips for finding a drop shipping supplier that you can trust:

Experienced Sales Representatives

Sales representatives are the first line of communication of a company, and these sales representatives are most likely those that the retailer will be working with most of the time. If these sales representatives are experienced at their job, they will most likely know how drop shipping goes, and the ins and outs of the process, allowing them to more easily handle any issues that come up and coordinate with the retailer to handle any issues that come up. An experienced sales representative will be able to put the retailer's mind at ease, as they are adept at communicating and will be able to make things move much quicker and smoother.

High quality products

Though an ecommerce store does not have the traditional brand hallmarks, it is still a brand that the retailer will wish to develop. After all, it is key to the drop shipping platform's success that the platform be recognized as a reliable place to buy high – quality products. A retailer is judged by the products that they sell and the quality of service that they provide, and the supplier handles both of those things, though the service to a lesser extent. If the supplier has high – quality products, customers will end up more satisfied, which means repeat customers and a good reputation, and good reviews and recommendations are one of the best ways to boost business and keep the retailer afloat. A reputation for selling low quality goods, on the other hand, is a quick way to sink any chance of success.

Technologically Capable

A good drop shipper keeps up with the times and is able to match the latest technological needs. Whether it be by having an inventory software that ensures that their stock availability is always up to date, or an efficient warehousing system to dispatch orders quickly, or even by simply having a well – automated order receiving system, it is important for a drop shipper to be capable. This will come in handy especially when it comes to scaling the business, in case the merchant wishes to expand, as they can feel secure that their trusted business partner will be capable of scaling along with their operations.

Punctuality and Efficiency

Drop shipping is not only about the products, but about a safe and efficient shipping system. If there is a drop shipping supplier that offers same day shipping, or at least shipping within twenty – four to forty – eight hours from receipt of the order, this will go a long way in making customers happy with the service. In a highly competitive market, any edge goes a long way, and a quick and efficient delivery system is a way to gain customers. One way of ensuring that the supplier is actually efficient with their order fulfillment process is to test them by ordering a few items, just to see how fast they are able to fulfil the order.

Where to look for Drop Shipping suppliers

If you happen to be an experienced businessman, or are friends with one, then most likely you will already have access to one or more reliable suppliers that are also capable of fulfilling drop shipping functions. However, not everyone is so lucky, and in case there are no contacts available, the best way to look for a drop shipping supplier in an area near you, funnily enough, is to simply Google it. There are many websites online, among them start – up incubators that provide directories of various drop shippers that provide various products. Once the retailer finds a few promising leads in a suitable area, it is simple to send them a quick and polite email in order to inquire about their services and a possible partnership. Sending an email over calling is preferable, as an email chain would allow you to keep a record of the conversation, as well as allow you to gauge how well and how quick their sales representatives do at replying to inquiries.

Drop Shipping fulfilment

While we have already gone over the basics of drop shipping order fulfilment, some aspects still need to be taken care of on the part of the retailer, such as whether some steps should be automated or not. Some components of the process such as the receipt of the order, the shipping information, and other such details can be automated, or can be handled manually, depending on the preference and resources available to the retailer. In case of multiple suppliers, the fulfilment process will most likely include sending the orders through email but finding the best supplier per product per order will likely rely on factors such as delivery location, shipping cost, and product availability. In this case, the retailer needs to find a way to ensure that these details are dealt with, either through using advanced software, or manually sifting through the orders to match them to the best – fit supplier.

Drop shipping Customer Support

As has been reiterated time and time again, good customer support can make or break a business. By now the reader should know that the majority of the contribution of the retailer to the customer shopping experience is in providing the platform and in providing customer support. Thus, it is in the best interest of the supplier to build and maintain the best customer support system it can in order to look good in the eyes of the customer and distinguish themselves from their other competitors.

Phone Support

One of the most classic methods of customer support is having a phone customer support system. Not only is it classic, but it is one of the quickest ways to get in touch with the customer, and it also works to the advantage of the retailer. The retailer can have an advantage when using phone support as a human conversation makes it harder for the customer to get mad, and it also makes it easier for a trained sales representative to defuse and manage the situation. It is also more immediate, and it allows customers to resolve their issues quicker, and allows the retailer to receive feedback in a more immediate manner. In a lot of countries, especially the more developed ones, the landline phone is becoming phased out, with more and more households opting not to get a phone in the first place. A retailer can still offer phone support through applications such as Google Voice or Skype, which will allow the benefits of voice communication while still remaining relevant and allowing people without landlines to call directly. However, this will take more internet infrastructure, as it will require the platform to have a messaging system in order to inform the customer support representatives that there is a customer that wishes to call.

Email Support

The phone support is the classic method of customer support, but in reality, most of the customer support interactions will most likely be done through email, due to its convenience and accessibility. In line with this, it would be best to have domain emails set up for your website, which would grant credibility and legitimacy, as it looks quite professional and helps in establishing a brand. In addition, email support is useful for both retailer and customer as it allows them to track what steps have been taken and they can keep a record of what has happened during the interaction. One useful software for email support is the Helpscout software, specially designed for customer support functions.

Social Media Support

Given the primacy of social media in our everyday lives, a lot of customers ask questions or direct complaints at the social media pages of brands and companies even before using official, more conventional channels. This includes posts on their page or direct messages, things that are done by customers because of the convenience, and because a large amount of the time, other customers have asked similar questions on the page, and they hope to find the answers there. In line with this, having a dedicated customer support representative handling social media will help with engaging the customers even during the times that there is negative feedback. A skilled social media handler will be able to do much with the company account, and this can help with the popularity of the brand and will help with establishing good faith.

Live Chat Support

Given the dominance of internet technologies nowadays, a lot of brands are including live chat functionality in their websites and platforms, allowing customers to have nearly – immediate access to a customer support representative, and this acts as a hybrid of a phone call and email method of customer support.

This is because the response is almost immediate, but there is a written record, and the customer can easily forward data such as pictures of a defective product, or a picture of the packaging, or the tracking number of their order. However, having a live chat function is difficult for a start – up with limited resources, and viable alternatives that serve a similar function are using the direct messaging services on social media platforms. However, integrated live chat support is a good option to explore if ever the retailer has the opportunity to scale up.

Sample Products and Test Marketing

In every business, the ideas you have, the products you think you want to sell, and the audience you picture who will want to buy them are all thoughts and premises that need to be tested. If you don't test them, they will remain in their state of untested reality where everything remains the same. It is neither good nor bad because it is not validated until tested.

With your Drop shipping business, you may have an idea for what you think is the coolest product on the planet, but when tested, it shows no signs of interest. There are also products that you will find when searching for trends and become surprised at some of the items that have taken off and have become top sellers.

It's easy to look at Amazon and see a giant of a company that is successful at every turn. But this didn't just happen. Founder Jeff Bezos runs his business based on hid theory that even if you only have a 10% chance of something paying off 100X, you should not only take that chance but take it every time because it will pay off in the long run.

Testing your sample products and conducting test marketing are both valuable parts of your Drop shipping business that should be conducted on a regular basis. Here is information on finding sample products and conducting the test marketing that is much needed to complete the process.

In Drop shipping you can test small batches of products to see if they will sell before you invest your time and get stuck with a large inventory of items that no one wants. It is important to not view a failed sample attempt as a failure. You should view it as giving you the information you need on your way to finding your top sellers.

When using social media platforms to test your products you are going to have to join forces with influencers who fit your niche. First, you will have to find the right influencers for your product, but once you do, you will be able to reach more people than you could on your own.

Here are some influencer platforms where you can start looking for the right ones for you: AspireIQ, Whalar, and Neoreach.

How to test your products on Instagram

1. The first thing you need to do is know the niche for the product you are going to be testing. When you identify that, choose around 3 pages around that niche.

2. Go to the Ads Manager section on Instagram. Go to Create and follow the information that is requested.

3. Find your influencer who will test your ad. Try to keep your costs down so you can continue to test more than one product.

4. Gather the information from your ad to see if you need to run it again or move on to the next product.

How to test your products on Facebook

1. When using Facebook one of the best ways is to create a Page Post Engagement (PPE) ad. There are YouTube videos that will show you exactly how to create this ad. It will ensure that it is shown to the best audience for your product. You will also get to see how many people liked this ad, how many shared it, and you will be able to read any comments they leave.

2. You will also get to see how many impressions have been left. The cost for the ad will be about $5, which is less than a regular ad.

3. Even though this type of ad costs less you are going to need to switch to a conversion ad. This type of ad is geared towards bringing you more sales, increasing sign-ups, and Facebook has a system of auto-optimization that is valuable.

4. Start with creating your Engagement campaign on the Facebook page. You may want to start with anywhere from 3 to 10 ad sets for the campaign. Set your budget at $5 and you can check daily to see how many impressions you receive until you reach 1000. The final cost should be no more than $25.

5. Check the response to see how many times people clicked on the ad, how many times they added items to their cart, and read any comments that were left.

How to get traffic to your Drop shipping store for free

While advertising costs money, there are many ways of using social media where you can get people to your site for free. Most of the usual places are consistently the best ways to draw people to your site.

Whenever you have the chance to join a support group that is based on your niche market, make sure to join the group or post a blog to the main page.

If your market deals with cooking products, showing a recipe using your own products would be a great step towards advertising your store.

Set up a contest or a giveaway for your current Facebook followers offering them a mall item in exchange for sharing your page or getting their followers to follow your page.

Ideas for advertising your Drop shipping store

You can start an Instagram page for your Drop shipping business to begin advertising your site. Here is a link with instructions on how to start one:

https://dodropshipping.com/grow-dropshipping-instagram-account/

If your Drop shipping store has items in the following categories you will want to start your own Pinterest page:

- Cooking
- Beauty
- Fashion
- Crafts
- Homemade items

The Pinterest audience is more than 80% female. Make sure you start a business ad so that you can reach the create ad section to advertise your site.

Check to see if you can find any influencers on YouTube who could help with your niche market or a specific product.

If you would rather handle your own advertising by creating your own YouTube ad, there is a link with simple instructions: https://www.oberlo.com/blog/youtube-ads-beginners-launch-first-campaign

You may want to start your own YouTube channel. You would be able to draw people to your channel and show them how to use many of the products in your store.

Facebook is always a great place to advertise your business and you can start with friends and family members and then move on to influencers.

Product Sourcing

Okay, you are ready to find the best products to sell online but where do you begin? It is suggested that you don't just purchase items based on what you like personally but you should keep your mind open and follow what is currently trending, popular, or selling well at other online shopping sites. It may not be your cup of tea but it might be a favorite item for a different group of shoppers. When you stop to think about everything that is out there to choose from it could be very overwhelming to even get started. So how do you begin?

- Once you find a product you would like to sell, that is great. But it is just the beginning. You need to learn everything you can about this product.

- Extensive research is required. Who would be your target market? Check out social media to better define who you are marketing to. Check ratings as well as actual sales. See if the product is trending or past its prime.

- What are the names of the companies you would be ordering from? Make contact with some of these companies and get a feel for each one. See if they could send you a sample of the product you want to sell. You should know this product inside and out before you commit to selling it.

- When you find a supplier you feel comfortable with, see if you can set up a sample order to see exactly how the process will work using their services. Don't be afraid to try more than one company. With a sample order you will be able to see how the product will reach your customer first hand. You will be able to determine if your customer is going to have a positive experience or if they are wondering why they even ordered the product.

Identifying Your Goals for Your Drop shipping Business

Figuring out exactly what you want to achieve with your Drop shipping business is a very important step that you should not skip over. How will you know if you are headed for success or just treading water?

The basis for setting goals in any area of your life is the same. You just have to adapt the steps to your Drop shipping business. There are a number of specific areas that you will need to address. The more specific you are with setting, adjusting, and re-evaluating your goals, the better chance you have of achieving them.

1. Your Product Line

   If you already know what you would like to sell, you are ahead of the game. Right now, just start thinking of items you might want to feature on your site. You should also take the time to check out other businesses that sell the same or similar items. Research what items are trending right now. Remember, it doesn't have to be your favorite, but there could be a specific sector that is always looking for certain items that could become top sellers for your business.

2. Staying Current

   This is a practice you should conduct on a regular basis. Evaluate your product line to see what is working and what is not. What is popular today may change by next week. Staying on top of the trends will keep your business relevant and help you retain your customer base and even attract new buyers. No one will frequent your site if you continue to carry the same items all the time. It would be like going to a restaurant that never runs any specials but has the same old menu all the time.

3. Your Financial Goals

   If you are just starting out you may have to look up businesses that are selling the same or similar items that you plan on selling and find out what their profits might be. If you are already in the Drop shipping business, look, up your earnings for each of the items you are selling and figure out how much you would like to increase them by. Most of the ecommerce sites that you are on or looking forward to using should probably have a listing that will show you the revenue you have made per number of transactions.

If you don't already have a financial plan set up you will need to make one. If you do, you will want to stay on top of it on a regular basis to make sure you are on track with your goals.

A financial plan for a Drop shipping business is fairly simple. Costs are low so all you will need to list is: the cost of your domain name; the cost of your logo and any other costs involved in designing and setting up your website; how much you pay monthly for your website; the cost of acquiring samples; and any additional costs you may have incurred or are currently paying for on a regular basis.

When you set financial goals you will need to figure out what it will take to earn the specific amount you want to build or increase your profits by. How many sales per week will you need to make in order to reach an extra $1000 a month? Will you be working with wholesale products or retail products?

What Are Wholesale Products?

Wholesale products are less expensive than retail products because they are sold in larger quantities. Wholesale items come directly from the manufacturer and are then purchased by retailers who in turn sell the items to customers. This process cuts out the middle man and the purchaser of wholesale products is able to buy the product at a cheaper price. Wholesalers don't have to spend money on fancy storefronts or advertising and generally work from a warehouse setting.

Products are shipped in bulk to single locations so there is not any extra work involved in shipping and distribution. This makes the resale of products to a customer a more profitable deal. When you work with wholesale products you are generally limited to specific products that the specified wholesaler carries. Items purchased from a wholesaler are priced to be resold.

What Are Private Label Products?

Private label products are developed so that one company can hire a manufacturer to sell their products according to their specifications and packaging. This creates a line of products that are all under the company's name developing their own identity. Private label products can usually be found in food items as well as personal grooming products, in the beauty and cosmetics area, and in fashion and apparel. Many cosmetics and skincare products have grown into profitable and reputable private label items.

One of the main advantages of private label products is they can prove to be just as good and sometimes even better than established name brand products but at a lower price. Target, for example, sells items under their private label, Archer Farms and Walmart sells products under their private label Great Value.

Sometimes a major company is behind a private label product but it is still sold at a lower price. If it is manufactured through the famous name brand it will usually identify itself on the label. This is considered a white-label product.

There are manufacturers who will produce products under a number of store brands and simply change the label to reflect each store's brand name. You would be surprised at what is behind some of the labels on generic products you buy.

Private label and white label products are sold at a substantially lower price than popular name brand items. It doesn't mean the name brand product is better than the private and white label products, it just means the name brands have to spend more in marketing, advertising, and branding to make money on their product line.

Plan of Action

Pick out 4 to 6 products you would like to be part of your product line.

- Learn everything you can about each product
- Who would be your target market?
- What other sites are selling this product?
- What price is it being sold for?
- Check to see if it is being sold wholesale.
- Contact the manufacturer to see about getting samples.

- Create a worksheet of all of the things you are paying for to start up and run your Drop shipping or Shopify business.

- Set your financial goals based on your expenditures. Break it down by week, month, and year.

- Check out what products are available wholesale.

- See if there are any private label items you want to add to your line.

- Set a day that you will review your product line each week.

- Decide on how many items you want for your product line.

- Keep a list of items you would like to check out to add to your product line in the future.

How to Identify and Work with Suppliers

Before you set out to look for suppliers, we value your business and would not want you to get cheated. It is essential to distinguish between valid wholesalers and retailers posing as such. We already differentiated in defining the two and the terminologies, feel free at to scroll back up to remind yourself of the differences. Note that there are retailers that claim to be wholesaler but actually are not. Legitimate wholesalers buy directly from manufacturers and offer much lower prices than retailers.

Here Is How You Identify Fake Wholesalers

Unfortunately, real wholesalers very rarely invest in marketing and are usually much concealed. This means that by the time you find a legitimate wholesaler, chances are you will come across very many fake ones. You also should be wary of swindling middlemen, but fortunately, you have us and we have you.

They will ask for ongoing fees: Have you ever been asked to pay an application fee to be accepted for a certain job? If yes, then you probably realized that you got conned. This is the same with such 'wholesalers'. They will ask you to pay a monthly fee to grant you the privilege of working with them.

Two words, RED FLAG! Real suppliers will never ask you to pay ongoing fees.

However, distinguish between suppliers and their directories. We shall take a look at directories shortly but they are likely to ask you to pay a certain fee, however, theirs would be legitimate and be reasonable.

Open to the public: Wholesalers do not sell to the public, and if this particular wholesaler does, they are simply a falsely poised retailer cheating the public with their hyperinflated prices. However, you need to be registered as a legitimate business and have a wholesale account. You also need to have been approved before you make your first purchase.

Here are some fees you will incur:

- Per Order: Many and most drop shippers will charge you a fee for every order you make. This will probably range somewhere between two and five dollars. It is all a matter of complexity and the size of the products that are being drop shipped. Note that you are not being conned, this is a standard of operation in this industry.

- Minimum order: Wholesalers will always have a minimum purchase number. This is done to ensure that they get rid of window shoppers who are a nuisance and people with small orders that won't translate to important business.

If you are drop shipping then this will definitely come with its own complications. What would you if a supplier has a minimum purchase of around six hundred dollars and your business' average order is two hundred dollars? In such a situation, your best option would be to prepay the supplier the six hundred dollars. This allows you to build credit with them.

Identifying Suppliers

Having the knowledge to know identify who's real and who's not, it's time to find you some suppliers. Live everything in life, there are a number of strategies you could employ to find a supplier that is in line with your goals. We listed the methods below basing them in the order of effectiveness and preference.

Contact Them: We highlighted somewhere above in this pile of words that phone calls work miracles. Call the manufacturer and find out what they have to offer by simply asking for a list of their products. Also, find out whether they drop ship or not. This is a basic.

Google: Google is indeed your friend. This is obvious, why didn't we start with this? Well, because, there are a number of things you need to keep in mind,

Carry out an extensive search: Let us again revisit and old point of wholesalers being terrible at marketing, but no offense to them. This means that your top searches will probably not what you are looking for. But look at this a challenge, when is the last time you clicked 'next page' on a Google search? Now you have a reason to.

Website aesthetics could be misleading: While how appealing a website looks like could be a good indicator for how serious a business is, this may not entirely apply to suppliers, especially wholesalers. Do not skim through a website and jump on to the next because that one did not look good.

Use as many modifiers as possible: I'm sure you've heard enough times already, so here it is again. Wholesalers do not invest in marketing and will not do any Search Engine Optimization. Try using as many words that will distinctively bring up exact results for what you are looking for, words such as a distributor, warehouse, bulk, and supplier.

The competition is your friend: Wait, what? Yes, your completion could help you identify a supplier. How do you ask? Simple. Place a small order with a competitor who is drop shipping. Once you receive your package, simply Google the returns address that is on the package. And bingo, you have identified who the original shipper of the package is. Contact them next.

Trade Shows: Trade shows offer one major advantage, centralization. Attending a trade show allows you to interact with potential suppliers all in one single spot. This only works, however, once you have already identified a niche market and know what product you want to deal with.

Directories: Here we are! We said that you should not confuse suppliers and their directories. So what are directories anyway? A directory is a database of suppliers, simple. They are usually sorted in accordance to market, niche, and items. Now comes the question, why should you pay for supplier directories? This is because most of the companies that run supplier directories are for-profit, thus will charge you to let you access you their database. However, to prevent monthly subscription and other expenses by supplier directories, ensure that you conduct your research and know from the get go what specifically you are looking for. Identify your market niche and products then it will require a bit of searching to find what is it you are looking for.

Here are some supplier directories that offer impeccable services; Doba, Wholesale Central, Worldwide Brands and SaleHoo.

Before You Contact Them

Now that we've taken through criteria of sorts for identifying potential supplier and are ready to contact them, there are a few things that need to be in check before you do so.

- Is your business legal? Is your business legal? As we have constantly mentioned, almost all wholesalers will require you to certify that your business is legal. They also tend to only reveal their pricing to legally registered businesses. If you just need basic information then that you shall get without any documentation, but to be fully incorporated in the system and get the inside scoop, your business should be fully legitimate.

- Understand your and the general reality: You need to know that supplier will not go any extra mile, not even an inch to help you out. Similarly, everyone else who contacts them makes promises and tells them how great their plans are. They've heard it before, they've heard it all. All suppliers need is credibility. Be definitive in your statements and answers, use terms like 'we have', 'we are'. Mention things that carry some weight and remember to mention any professional experience you have. Avoid using phrases like 'I think." Do not ask for favors too soon and be as convincing as you possibly can.

- The phone is your friend: The idea of making phone calls especially to people who are deemed as our superiors is always frightening. But, phone calls are a very efficient way of getting things done. Phone calls are not as scary as you think. Suppliers are also accustomed to receiving phone calls thus you definitely will be attended to.

Attributes of Good Suppliers

- Expert Staff: One good indication of a credible supplier is its staff. Good suppliers will have representatives who understand the industry quite well. You can tell this from how they answer questions.

- Committed support: Essentially, suppliers are supposed to allocate you're your own sales representative for a streamlined flow of business. The sales rep is supposed to take care, handle and fulfill your needs. It is very frustrating to have to call suppliers and nag them to fix a certain issue. Therefore, the sales rep acts as the bridge between the two entities.

- Technology: As time goes by, the key to remaining successful in the industry is adaptability. This is an easy way to know what kind of supplier you are dealing with. If they are invested in technology then they will be a pleasure to work with. They will offer you real time feeds on inventory, shipping, catalogs, and the like. Imagine a supplier that still handles all that manually.

- Accepts orders through email: This may sound minor and negligible but some suppliers do not accept orders via email. Pause for a minute and think about having to place every single order via phone and whether that system sounds effective to you.

- Location: In this business of drop shipping, location is one of those factors that carry a lot of weight. Find a supplier that is located in the middle of the country, especially if you live in a big country such as the United States or Canada. Why? This is because, if a supplier is located at one end of the country, it will take too long to get orders to the other end fulfilled. The ideal fulfillment period is two to three days, keep that in mind.

- Efficiency and organization: This one is difficult to measure and calculate. How do you know whether someone you have never worked with is organized and efficient? Simple, work with them. How? Place an order or two and be the judge. This will tell you a lot about a drop shipping supplier.

How to Pay Suppliers:

There are two ways in which suppliers accept payments:

- Credit cards: Most suppliers will require you to pay using a credit card as you're starting out. As your business grows and flourishes, credit cards are still the best option for payments because they can rack up a lot of reward points.
- Net terms: Net terms means that you are provided with a number of days to pay for items you purchased. For instance, when you are on 'net 40' terms, this means that you have forty days, which are counted from the date of purchase to pay for the goods, either by check or bank.

Here is a recap of the chapter:

- Fake drop shipping suppliers will: Ask for ongoing fees and sell to the public.
- How to identify suppliers: Contact them, Google extensively, order from the competition, attend a trade show and use supplier directories.

- Before making contact: Your business should be legal, understand the realities and do not be afraid of the phone.
- Characteristics of good suppliers: Expert staff, devoted support, invested in technology, accept email orders, are located centrally and are organized and efficient.
- Payment options to suppliers: Credit cards and on net terms.

Starting Your Own Store

While third-party marketplaces often have the benefit of requiring less marketing efforts and less content creation, the end game is to draw a lot of traffic to your products, and this is best done by creating a niche-based online store coupled with a blog, social media outreach, and any added value you may be able to give your potential customer.

Creating Your Own Website

You have a lot of choices when it comes to solutions for creating your own website. That said, there are generally two approaches.

1. Pay for hosting, and have a website built by a designer from scratch. There is a time and place for this type of approach, but it is going to be expensive to have an online store put together from scratch, and you need to work with graphic and website designers that understand the intricate nature of search engine optimization, branding, marketing, and ensuring that security is in place to protect your consumers. For the vast majority of dropshippers, this approach is probably more money and headache than it's worth.

2. Use a full ecommerce solution service. This could be those "other third-party" marketplaces we've discussed,

but they do not offer a full set of tools for improving our reach to your target market. Perhaps the best solution available today is Shopify. Unlike these marketplaces, Shopify helps with search engine optimization, adding a blog to your page, creating a dedicated website with an attractive design, and keeping down the losses per sale associated with fees. I cannot stress this enough: you really should be using Shopify unless you have special requirements that require custom coding.

Using Shopify to Simplify Your Life

I am not going to walk you through the entire process of setting up your store right now, but I encourage you to learn this process online or by reading my books on the subject. For our purposes here, let's discuss what Shopify can offer and how to set yourself up for Drop shipping success with this platform.

To being with, there are a few things to consider about Shopify:

- *It's not free.* They offer several plans based on the size of your online store, and $29 is the minimum. You will be able to upgrade your store and have access to extra tools as your business grows.

- *It is not a marketplace.* Unlike the other "store" creation options we've discussed, there is not a search bar on Shopify's website for consumers. However, because Shopify has a strong emphasis on helping you improve your search engine optimization and integrates into Google shopping, people CAN still find your products when searching.

- *It has a robust app store* with free and paid ads that can dramatically improve your ability to customize your website, store, and processes. This includes tools like Oberlo, which integrates Drop shipping Aliexpress items where it handles most of the work on your behalf, other than

- *It is a full website solution,* not only a solution for a store. This includes pages and a blog. Unlike other options, when someone is on your Shopify store, it just appears to be a standalone online store. It is your own website through and through, which gives you the freedom to create the experience you need for your consumers with a far greater amount of ease and less costs than other methods.

- *It offers superior security and customer service* that running a website on your own simply can't.

- *It is very user friendly and intuitive,* making it ideal for those without a lot of experience with technology, website design, and search engine optimization.

For a beginner, the method setting up a Shopify store for Drop shipping is fairly simple. While you'll need to build on this basic model, it can be broken down into a few simple steps:

1. Sign up for Shopify. You'll need a great store name! You can use their free 14-day trial that will give you time to setup your shop prior to going live with the paid version.

2. Purchase a domain name. This should be as close to your store name as possible without using misspellings. Shopify sells domains directly on their site, and they cost roughly $15. Shopify will prompt you to direct all

your new traffic to that domain name, which you should accept.

3. Select a theme. Now that you have signed up and purchased your domain name, you can choose the design for your store and website by clicking on "Online Store" on the menu and choosing, "Theme Store." There are free and paid themes, and you will want to adjust this to fit the demographic and product category for your store. Free themes are alright, but many websites use them.

4. Build the bones of your website. This includes your home page, about page, contact page, and anything else that is paramount. If you're uncertain at all, look at reputable online stores for some ideas of how to approach this. You can of course hire help to create great content for these pages as well.

5. Begin adding products. Once you have the bones, you are already at the point of inserting items. There are a couple ways to handle this process. The most obvious is to use their inventory tool and fill out the appropriate fields with great, original sales copy and images.

6. Use the theme design tool to implement any pages and products to your menus, home page, and organize your website.

7. Start a blog with their blogging tools. We'll discuss this more in the marketing chapter.

This may be a grossly simplified overview, but it is essentially all you're looking at to get started. From here, we still need to take our time to work on finding our suppliers and products, so taking advantage of that 14-day trial is a good idea, since we want some time to put together a store before launching it into the world and beginning in earnest on our marketing.

Build Your Site Up

You will quickly find out that Shopify is very user friendly, and while there are many considerations that simply cannot be automated, it takes a lot of the learning curve away from the process of creating your own online store. As you learn more about leveraging their many tools, apps, and the benefits of their emphasis on solid search engine optimization, it will become easy to continue putting together a great website. Any time you're feeling uncertain how to improve, take the time to find your competitors and see what they appear to be doing well, duplicate it, and improve upon it.

Marketing Your Business

Unless you're only using third-party marketplaces, which isn't recommended for those aspiring to make very large incomes with dropshipping, then marketing your Drop shipping business is going to become an important part of the equation. How do you reach the target audience for your niche? Furthermore, how do you manage this without completely breaking the bank starting off and maximizing on your investment even if you have plenty of money coming in to justify the cost? While there are a lot of benefits to paid advertisements, the best advertisement is having a platform together in your many interactions online.

Search Engine Optimization

We've mentioned search engines optimization quite a bit, especially in regards to keyword research, and it cannot be stressed enough how important it is to play nice with Google. Ultimately, it is my advice to pay an SEO expert to give your site an once-over and give you a plan of action to improve SEO after you have some content available already.

There are a number of things that Google looks for when trying to rank your website within the search results:

- *Create content.* Having content is key to Google actually indexing your website. Not only do you need content on your site, but you need this to be original content that is not duplicated from other parts of the internet. The more content, the more Google can index, and the more this is original, the less you're penalized for potential plagiarism.

- *Keywords.* Google looks for keywords and key phrases for obvious reasons, but how you handle these can matter a lot more than you might think. It is important that you're not overusing keywords in an unnatural way. Use a keyword no more than once per 100-300 words, especially if it's unnatural for it to be used so much in the content.

- *Images and videos.* With Google, images and video will work with their image/video searches if you've utilized them well. This can create an added method of people finding your site, and that also helps your site itself go higher in the page rankings for search results.

- *Backlinks.* A backlink is any link to another website. The more reputable and higher in the page ranking for Google the sites that link your page, the better these help you reach higher into the page rankings as well. There is a lot of confusion about backlinks and people will very often have links blasted out to any websites possible. This process is sometimes detrimental to your website, as cheap services for this will often rely on old styles of SEO that no longer apply and end up putting your website links on sites that aren't helping you at all. It is wise to only gain organic backlinks or at least work with a SEO professional.

- *Technical stuff matters.* The great thing here is that Shopify has their technical aspects together. If your online store is not with Shopify, you will really need to hire a SEO specialist that knows about web design to help you determine if there are any poorly coded portions of your website that need to be updated to allow for the best overall experience for the user and search engine optimization.

There is a lot more to SEO than just understanding these terms and utilizing them, but the general thing to take from this section is that you need original, high-quality content that utilizes images, videos (if possible), and is highly compatible with various web browsers and operating systems. SEO is an organic way to drive traffic, but it is more of a long game than paid advertisements.

Blogging

Adding a blog to your operations is a great way to help add a lot of content to your website, host product reviews, and engage with your demographic. Blogging is an excellent place to utilize SEO, and it gives customers a personality behind the company if done well. The approach you take to blogging can vary. Some will post several times a week, some post only once a week, but the key here is consistency. It makes sense to have a publishing schedule, or it is all too easy to not publish anything at all.

Establishing a blog within your niche that is an authority on related topics is a great way to draw people into your website and thus into your store. It gives you a chance to offer people value even before you ask them to buy anything directly, and it allows you introduce yourself into the community. For a niche that you're not truly familiar with, or if you're a shoddy writer, or if you simply can't make the time, you can always hire a contractor to help write your blog posts. My advice here is to find one that provides an intermediate price for great writing and has some personality that can be interjecting into all the posts. If not using a single writer, then the ideal situation is having a single editor instead, but a very good blogger for hire may not even require much editing, so it's worth paying a little more to avoid low quality content.

Social Media

Social media is almost a requirement for businesses these days, and you would be foolish as a niche store owner not to utilize social media in some manners. The ideal situation is that you will be able to integrate into the online community for your target audiences, either by joining it or working to create a place for them. Creating a place for them, such as a Facebook group, may be the better option, especially if you're great at engaging people over the internet.

Not only does this help you gain some insight into your demographic and feedback on your business, but it also helps establish you as someone that cares within the community, should that apply. This can be a lot of work, but slow and steady is the secret to making it function largely on its own. Like other platforms, you can always hire a contractor to help with this.

At the end of the day, you have to remember that content is king. You cannot simply spam and make snarky comments and expect too much in return. You need to help to provide value first and foremost, and then you can promote your business.

Email List

Having a mailing list helps to send out messages to customers that were willing to sign up for a mailing list, and it has long been touted as one of the most popular ways to gain and keep an audience online. You can promote your mailing list on your blog, on your store page, and of course on social media. The easiest way to gain mailing list subscribers is to offer them some type of value. This can be a coupon code, a free eBook, exclusive deals and content, etc.

Handling your mailing list is best done through services like ConstantContact or MailChimp.com, which are not going to be free, but are much more powerful than attempting to copy and paste a ton of email addresses into your Gmail account.

Product Reviews

Product reviews can make or break a sale. Allowing these on your ecommerce store and making sure to stock great products is a key way to encourage customers to help do the selling for you. Just remember that it is not savory to pay for fake reviews.

Paid Advertisement

Perhaps the easiest and often most effective way of advertising is paying for ad placements within search results, social media, and on other websites. This can be an expensive route to go, but a well-crafted ad campaign can often bring in traffic you simply cannot gain from other methods. Paid advertisements deserve a book to themselves in their complexity, and if the money is there, paying a marketing expert to help with these may actually be cheaper than trying to guess and check on your own.

The number one method for creating a good ad campaign is to create several ads and compare them to one another. The ones with better results get tweaked further and tested again. This is often referred to as "A/B Testing." These ads may only be slightly different from one another, but the results will speak for themselves.

The most common advertising services to use are Google AdWords and Facebook Ads. Obviously Facebook Ads places ads in front of people in social media context, and in many ways this is a great benefit because it is easier to target people that have listed specific interests, ages, and other demographic information. Google AdWords can propagate your ads across search results on the world's largest website, and it also places ads for you on other websites that are relevant to your content and products.

Outside of these two ad services, there are others that are widely ignored by the less experienced. This includes most notably Bing Ads, which works to place your advertisements on search results for both Bing and Yahoo, as well as websites like Google AdWords does. While the direct reach may be less than more popular methods, the cost per click or cost per results are much lower in many instances.

Those keywords that you have learned about along the way are going to be of great use during setting up paid advertisements. With the Google Keyword Planner, the level of competition and the average cost per click is given to you directly for these keywords, helping you understand how the search volume and your placement within those search results is going to help you gain exposure.

There are many other paid advertisement methods worth looking into as well, and ultimately, as long as you're striving for high-quality content, great products, and a pleasant user experience, advertising your entire store or specific products through this method is the fastest way to see results. If your sales content is sales-worthy, it will be greatly worthwhile to invest in advertisements.

Don't Spam

The one major lesson you must understand is that spam does not usually make sales, and it's technically illegal to attempt to be disingenuous with your marketing efforts. Posting comments on every Facebook post isn't going to drive that much business. Posting in forums only to promote a store isn't usually going to work either. If you're going to use these routes for promotion, you need to truly be involved and engaged with those in the community that constitutes your market.

While there is a lot more to marketing than these general overviews, this is going to set you up for putting together a marketing plan that will work for your budget, your target audience, and your goals. I do not suggest relying too heavily on only paid advertisements, just like I don't suggest only focusing on SEO. A well-rounded approach to marketing and engaging the consumer is the best way to move forward.

Establishing Your Brand Through A Marketing Plan

Once you have established your supply chain and your website is up and running, it will be time to establish your brand. You do this by developing a smart marketing plan and scaling that plan to fit your estimated growth rates. The last thing you want is to create a great marketing strategy only to end up overwhelmed. That can cause you, and your business, to crash.

Scaling Up Your Business

At this point, you definitely want to know what scaling is so you feel like less of a newbie.

Scaling means that you are creating new revenue at a much faster rate than you are increasing your costs. If your costs increase with every single new income stream, then you are not really becoming profitable.

Smart business owners want to scale their business just as much as they want to grow their business. To do this, you need to have the foresight to look ahead. Scaling is tied directly to your marketing plan. Your marketing plan should give you a good idea of how fast you could grow and what you will need to have optimized to ensure your business continues to grow in profitability without picking up just as many expenses.

The primary goal here is not to eliminate costs because frankly, that is impossible. No matter how you look at it, every business has costs and overhead. What you are trying to do here is to make sure that your business has more profit than costs. You also want to be careful that you aren't working so hard for so little that the business is no longer worth it for you. In order to do that, you will need to create a system that helps you deliver your products in services in an efficient way that can be replicated and used over and over again for little cost. This will tie into your supply chain and website. Your supply chain needs to be able to keep up with order demands. If it can't, you need a new one. Your website needs to be optimized for high volume traffic. Things as simple as you create an easier system for payment can help scale your business.

Although scaling is important, and it is a key piece to the puzzle that is a successful business, you need to strategize and scale proportionately to the business itself.

To scale to quickly could be as detrimental as not scaling, or scaling too slowly. If you are only bringing in one thousand dollars a month, you aren't going to spend five thousand dollars on scaling your operations for those sales. That is a fast way to spend too much money too quickly.

What it comes down to, essentially, is that scaling allows you to run your business efficiently and smoothly. If scaled properly, there will be no need for you to be working twenty hours a day to problem solve.

You will be able to trust that your website is running s\
and efficiently. You will know that the ads you have i.\
are bringing in a steady stream of customers. Those customers will be happy because you have ensured that your supply chain could handle the growth in sales.

That is the point of scaling. It makes your life easier, and your business runs smoothly. Without scaling you would end up frustrated and overworked. Your customers would become unhappy. You may end up with a lot of growth but you will not be able to sustain it because the business is not scaled to serve that many people.

Scaling vs Growing

Growth is when your business is creating new business, but also incurring costs to match. You are bringing in customers, you are making sales, and you can see clearly that your business is increasing in size.

Whereas you used to only need to check-in and see how your store was doing once a day, you are now fielding questions and putting out fires all day long. Here is the problem: in order to see this growth you have probably spent a great deal of time and money on trying to market these products.

In the Drop shipping world, you are not making or dealing directly with the products, which is already helping you to scale. However, you still need to market and your products which will require a lot of work and a lot of money. You also need to get the orders, check that the orders are correct in your system, and get the orders to your supplier. Then, you need to be able to trust that your supplier is shipping out the products as promised when promised, and with the quality promised.

You have already read how a good, solid supply chain is one of the most important aspects of your business, but as it relates to growth and scaling there are some considerations to take a second look at.

You also need to look at how you communicate orders to your supplier.

If you are experiencing high growth and gaining customers quickly but your supplier can't deliver that quickly, you could end up losing money.

Let's say you gain one hundred new customers in less than a week and they generate you another one thousand dollars. So now it is two weeks later. Fifty of your customers got their products with no problems. They got everything on time and with no defects. You don't need to worry about those customers.

The other fifty did not have the same luck. Some products may have been late or not shipped. Maybe you missed ten of them because you have not scaled or optimized the part of your business that involves sending orders to the supplier. So you refund them.

Twenty got defective products. The other twenty got the wrong product altogether. Either way, you just lost five hundred dollars, or more, because you now need to refund or replace the items.

Had you scaled, the results would be different. You would have had an ordering system in place that automated the orders and you would not have missed that first ten.

That same system would record exactly what the customer typed and/or clicked on so you are no longer attempting to manually order everything. In addition, you would have a reliable supplier who can handle large orders so the customers would have gotten the correct items.

You may still end up with a few whose items were damaged in transit, but those customers would only make up a small percentage.

Scaling Business Culture

No matter what type of business you are running company culture is important. It sets the tone for how you and your employees treat customers, vendors, and each other. Having a company culture that involves respect, kindness, and putting the customers first can make the difference between your company thriving or failing.

Company culture starts with you. What do you want the culture to look like? How do you want the employees to treat each other? How do you want them to treat customers?

Let's say you want the culture to center around respect for employees and customers. You also want your employees to be driven and innovative. That is your culture. That is what you include when you are training new employees.

This may seem simple. Drop shipping companies usually start with just one person starting their business. However, you will eventually need employees to help with customer service and marketing at the very least. You may need more than that. The first few employees may be easy to train.

It is easy to take one or two people and say hey, this is the culture. This is what I mean. This is what I want. It will not be so easy with twenty employees. It will be even harder with fifty.

So how can you maintain your companies culture and reinforce it? How do you ensure that your employees continue providing quality customer service? How do you ensure that the employee morale stays high and you don't end up with a high turnover rate or terrible customer service?

You are the key here.

The first thing to remember is that this is your company. You need to model these behaviors. Anytime you are around your employees or talking to a customer you need to demonstrate the same qualities you are asking for. Be patient. Listen to the customer. Speak to them kindly and do all you can to resolve their issue. This shows your employees that you are not only asking them to show customers respect and kindness but that you are willing to practice what you preach.

There are many other things you can do. No one thing is enough. Make sure your managers are on board. They deal with the rest of the employees more than you do, and the more employees you have the more managers you will need. Always model this behavior to them, and talk to them about doing the same thing.

Reward employees who show the qualities you are looking for. Did Jennifer in your customer service department handle a particularly rude customer very respectfully and kindly even though you could tell she was stressed? Tell her what a great job she did. Let her take a break. Occasionally have company-sponsored luncheons or parties to thank your team.

You can also put posters and graphics around the office, and set up learning materials through the employee portal. Make the company culture a priority. Happy and cohesive groups work better and more productively than groups who feel ignored and unappreciated.

Things to Look At When Scaling Your Business

There is no shortage of considerations when you are trying to decide on what to look at to scale your business. There are so many moving parts to any Drop shipping business.

It may seem simpler than a traditional business, and in some ways it is, but in some ways it actually much more complicated since you do not control the products or shipping yourself.

The first thing you need to look at is your marketing plan and your projected growth. Assume that your business with double within a month. Could you handle that? If all of your projections have you making two hundred orders a day within the next two months, how would you handle that?

Let's start with the basics.

Are you using a quality website platform? Have you ensured that your platform, in particular, has shown that it does not crash with heavy traffic? Is it fast enough?

On average, if a website takes more than two to four seconds to load, almost a quarter of the potential customers would leave the site. You need to have a high-quality provider to guarantee your site can handle heavy traffic and fast load times.

How are the payments being processed? Do you offer enough options? Do you accept all major credit cards and payment apps? The more payment types available to your customers the more likely they are to buy.

If person A only uses PayPal for online shopping and you do not have a PayPal option then you just lost a customer.

Once you have the orders and payments, how are you communicating those orders to your supplier? Do you have an automated system in place?

Having a close working relationship with your dropshipper is always the best way to handle things like this. That way, if you choose to make life easier by automating your system, you can still make sure that if there are any issues you will know about it right away.

Do all of your systems work well together? If you have an automated payment system, an automatic ordering system, and systems controlling your bookkeeping and more, do they "speak" to each other? The more automated all of your systems are and the more they can share information with each other the better.

Finally, let's talk about employees.

Will you need more? Having a tech on call is a good idea, of course. What about an assistant? Maybe someone who is more experienced in marketing? Remember, you want to scale, not just grow.

Hire who you need to for business to run smoothly, but not before you need them, and automate as much as you can so that you only need a few employees.

For example, if you are up to a thousand orders per week, you can have three employees. One tech, one marketing expert, and someone that helps you to field customer calls. Your automated systems handle the rest.

How to Scale Your Drop shipping Business

So far you have learned what scaling is and why it is important. Now you can learn what you can do to scale your Drop shipping business in a way that makes sense and works for you.

Let's assume you have already gone over all of the details in the "Things to Look at When Scaling Your Business" section. So now you want to know what to do once you have evaluated your business and looked into all of the different things you could streamline.

Start by once again combing through your marketing plan and your current growth rate. How many new customers and new sales can you expect for the next month? How about for the next six months? How about for the next year? Project your growth, and work backward from there.

Do not hire four employees to take customer calls when you won't have more than a hundred orders in an entire week. It is unlikely every customer would call, and even if they did, one employee could handle one hundred calls in a week.

Talk to your suppliers. This can not be said enough. Your Drop shipping partner is the person who supplies all of your customers with the products. They keep the stock, they take the orders from you, and they pack and ship all of your orders.

You can have every perfected system in place. You could have the absolute best advertising and the most amazing website. The entire business will fail if you do not communicate with your suppliers.

Let them know what the projected growth rate is. Make sure they know how much inventory you think they may need. Let them know that orders will be increasing so they can decide if they need to add people to their team to keep up.

Also, attempt to make your costs lower. If you are reaching a certain benchmark, try to talk to them about taking off a percentage for so many bulk orders.

Get a freelancer or hire a techie who is experienced in building entire business systems. You need someone who can optimize your website. They should also be able to set up your payment systems, your ordering systems, your phone systems, your bookkeeping software and more.

Get a professional who can automate as much as they can and then tie it all together so they work well together. Keep that person on retainer in case anything goes down. This person will be invaluable. The right systems save you time, money, and stress.

Speaking of money, pay attention to your accounts!

Some banks and payment apps will flag and block funds if they feel something is fraudulent. They don't necessarily know you are running a business. Communicating with them and heading off any problems before they start can go a long way in preventing any accounts from being frozen or blocked.

As your business grows you will need to hire customer service representatives. You cannot spend twenty-four hours a day awake and taking calls and responding to emails.

It is important to deal with customers, but you are a busy person and no matter how much you'd like to, you can't take fifty calls and a hundred emails in a day by yourself on top of running everything else.

Hire an assistant to help you manage all of this. Have someone responsible you can trust working directly with you to help with anything you need. They should be able to do anything from grabbing you a coffee to handling calls to your supplier if you need them to.

Throughout all of this, treat everyone who works for you well and always do your best to model the company culture you want to create.

Why a Marketing Plan is Essential when Scaling Your Business

Your marketing plan is probably the most important part of your overall business planning. It outlines your products, how you plan to market these products, and who you are marketing to.

The marketing plan is your go-to when trying to make decisions in your scaling operations.

Your marketing plan is created based on data. You will have done research and looked into every single detail of your business and projected growth. This data will then be compiled and analyzed at which point you will put it all together in a cohesive way.

It will include your overall plan along with sections outlining how much money you plan to make, how you plan to make it, and when you plan to make. Your goals will be set and you will have data to support your projected goals.

When scaling your business your market plan will be your most important tool. This will be your guide. It will give you a clear timeline. Scaling is a process. It is not something that you can do overnight. You need to make strategic changes and decisions based on your marketing plan's projected goals and timelines.

For example, if you have planned and projected that at three months you want your website to have two hundred and fifty thousand visitors a month then you will need to scale to meet that goal. Which means you will need to scale your advertising. You could choose to hire someone for that goal.

You can use sites such as Upwork and Fiverr to find freelancers to write your copy for you and create social media content, or you can choose to do it yourself.

In the meantime, if you have grown your website traffic by that much you will have also built your sales way up. This means you should also ensure that by that three-month mark you have also set up all of your payment and ordering systems so that the process is streamlined for you, your customers, and your dropshipper.

You would have hired a programmer to set all of that up for you and a customer service rep to help you handle any incoming customer problems.

Throughout all of this, you would have talked to your Drop shipping partner about the projected increase in product needs. That way you could make sure they can handle the influx on their end as well.

This is just an example of why a marketing plan is essential to building your business. Because for each milestone you have outlined in your plan you can already have a solid way to ensure you hit it by properly scaling in accordance.

If you do not use a marketing plan, your company may grow, but you will not have planned out how to grow all of the moving parts with it. So how do you create this all-important marketing plan?

Creating a Great Marketing Plan

A marketing plan can be time-consuming to create, but it can save you time and thousands of dollars down the line. The very first thing you need to do is sit down and detail where you are now and decide what your goals are and why you chose those as your goals.

Remember to keep these goals clear and concise because later you will need to flesh it all out. You also need to have the data to work with, such as what types of ads and content attract the demographic you are targeting.

For example, you would not write "gain a million twitter followers". This is vague and not based on any type of data set. You would write "gain a million twitter followers by hiring an experienced writer to write articles specific to "my niche" and targeted customer demographics. I will post three articles per day every day, and ensure the writer uses set keywords in the articles. I will gain one hundred thousand followers every two weeks until I hit a million"

Customer demographics will be a large part of your overall marketing strategy, so you want to include as much about them as you can. Do as much research as you can possibly afford to do when studying these demographics.

If you are selling gaming headphones, for example, you would need to do studies and research to determine the people most likely to buy them. Let's say that the research shows that these headphones will primarily sell to young males between the ages of sixteen and twenty-five.

You need to know all you can about males between sixteen and twenty-five in order to cater all of your marketing content to them. Targeted marketing works better than any general marketing you could do.

Now that you have your current standing and goals outlined, your timeline, and your scaling strategy to match, you can fill in the rest of your marketing strategy. Include demographic details.

Write a solid but to the point executive summary outlining who you are and what type of values you want your company to represent. Research your competitors and find out what works and doesn't work for them.

Outline your overall marketing strategies and how you plan to track all of your growth and changes so you can continue to scale in advance.

Ultimately, your marketing plan should be clear, concise, and informative. Make it attractive to look at so anyone who needs to see it wants to read it. Keep your executive summary to the point while still giving the reader a clear idea of what you want to convey. Make your goals and the plan of execution to those goals clear and detailed. Make sure the reader can clearly see who your targeted audience will be, and how you will keep track of all of your progress.

This marketing plan will be your guide. You will refer to it to make any changes necessary to scale your business. You will refer to it when talking to any investors or at any meetings with other business owners. You will use it to inform your employees about the overall strategy and goals of the company and what you need from them.

This plan will be something you look back and follow for years to come, and a good marketing plan will cover ten years or more. You can always go in and adjust it based on new data.

Most importantly, this marketing plan is what will help you securely establish your brand in a strategic way.

The Supply Chain & Order Fulfillment Process

The term "supply chain" is one that describes the path that goods take from their conception, to their manufacturing, then to the delivery, and eventually into the hands of the end – user. Supply chain specialists, when discussing supply chains and their methods, will talk about the very beginning of the supply chain, from the sourcing of the raw materials needed in order to build the products in the first place. However, that is too in – depth for the purposes of our discussion, and in order to learn about the drop shipping supply chain, we really only have to focus on the most applicable components, which in this case are three: manufacturers, wholesalers, and retailers. Now let's define these terms before we move on in our discussion.

Manufacturers

Though we discussed manufacturers earlier, it's better that we refresh our memories and update the definition a little bit. As we know from earlier, manufacturers are those entities that develop and / or produce the actual products themselves. They are the source of the products, and more often than not, sell these to wholesalers or vendors, who then re – sell these products to retailers. Purchasing from these manufacturers will most likely be the cheapest way to purchase products in order to sell, but these manufacturers also often have minimum purchase requirements, meaning the buyer will most likely have to buy in bulk, and will have to take care of storage and shipping in addition to buying inventory. However, there are some manufacturers that have drop shipping services, which is a boon to any drop shipping retailer. Otherwise, drop shipping retailers will most likely not be able to buy directly from manufacturers.

Wholesalers

Just like with manufacturers, by now we should have an idea of what wholesalers do – buy products in bulk from manufacturers, and re – sell them for a higher price, most often to retailers. Wholesalers have to store the inventory that they buy from manufacturers, which is why the mark – up on these products can still be fairly significant when compared to the price from a manufacturer. In addition, many wholesalers stock products from many different manufacturers in a specific category, which means they can have an appreciable catalog that retailers can choose from. These wholesalers also have purchasing minimums a lot of the time, but these minimums are usually much lower than the ones that manufacturers require to buy directly from them. A lot of wholesalers operate solely on the wholesale level, meaning that they sell to retailers only, not to the public at large.

Retailers

A retailer is defined as any entity that sells goods or products directly to the public at a marked – up price. For the purposes of our discussion, running a business operating on the drop shipping model and fulfilling orders through suppliers will qualify one as a retailer.

Drop shipping as a type of service

This guide is about drop shipping but note that there is no "drop shipper" on the supply chain, and it is not included in the definition of the three major components in the drop shipping supply chain. This is because any of the three components is capable of acting as a drop shipper. One thing to remember is that a "drop shipping supplier" means that the supplier will ship products on your behalf and will sell to you on a per – unit – ordered basis, but this does not necessarily mean that they are a manufacturer or wholesaler, as even retailers can have drop shipping services. This means that not all those who have drop shipping services are offering wholesale prices or manufacturer prices, as we remember that drop shipping is simply sale on a per unit basis and delivery to the customer. As such, it is of extreme importance that the drop shipping business owner choose the right supplier in order to get their business to work.

Drop shipping in Action: The Order Process

Now that we have a basic overview of the roles in the drop shipping supply chain, we should now take a look at how drop shipping actually works through a step – by – step run through of a drop shipping order. For the purposes of this example, we will be using an imaginary store, Shirt Shop, which is an online retailer that is dedicated to selling differing types of shirts. All the products of Shirt Shop are drop – shipped from the wholesaler Wholesale Clothes. With this in mind, let's get started.

First Step: The Customer places an order with the Shirt Shop

Customer A needs a new gym shirt, so he goes to the Shirt Shop's online platform and looks for a shirt that he likes. Once he finds a suitable shirt, he adds it to the shopping cart, places his billing information, and confirms the order. Once the order has been received and approved, both the Shirt Shop and Customer A will get a procedurally generated email confirmation of the order. Customer A's payment that was placed during the check – out process will be received and deposited automatically into the bank account of the Shirt Shop.

Second Step: The Shirt Shop places the order with Wholesale Clothes

The Shirt Shop then places Customer A's order with Wholesale Clothes, which can be done by simply forwarding the procedurally generated email to Wholesale Clothes, though some more advanced drop shippers support XML uploading or other methods of transmitting orders, but e – mail is a very common method due to the ease of use and accessibility. Once Wholesale Clothes receives the order, it then bills the account of Shirt Shop for the price of the unit and the delivery fee pursuant to the terms of their prior agreement.

Third Step: Wholesale Clothes Ships the Order

Once Wholesale Clothes confirms that the item is available, and once they have successfully billed the Shirt Shop's account, they will now box the order and ship it to Customer A, using the delivery address provided by the Shirt Shop. Note that though the shipping will be handled by Wholesale Clothes, the Shirt Shop's name and business address will be on the return address, and the logo of the Shirt Shop will be the one on the invoice and packing slip. Once the shipment has been completed, Wholesale Clothes will forward a copy of the invoice and tracking number to the Shirt Shop. Note as well that contrary to what a lot of people may think, the turn – around time on drop shipping may happen extremely quickly, and many suppliers are capable of shipping the order within a few hours of receipt of the order email, which allows retailers and online merchants to advertise same - day shipping capabilities, though they make use of drop shipping services.

Fourth Step: The Shirt Shop Alerts Customer A of delivery

Once the Shirt Shop receives the invoice and tracking number from Wholesale Clothes, they forward this information to Customer A, most likely making use of the online store interface. Once this is done, all that is left to do is for Customer A to receive the delivery, then the order and fulfilment process has been completed. Note that the profit margin of the Shirt Shop will be the difference between what Customer A paid at the end of step 1 and what Wholesale Clothes billed them at the beginning of step 2.

Invisibility of Drop shippers

Though drop shippers are integral to the entire business process, the drop shipping supplier should be wholly invisible to the customer during this entire process. When Customer A receives the package, the Shirt Shop's name, address, and logo will be on the shipment, not Wholesale Clothes'. If in case there is a problem with the order, such as the wrong item or damaged goods, Customer A would then contact the Shirt Shop, who would then coordinate with Wholesale Clothes to rectify the situation. When done properly, the end consumer will never see the drop shipper during the process. The drop shipper simply stocks and ships the goods, and the drop shipping merchant is the one that handles all interaction with the consumer, from marketing, to platform development, to customer service.

How to choose the best–suited drop shipping products

In order to have a successful online business, or even businesses in general, the businessman has to find the proper products to sell, as the entire business depends upon being able to successfully market and sell the products. There is no way to predict with one hundred percent accuracy as to what the best product for the chosen market will be, but there are some ways to make sure that the product will at least appeal to the customers that the retailer has in mind. The first step in deciding what product to sell is to list down all the product ideas you have and shortlisting these ideas, using a set of criteria to winnow out the good ideas from the chaff. The following may serve as a good set of criteria in order to determine the suitability of a product for a drop shipping business.

Price

One of the most crucial things when it comes to being able to sell a product is the price. In order to get a product flying off the shelves, the retailer needs to be able to set a price at a sweet spot, as pricing too low may lead to more sales but little or no profit margin per unit sold, and pricing too high would lead to more profit per item sold, but much less in terms of sales volume. Finding the proper balance is key to being able to sell a product well. Choosing an item based on how much it would cost is a way to filter product idea lists, as it's easier to sell more lower – cost items. Given that the general profit margin of drop shipping is between fifteen percent (15%) and forty – five percent (45%), it may be better to choose products that retail for about fifty USD to a hundred USD, as people are more likely to buy more smaller items than big – ticket items online.

Size and Weight

The size and weight of a product is relevant when it comes to choosing what to offer for sale on the retail platform as shipping costs are dependent on the dimensions of the product and how much care and effort has to be taken when shipping products. So when it comes to choosing what to sell, smaller and lighter products may have an advantage as shipping costs are less, and there is a lesser chance for these items to be mishandled, and in the case that one of them ends up damaged, the cost to replace is much lower, allowing the retailer to guarantee delivery without worrying about loss.

Complementary Products

One of the better methods to choosing what products to sell is to consider offering a catalog of inter – related products, which would encourage customers to purchase more items in one order, such as phones and their accessories. It would be best to consider inter – related products in a certain niche, such as if selling art supplies, whenever offering easels as a main product, it would make sense to sell other items such as canvas, paints, paint brushes, and other types of art supplies that someone buying an easel would logically need. It may even make sense to sell a main product at a very small profit margin and make up the difference by selling other components of the product or its accessories at a higher profit margin, as customers are more likely to buy related products from the same store in the interest of convenience and saving time.

Durability

When we talk about durability, it is more about the inherent consumability or renewability of a product, not the quality or make of the product. If the goods that are sold are inherently disposable or renewable, or are consumed by use, such as the aforementioned art supply example, then there is a higher chance that customers will buy from the store again as it is used. Depending on what product is being offered, having a subscription service that offers a discount may even be an attractive option for customers, and may keep them coming back to your retail platform, driving up sales and traffic.

Turn – Over Rate

Another good criterion to keep in mind is the turn - over rate of the product that you are thinking about selling. The turn - over rate is how often that particular product is substantially changed or updated, or given discounts, etc. As an online retailer, one big part of running the business is keeping the catalog updated, and this includes product photography and content relating to the product, which will give customers an idea of what they would be buying. If the turn – over rate of a product is high, then a lot of time and resources will have to be spent taking more photos of the product and updating the catalog, and possibly even re-writing content to take the changes into account. Unless the product is particularly popular, it may not be worth it to add too many items that have high turn – over rates to your online store's catalog.

Common Mistakes to Avoid When Drop shipping

People say that making mistakes is one of the best teachers, but it's also possible to learn from others' mistakes instead of having to make your own and suffer for them. As such, here are some common mistakes that many beginners and even some experienced businessmen make:

1. Do not base what products you will sell based on your own personal taste. Not everyone likes what you like, or dislikes what you dislike. The decision of what product to sell should be based on market research, facts, proper evaluation. Due diligence must be taken when selecting a product, as this is one of the key components of a successful business.

2. Never sell fake merchandise such as knock – offs or "true copies". These copies are often low quality, and your customers will end up complaining and feeling cheated. In addition, these knock – offs violate intellectual property laws around the world and are very illegal and expose the seller to liability for fines and in some cases, jail time.

3. Never base product selection just based on bandwagoning. Just because it is currently popular and seems like everyone is selling a particular product or a version of that product, it does not mean that selling that product is also a good choice. For one, the market for flavor of the month products is most likely extremely saturated, so it would be difficult to make or sell a product that would differentiate itself. This does not mean, however, that just because a product is trending, the merchant should avoid it. Rather, this means that due diligence should be taken to check as to whether or not the popularity of the product is likely to continue or to fall off, and if offering the product would be the right thing to do.

Finding your target market segment and niche

In order to do well in business, the target market should be clearly identified, in order to better target product choices and marketing strategies. In order to do this, the seller should do proper market research to get a better idea of what they have to do. The following are some tips for the seller to aid them with their market research.

Measuring Demand

The first step in undertaking market research is to measure the demand that your product is currently undergoing in the market. There are tools online, both free and paid, that allow the user to check how often the product is ordered, or even how often the product or key words related to the product is searched on popular search engines like Google every month, which would be helpful when it comes to checking just how the current demand is, and how the market is trending in relation to that product, or that type of product. Ideally when researching a product, a few thousand "hits" on a product's name or key words would be ideal when finding a product to build a business around. However, remember that in some cases, such as an emerging product or in an emerging market, some products may not yet be well – known, though they are beginning to gain traction. In these cases, key word "hits" may not be the best method in measuring demand.

Understanding Seasonal Patterns

Not everyone buys the same things at every point in the year. Not every product sells well at every point in the year. Some products are only associated with certain times of the year, and as such, are only sold on certain periods. While not a drop shipping product, one popular example would be pumpkin and pumpkin – related foods around the fall / Halloween season. Halloween costumes themselves spike in popularity in September and October, but the demand during other months are low. These commodities and products are seasonal, so it would be important to keep this in mind when selecting what products to feature on the online platform. Some tools such as Google Trends may be helpful in analyzing data and looking for the peak periods of searches for certain products.

Observe the Competition

Keeping an eye on competitors is a classic move of businessmen, as there is always something to learn by watching others. It may be useful to check out websites in order to see what other retailers are doing, and by studying their websites, the retailer can learn what they are doing right, and what things they may need to improve upon, and these lessons would come in useful when constructing or revising their own platforms. In addition, examining the websites of competitors would come in handy when needing to find out what gaps there are in the market, and it would help when deciding whether or not to specialize in a particular product or not, as fulfilling unmet market expectations is one way to become successful.

Analyzing Sales Outlets

Congratulations for making it this far, let's run through a quick checklist of our business so far: Market research was done, our business is legal, up and running, we settled of products to sell and have suppliers on board, what's left? It's time to actually start selling! All you now need to go is present your product to potential clients. This will be done through either one or a combination of eBay, Amazon or your own online store. Let us dissect both.

eBay.

Pros.

- *Easy to start:* All you need is simply to create an account and list your products. That's it, you are officially in business.
- *Audience:* eBay being an ecommerce giant, has millions of online buyers who frequent the site. This means that your listings will receive a lot of views and it is highly unlikely that you will not find customers out of it.
- *Free Marketing:* I mean, this is eBay we are talking about. You get to piggyback of off its platform and never need to worry about marketing or paying for traffic or even search engine optimization.

Cons.

- *Listing fees:* In the drop shipping business, margins are crucial. Listing fees are the biggest shortcoming of selling on eBay as they consume fairly large chunks of the profits.

- *Re-listing:* eBay has been likened to an auction house marketplace. This means you have to keep on monitoring your products and re-list them. The process can be automated but is not as straightforward.

- *Lack of customization:* Your listings have to follow designated eBay templates. Thus you cannot stand out.

- *One time customers:* If you are extremely likely, you will have one or two repeat customers, buts most of them will only buy from your once. The platform focuses more on the products than the sellers.

- *It cannot be termed as an asset:* When establishing a business, keep in mind that you are building an asset that has a value and can be sold later on. On eBay, you are significantly restricted and are not creating a personal brand of any sort that has value hence it cannot be sold in the future.

Amazon.

Pros.

When it comes to advantages, Amazon and eBay have pretty much the same to offer, so refer to the pros listed above and simply replace eBay for Amazon every time it pops ups. Therefore, we shall immediately jump into the disadvantages.

Cons

Similarly to pros, Amazon and eBay do share disadvantages: Amazon also charges listing fees, does not offer any customization and most of the customers are one off buyers. But here is one unique Amazon shortcoming.

- *Sales data:* Amazon is able to access and view all of your sales data. Merchants have complained that they use this to their advantage and identify great opportunities and improve on their own, eventually running third party sellers out of business from their platform.

Your Own Online Store.

If the thought of third party sites does not appeal to you then the best alternative will be to run your own online store.

Pros.

- *Control:* Since it is your online store, you are fully in control and can make decisions in regard to the shopping environment you wish to control and how to bring and add on to value to your customers.
- *Design:* Setting up an online store is absurdly easy. With platforms like Shopify, Weebly and strikingly, you can quickly customize it, add your products and voila! This could even take just one single day to set up.

- *Mobile Ready:* Almost 30% of all online buys are made via mobile. One shortcoming of eBay and Amazon is that they are generally unresponsive via mobile. A respectable online platform, Shopify for instance, will not only be responsive and look good on mobile but allow you as well to manage the business from your mobile device.

- *Fees:* A hundred percent profits. You can forget about third party fees with your own online store.

- *Value:* This here can be termed as a real business and appreciates in value over time. Which means that it could be later on be sold.

Cons

- *Traffic:* With your own online store you are entirely responsible for creating traffic towards it. This should be through extensive marketing, search engine optimization, and pay for advertising. This will definitely cost more and be long term.

We hope this chapter has helped you evaluate the available options for sales outlets. We would advise you, however, to build your own ecommerce store rather than depending on third party platforms.

The Main Players

There are several suppliers which have been Drop shipping for several years and are well established. Some of these have managed to dominate large market sectors; they can be the best way to get started in the industry as you will be selling products which are already recognized and respected. Of course, this will come as a trade off against profit margins or even restrict the method by which you can operate. You must read the terms and conditions for each supplier thoroughly to know what you are undertaking when you sign up with them. They can provide you with a doorway into the business and you can diversify or even specialize once you are established.

There are a variety of options available when establishing your business; the following four options are just some of what is possible:

Shopify

This is currently one of the biggest eCommerce sites in the world and has sections of its website dedicated to Drop shipping information; this should help anyone establish an account with them. They offer you the opportunity to set up a Drop shipping store with them and will create your domain name and hosting, allowing you to be ready to start trading in less than half an hour. You can then choose your own suppliers; including linking with Amazon or eBay and promote these products in your own site.

Shopify have their own eCommerce module and a wide range of payment options which ensure you can take payment from your customers by whichever method suits them. Shopify has been established for many years and now provides a comprehensive package which will allow you to create your own website in minutes; this site can be used to list your own products as well as for Drop shipping purposes.

It is easy to get started with them; simply visit their website and choose between a free hosting and a paid hosting; you can always upgrade later. They will then provide you with step by step instructions to create your site and get started. Alternatively you can use the eCommerce products supplied by their website on your own site, hosted elsewhere; this will allow you to take funds quickly and easily from any customer, it will also cover all the legal requirements regarding data storage and personal information.

It started in 2004 and has grown to become one of the best platforms in the world to run your own online store from; it is even the preferred service for Amazon merchant users. The site has been complemented many times thanks to how easy it is to use and how well the site functions. You can customize almost any part of it by simply dragging and dropping; allowing your site to be genuinely unique. Perhaps, most importantly when starting your Drop shipping business, this payment collection service can be integrated with a Shopify website and provide you with a professional looking and welcoming website without the need to set up your own website. Shopify is capable of dealing with all your customers needs; whether Drop shipping or selling your own products.

Private Label

This is a clever part of the Drop shipping business which makes it easier for both the wholesaler and you. If you are just starting out in Drop shipping you should be looking to build a well recognized brand; one that is respected and known by thousands of people. The first step in doing this is sourcing quality products to sell; these are products which will provide satisfaction to the buyer and will not break easily.

The second, most important step in this process is to make your name known to your buyers and prospective buyers. The more people who know your business name the better in terms of sales. This can be aided by your chosen Drop shipping firms sending items via 'Private Label'. This system allows your customer to order from you; the order is then sent to your wholesale supplier who sends the product directly to the customer. Private label refers to the fact that the product is sent with your address details; the customer will believe that you have sent them the parcel and, if they have any issues, they will contact you. Perhaps the best part of this system is that you can build the name of your business; people do not need to know where exactly the product came from. Providing they believe it was from you and that you offer excellent customer service.

The supplier, for their part, is happy to promote this method of shipping as you will need to deal with customer issues and they will not have to become involved.

Private labelling is also a useful tool to those who are building their own inventory; it is possible to order make-up, skin care products or even phone charger cases which are blank and can have you own logo put onto them. This will allow you to sell your own stock, with your own brand name and build a reputation for yourself. Of course, you will need to research and confirm that the product is of good quality and represents good value for money. This option moves away from the traditional Drop shipping model and means you will have to expend funds on packaging and storage, as well as buying up front. However, it can be a useful addition to your Drop shipping business; either as an additional sideline or even to help promote your business by sending a self branded product as a reward for loyalty. The product could be sent with the third order from a customer and serve to remind them daily if your business products they can get from you.

Most Drop shipping wholesalers will offer a private label service and it is well worth using; after all you need brand recognition in order to build your business.

Amazon FBA

This is Amazon's offering to anyone building a business or even running an established business. It provides an opportunity to utilize Amazon's reputation for world class service without having to pay directly for it! However, this service is not designed for dropshippers. To use this service you must be able to send a number of your products lines to Amazon. When an order is placed, Amazon will be able to send out your products for you; directly from one of their fulfilment centres. The FBA stands for Fulfilled By Amazon and is designed to allow you access to Amazon's delivery service as well as their reputation for excellent service.

Only items which you have already dispatched to Amazon can be included in this scheme, but, the scheme will allow you access to a variety of benefits:

- All your products can be dispatched under the two day Amazon promise making them appear much more appealing to Amazon Prime customers. The great part of this offer is that an Amazon prime members get free shipping, Amazon cover the bill for this shipping so you increase the likelihood of a sale without any additional cost!

- Listing products with Amazon Fulfilment will also allow you to access the markets in Mexico and Canada; potentially opening up a whole new customer base.

- All listings display the Prime logo which allows customers to know that it includes free delivery and that all packaging, deliveries and even returns are handled by Amazon; this gives the customer more confidence when making their purchase.

- There is no minimum amount of stock you need to carry with Amazon, so although you will have to outlay in stock it does not need to be a significant amount. This is especially beneficial during the early days of any business when costs can be exceptionally tight.

- Your sales do not need to be on Amazon to benefit from the Amazon packaging and delivery service. This means that if you do need to keep an inventory at least it can all be kept at Amazon; reducing the costs of you storing your products.

- Amazon will charge you fees to cover storage and order fulfilment. The value of this will depend upon how many orders you have sent through Amazon and how many products they are looking after for you. These fees are charged as a pay as you go option which ensures you are only charged when an order is dispatched.

FBA is an excellent option for anyone establishing their own business and selling a physical product which they have purchased to resell. However, it offers little benefit to the dropshipper as it requires the purchase of stock; something that most dropshippers would not choose to do. Of course, if you are already running a business or are looking to have a more traditional retail model running in parallel to your Drop shipping model then this could be the perfect answer as it takes much of the uncertainty and stress out of running your business.

There are thirteen fulfilment centres across the United States; once your products are in any one of these centres you will be able to benefit from this Amazon service.

Retail Arbitrage

This is another system which is not directly dropshipping. The art of retail arbitrage is looking for bargains which can be sold on for a reasonable profit. This requires capital upfront and an affiliation with a good delivery firm. This is one option which can be used with Amazon FBA to save time and space; in fact, it is even possible to purchase items from Amazon to add to your own inventory; providing the price is right.

Items can be purchased from anywhere; direct from a wholesaler, online supplier or even in a physical shop. You will require the capital to purchase the stock and you will also have designed a website or suitable online store to enable you to sell the products on. The real trick to successful retail arbitrage is finding the right stock to buy at the right price. If you are considering this option the following few tips may be beneficial:

- Amazon Price checker – this is an app you can access on your phone or tablet and check what price a particular item is selling for on Amazon at the moment. This will help you to decide what price you can afford to pay for a specific product and how much profit you can expect to make on it. You should also pick up an app which will alert you to items which are restricted; there is little point in buying something for a good price if you are not allowed to sell it!

- Consider where you can purchase stock; it is unlikely you will be able to go directly to a manufacturer and get the product for a better price than a mainstream player. However, you can look at the auction companies and the same Drop shipping wholesalers that you would use to start a Drop shipping business.

- Online reward and loyalty programs will reward you for shopping with them. If you can tie in some of your retail arbitrage purchases with one of these schemes you would be able to obtain rebates through the reward scheme which can equate to a significant amount of money; effectively helping your profit margin.

- Offers and incentives; many businesses have special days when items are reduced for only a limited period. They may also have a variety of coupon codes which can be used to reduce the price of a goods or you can even get discounted gift cards; allowing your funds to go further.

- Finally, it is essential to consider where you will sell your stock. This may be dependent on what stock you purchase or are selling. If you are dealing in new items then Amazon is a good place to market your products, pre-owned or worn items can get a better response on sites such as eBay.

Choose you products carefully and don't be afraid to start with what you have. Drop shipping and retail arbitrage can work well together.

Different Methods of Drop shipping Business

There are many ways that you can do Drop shipping but, in this chapter, we will look at the most effective methods that you can try in 2020.

1 - Focus Your Time in Marketing

Many of the aspects in Drop shipping retail are automated which frees up your time in focusing solely on branding and marketing your products as well as optimizing your site.

Marketing is a money maker so from the logo, website look and feel to the tone of voice - you want all these things to sync in well so that you can convert your traffic to sales.

Learn to master the use of ads and optimize your website with specific keywords. These elements drive more traffic to your store and convert at least 2% of customers on a daily basis.

Your objective is to get more traffic to your site so that it can generate a good percentage of sales. SEO can help drive long-term sales simply by having you rank high on search engine results.

You can do this by:

1. Creating blog content
2. Optimizing your product pages
3. Updating your pages and keep it fresh

4. Using social media to optimize being found online

2 - Create Fantastic Offers

Sales, bundles, and offers are something EVERYONE loves! It not only makes you noticeable but also increases traffic to your site! If no products on your site are for sale, customers visiting your site will lack the motivation to purchase your products. However, the right product with the right deal will more likely make them purchase on your site.

Tie offers with celebrations, holidays or even create bundle packs. When customers love a product from your site, they will likely want to purchase more of it. The hardest part is to get them to purchase - after that, it is uphill all the way!

3 - Avoid Underpricing Your Products

In dropshipping, the cost of products is usually close to wholesale price and it allows you to sell your products at market value and get a nice profit. If the cost of your product is $5 then you should be selling it for $20 so you can profit.

If your prices are fair and within market value, you should be able to gain a sizeable profit from each order made on your website. Do not undercut your prices even when other retailers are doing so unless you are giving an offer or discount or a sale. Create strategies that will allow you to make more money overall.

4 - Choose ePacket

ePacket shipping is currently the fastest and most affordable Drop shipping method. It ensures quick delivery without high costs. An ePacket shipping on average would cost you under $5 for most products so this will allow you to make a profit when you sell your product at a market value.

ePacket deliveries reach customers within 7 to 10 days from the date of purchase and are by far one of the best delivery methods for dropshippers to use.

5 - Go the Extra Mile with Customer Service

Ask anyone going to a restaurant if they would go back to a restaurant if the food was mediocre but with exceptional service. Chances are that the answer would be yes. People remember more of how you made them feel and the same applies to e-commerce as well.

Offering great customer service is one of the best ways to stand out especially if you are selling the same products as other merchants out there. Your customer service can be in the form of thank you cards included in the shipping packages or it could also be points that they have accumulated from multiple purchases which entitle them to a free gift! It can also be simple things like speedy response to their issues or complaints.

Whatever you do, make your customers feel valued and appreciated - it is because of them that you are a success.

6 - Stay Active on Your Channels

You need to put in effort on a consistent and daily basis. While you do not need to spend eight hours a day working on marketing and promoting your site, you still need to commit several hours on a daily basis to ensure that your store is updated, relevant and active.

As your business grows, so will the number of hours you need to commit to processing orders, speak with your suppliers, ensure shipping is in route and orders arrive promptly to your customers.

You will also need to ensure that your marketing efforts are in line with your products and social media is one of the best ways to stay current and relevant, ensuring that you appear at least once a day in the minds of your customers.

7 - Start With at Least 30 Items on Your Site

Don't make the mistake of importing hundreds of items to your site. While it can be exciting, the problem is that adding too many products too soon may be deadly to your site. For each product you add to your site, you need to have a few quality images, product descriptions, and keywords. Doing all of this in a short span of time can be time-consuming and exhausting, especially if you are still stuck in your day job.

Adding the product incrementally, starting with 30 would be best as you can write quality descriptions and maintain focus to start your sales and understand how your audience reacts on your site. You need to get one great product to land a sale and not 100 products. Stay focused and start small, building your way up.

8 - Monitor Your Competition

As always, you need to keep your friends close and your enemies closer. Monitor your competition's social media and their websites regularly. Like their page and you'll also receive updates on their products and the promotions they have.

By paying attention to what they do, you'll also have a better idea on how to sell your products on your store. Do not rip-off content but use it as inspiration to understand what makes or breaks attention. This not only helps bring in the audience to your site, but it also helps you make you do better in marketing your own products.

Conclusion

Remember, the methods in this book, when followed correctly, can yield you amazing results when it comes to making money. However, you need to act on these methods as soon as possible to ensure that you make a great living from it sooner than later.

The last thing you want to do is to procrastinate, that will only hold you back from achieving optimal results. Once you have read and understood the chapter, act on it as soon as possible so you can get going. You will be in a much better position if you act on it as quickly as possible, as compared to waiting for the perfect storm. There will be no ideal time to act on your dreams and goals than now, so make sure you start that business and learn as you go. That is the only way to succeed.

You can read all the books that you want, but if you don't take action, then you will never perfect the skills that allow you to make money. Go ahead and pick a method from this book and start working on it. I am sure that you might fail a couple of times, but eventually, you will succeed. Remember, the difference between a winner and a loser is how many times they have failed. Both have failed, but the one who got back up is the real winner.

Amazon FBA Guide

A step-by-step beginners guide to selling on amazon using retail arbitrage.

Create your personal e-commerce to generate passive income and make money online.

Table of Contents

Description

Amazon FBA is an incredible business model that has the capacity to allow everyday people to get into a profitable home-based business for relatively cheap. Due to the improved services being made available by both Amazon and suppliers like Alibaba, getting involved in a business like this is easier than ever before.

Depending on how you want to run your business, you can be as hands-off or hands-on as you want with Amazon FBA. You can choose to have Amazon completely run everything by having them manage fulfillment and paying them to manage your advertisements if you wanted. In this case, all you would have to do is purchase products and upload your product descriptions, as well as manage your advertisements. Or, if you wanted to be more hands-on, you could take advantage of all of these features and run your own organic promotional efforts through social media. There truly is no limit on how you can run your business and how involved or passive it can be.

One of the greatest things about Amazon FBA is that it is a business that you can start on the side of whatever else you are doing in your life. Because so much of the heavy lifting is being done by Amazon, you can begin your business while you are still working full-time elsewhere or even while you are running your own business completely separate of your Amazon FBA business. The versatility here is incredible and offers the opportunity for many people to shift their income from being primarily linear or earned from a job to being primarily online or earned through Amazon FBA. Many people even quit their jobs and other businesses entirely as they earn $10,000+ per month through Amazon FBA, which results in them not truly having to do anything else anyway.

This guide will focus on the following:

- Ideas and validating them
- Why choose amazon to sell your product?
- Identifying products to sell
- Sourcing products
- Private labeling with amazon
- Setting up a seller account
- Understanding seller central and FBA fees
- Listing products on amazon seller central
- Launching products with amazon
- Understanding seller central and FBA fees
- Fulfillment by amazon
- Using platforms to sell products through amazon FBA
- Increasing sales with marketing... AND MORE!!!

Introduction

With all the big buzz of Fulfillment by Amazon, some sellers may be wondering: FBA is just another fulfillment method, isn't it? What's all this talk about the use of FBA? Basically, What's the big deal about FBA?

FBA becomes a big deal once you realize the amount of support it can place on your online business. For some, it becomes a major decision in their business in terms of profit that they will be making during their online career.

Those who may get to feel the best effect of the FBA are those who are small business owners, these people may not have the most efficient fulfillment systems in their arsenal and may not want to risk any potential negative effects from a poor customer experience.

Although there are plenty amounts of benefits that a seller can gain from using FBA, you should also never forget the following:

•   Not every third-party seller should use FBA; it all really depends on the individual seller's financial resources as well as the nature of his or her business.

•   Sellers should look at FBA as another weapon in their arsenal and not as a blanket resource. Sellers should either be

100% FBA or 100% FBM (Fulfillment by Merchant), although most professional sellers have become a hybrid of both

Not all the products that have been submitted for FBA will end up being a good candidate for a number of reasons, mainly size, performance of their sales and their margin.

The reason why this guide might sound philosophical is that the only way you will see success with this Amazon FBA is if you do it consistently. For you to do that, you need to change your current lifestyle by being more productive and disciplined. You have to remember that healthy eating is for more than just an Amazon FBA; it's a lifestyle.

Plan your day ahead

Planning your day ahead of time is crucial, not only does planning out your day help you be more prepared for your day moving forward, but it will also help you to become more aware of the things you shouldn't be doing, hence That are wasting your time.

Moreover, planning your day will truly help you with making the most out of your time. That being said, we will talk about two things:

- Benefits of planning out your day
- How to go about planning out your day

So, without further ado, let us dive into the benefits of planning out your day.

It will help you prioritize

Yes, planning out your day will help you prioritize a lot of things in your day-to-day life. You can allocate time limits to the things you want to work on the most to least, for example, if you're going to write your book and you are super serious about it. Then you need a specific time limit every day in which you work on a task wholeheartedly without any worries of other things until the time is up. Then you move on to the next job in line, so when you schedule out your whole day and you give yourself time limits, then you can prioritize your entire day. The same thing goes for your Amazon FBA, make sure you allocate time for prepping your plans for the next day, which will allow you to have goals ready for you when you need it, hence making it easy for you to continue on with your Amazon FBA.

More focus on the task on hand

This point is quite similar to the previous point, as once you have started to plan out your day you have become more aware of the things that you are about to do. With the time limit on all tasks that you do daily, it will create an urgency to get as much of the job done as you can before time is up and you are moving on to your next appointment. Which will help you be more focused on the task at hand and get more things done. Many people consider planning your day out to be time-consuming, which it isn't if you prioritize your time the right way. If you plan your goals the day before, then it should not be a problem.

Work-Life Balance

You see, once you start planning out your whole day, you become more aware of your time and how to balance it out. Once you begin to write out your entire day ahead of you, you will know precisely what you are doing that day so you don't have to do anything sporadically throughout the day. Always plan some time for yourself every day where you can wind down, read a good book, meditate, or maybe hang out with your friends. You will feel refreshed the next day. Having to wind down and "chill out" will only make you a more productive person.

Planning out your whole day ahead will not only help you prioritize better. It will also help you be more focused on your task on hand and will help you have a better work-life balance. This will help you to stay motivated with the Amazon FBA that you are following. So now that we have discovered the benefits of planning out your day, let's dive into the how-to's when it comes to planning out your day.

Summarize your Normal Day

Now, before we start getting into planning out your whole day, you need to realize that to plan your entire day, you need to know precisely what you are doing that day. Which means you need to write down every single thing you do on a typical day and write down the time you start and end. It needs to be detailed in terms of how long it takes for your transportation to get to work, etc.

Now after you have figured out your whole day, you can decide how to prioritize your day. It could be cutting out a task that you don't require or shortening your time for a job that doesn't need that much time. After you have your priorities for the day, you can add pleasurable tasks into your day like hanging out with your friends, etc.

Arrange your Day

It is crucial that you arrange your day correctly, so the best way to organize your day is to make sure you get all your essential stuff done earlier in the day when your mind is fresh. After that's done, you can have some time for yourself to relax and do whatever it is that you want. But make sure you get done all the things that need to be done before you move on to free time for yourself. Another thing that will help you is to set time limits on each task, and once you start setting time limits, you will be more likely to get the job done.

Remove all the Fluff

So, what I mean by that is to remove all the things that are holding you back from achieving your goals. Make sure you remove all of the things that are holding you back from getting on with the things that you need to be doing. If you have time for the fluff, do it; if not, then work on your priorities first. In conclusion, planning out your day will help you tremendously! Make sure you plan out your day every day to ensure successful and accomplished days.

Be Grateful

We will be talking about how to be grateful and what the benefits are of being thankful for what you have! Now, believe it or not, being grateful every day will help you get more things done while keeping your mood elevated. See, when you're thankful for the things you have, you will start to feel like your mind is full of peace and joy. When your mind is in order and comfort, you will be more productive with all the tasks ahead of you that day. Being in a grateful state of mind will help you become less stressed and more positive, which will help your work quality tenfold. So, it is pretty essential that you stay grateful not only for better work performance but to also to be in a peaceful state of mind. This will also help you to do more positive things with your Amazon FBA. Let's discuss the three main benefits of being thankful.

Helps you start your day

Of course, if you start your day in a happy mood, you will more likely be keen to do more stuff and be more productive. If you read up on the most dedicated people and their day-to-day lives, you will know that successful people tend to practice the same habits which I am going to be talking about in this chapter. The benefit of saying things you are grateful for first thing in the morning will boost your positive vibes. When you talk about the things you're thankful for, you will complain a lot less and attract fewer negative vibes which is something we don't want! You always want to be in a positive mood as much as you can. To make sure you are in a positive vibe, write or say things you are grateful towards.

You will become more approachable

Yes, being grateful will make you more approachable! Believe it or not, people do sense your "vibes" when you walk in through the door. When you're more thankful about life, you are happier and more positive, which is what people want to be around. Who knows, the next person you see could be an opportunity for you to grow your business or get a new job! So, always make sure you are in a great mood and counting your blessings still, as good things will come to you.

Lowered Stress Levels

I think this point is very self-explanatory. Let me ask you this - what are most people stressed about? Lack of resources, plain and straightforward. A lack of resources creates 99% of the stress. Once you start counting what you have rather than what you don't have, you begin to become a lot less stressed, which is suitable for your physical and mental health! So, make sure you always stay in a grateful mood. If you want to understand more about how being grateful can change your life, I recommend reading "The Magic" by Rhonda Byrne.

So, all in all, being grateful will help you to live a better life and be more successful. Now you might be wondering how to be thankful throughout the day since it is so hard to block out ungrateful thoughts. Well, I'll show you three techniques that will help you combat your ungrateful thoughts and keep you in a grateful "vibe" most of your life.

Write ten things you are grateful for every morning

You see, writing what you are thankful for will make your life a lot easier and help you start your day in gratitude. What I want you to do is first get a notebook/diary, and as soon as you wake up, I want you to write ten things you're grateful for. This could be anything from something as small as having water to drink to having a nice car. The whole point of this is to make you start your day in gratitude as the way you start your day is the way your entire day is going to be, most of the time. So, make sure to start your day on the right foot by writing down ten things you're grateful towards.

Don't forget the 1:5 ratio

This is something I came up with, and it works great for me. You see whenever I say something I am angry about or not grateful for, I always say five things I am super thankful for right after to get myself into the grateful "vibe." In the beginning, this method will be your best friend as it will save you from killing your "vibe."

Cut out negative people

This task might be the hardest to do, but it is quite essential as the people who you are around are the people who will create your personality. So if you are around negative people, you will develop adverse circumstances for yourself, so if you are around people who are not upbeat about life and who find everything wrong and never see the good in anyone, you need to cut them out and be around people who are happy and ready for what life has to offer. Now I get it, some cynical people can be your family members, and you can't cut them out, the best thing to do is make them understand what they are doing wrong and show them how they can change their life. And if they still want to remain the same, then keep your distance.

In conclusion, it is essential that you are in a grateful "vibe" as it will not only help you with your mental and physical health, but it will also help you attract better people and better circumstances. Don't forget to practice the three methods we discussed in this chapter to be in a grateful 'vibe" throughout the day and life! That being said, I hope this chapter sheds some light on the importance of being grateful and how it can make or break your life. Also, I hope you don't take this chapter lightly because being grateful is the most critical thing you can do to turn your life around. So be thankful!

Now that we have covered the part of being grateful and how it can help you with your day-to-day life let us give you some concrete ideas on how to change the way you live your experience and how to make it better.

Stop Multitasking

I think we are all guilty of this at a time, and if you are multitasking right now, I need you to stop. Multitasking could be a lot of things. It could be as small as cooking and texting at the same time or it could be as big as working on two projects at the same time. Studies are showing how multitasking can reduce your quality of work, which is something you don't want to do if your goal is to get the best result out of the thing that you are doing. That being said, there are a lot more reasons as to why you shouldn't be multitasking, so without further ado, let's dive into the primary reasons why multitasking can be harmful.

You're not as Productive

Believe it or not, you tend to be a lot less productive when you are multitasking. When you go from one project to another, you don't put all your effort into your work. You are always worried about the project that you will be moving into next. So, moving back and forth from one project to another will definitely affect your productivity. If you want to get the most out of your work, you need to be focused on one thing at a time and make sure you get it done to the best of your abilities. Plus you are more likely to make mistakes, which will not help you work at the best of your ability.

You Become Slower at your Work

When you are multitasking, the chances are you will end up being slower at completing your projects. You would be in a better position if you were to focus on one project at a time instead of going back and forth, which, of course, helps you complete each project faster. So, the thing that enables you to be faster at your projects when you're not multitasking is the mindset. We often don't realize how much mindset comes into play. When you are going back and forth from one project to another, you are in a different mental state by going into another project which takes the time to build and break. So, by the time you have managed to get into the mindset of project A, you are already moving into project B. It is always best that you devote your time and energy to one project at a time if you want it to do it at a faster pace.

Affects your Creativity

This is a significant disadvantage of multitasking. Studies are showing that multitasking can negatively affect your creativity. When something requires too much focus from your end, it becomes harmful to your creativity, and you need a lot more attention when multitasking when compared to working on one thing at a time. If you want to succeed and live a better life, then you need to be creative, so if multitasking affects your creativity, then you need to stop doing that.

By now, you can see how multitasking can hinder the ability for you to work at your best. These three things listed above are a no-no when it comes to living a better and more productive life; not only does multitasking not help you to be prolific, but it also makes you slower and less creative. So, all the benefits you thought you were getting multitasking were not accurate after all. Nonetheless, by now, you might be wondering how to go about working most efficiently. Well, the best way to put it is to work on one project at a time. I want you to put all your time and energy into the project you are doing currently and not worry about other projects. Make sure you set goals when you start the project which will help you be more efficient and faster at your work. An example would be "you will not move on to another project until project A has been completed" or you have managed to hit a certain threshold at that specific project.

So, to sum it all up:

- Do one Project at a Time
- Don't move on until it is completed or you have managed to hit a certain threshold.
- Set yourself a goal (time, quality, etc.)

All in all, multitasking will do you no good. It will only make you slower at your work and make you less productive. Making sure you stop multitasking is essential, as it will only help you live a better life. One thing to remember from this chapter is to put all your energy to one thing at a time, and this will yield you a lot of better projects or anything that you are working towards to be great. If you want to be more successful and live a better life, you need to make sure your projects are of a high quality as I can't stress this point enough. You are probably reading this book because you want to get better at living your life or achieve goals that you just haven't reached yet. One of the reasons why you are not living the life that you want or haven't reached your goal could be a lot of things, but one of the items could be the quality of your work which could be taking a hit because of your multitasking. So, review yourself and find out why you haven't achieved your goal and why you are not living the life that you want.

Then, if you happen to stumble upon multitasking being the limiting factor of the quality of your work, I want you to stop multitasking and start working on one project at a time while giving it your full attention. What you will notice is that your work will have a higher quality and will be completed in a quicker amount of time following the steps listed above, which will change your life and help you to achieve your life goals in a better more efficient way.

After reading this chapter, many might be thinking that this is more of a self-help book than it is an Amazon FBA book. The truth is that we want you to understand how to live a better life by changing the habits that you are currently following. Truth be told, following an Amazon FBA and making it a lifestyle is a lot more work than you think it is. For you to make it easy, you need to understand that you need to change your habits in order to be successful at this Amazon FBA, which means you need to change the way you move, the way you think, and the way you perform. This chapter gives you a clear idea on how to start living a better life by changing up your habits. Once you do change your practices, you will notice that following the Amazon FBA as a whole will be very easy for you. The reason why it will be straightforward for you is that you will change the way you move and change the way you live your life in general. Changing the way you live your life will not only help you get better results, but it will also help you to follow this Amazon FBA as a lifestyle. Many people think Amazon FBA is not being a part of a lifestyle, and it is not something that they're supporting to better their health. But the truth is that when they're following an Amazon FBA, they don't realize that it needs to be a lifestyle for it to be a health benefit. If you want to be healthier, then you need to make sure that you're taking care of your health 24/7 365 days a year.

You need to make this a lifestyle, and for you to make this a lifestyle, we need to understand some self-help techniques to keep it sustained for a more extended period. This is why this chapter is more self-help oriented.

We wanted to make sure that this book is different than any other books that you've read when it comes to following the Amazon FBA.

With that being said, I hope this chapter was helpful to you.

Chapter 1 Ideas and Validating Them

We've explored some simple ways in which you can get those creative juices flowing, and how to generate your potential Amazon product ideas for the next step in the process. Here we'll see if your idea has any value, or if it is better to let others take their chance on them. This will be the final step in accepting your idea for your niche and entering the market.

Assessing ideas offers background research you perform in determining if your ideas do have value.

To do this, there are a number of criterions used in assessing your ideas such as:

- Demand
- Profit
- Passion
- Competition
- Customer Lifetime Value

Product Demand

This is the first criteria, and is one of the most important. Actually, no demand means no customers are searching for the product, and you'll find it nearly impossible to make a profit if this is the case.

The best products to supply are ones which have a high demand, and this is where there are a vast number of people who are searching for the exact same product. If you finally end up providing one of these high demand products which users use in everyday life, you'll quickly see your business becoming successful.

Everything begins with demand, and that's why it is the chief criteria. When you take a look at demand, it can be broken down further into three other criterions, which helps determine the demand for the product. The first demand criteria is revenue, which is earned from your product, and you can decide if any chosen product is in high demand if it's making sales for your competitors.

If sales are being made in the niche, it means there is still a significant profit to be made when selling that specific product. If there happens to be another seller entering into the niche, such as yourself, you should be able to take a piece of the action and a share of the market, unless it's totally swamped.

Uptrend data is the next criteria where specific niches will experience an increase in sales, as well as downward trends in the popularity of a product throughout a year. Some products are hot sales in the early months of the year, only to be sat waiting for buyers over the next few months. An excellent recent example of this is the fidget spinner, and during the middle of 2017, they were immensely popular. Many resellers jumped on the craze to make money from the trend, only to find this craze waned, and so they were left with too much stock which could not be sold.

It shows that many of these resellers might not have focused on the downward trend toward the year's end. Much is the same with seasonal products being stocked. A primary example here, being: items which are popular in the lead up to Christmas, but at other times sales become flat. It's crucial you keep an eye on these trends and see how they react over a period, and you need to consider how long a trend would remain in force.

The next and final criteria can be a way of validating the previous two as a way to determine the overall demand for a product. If you use the 10-4 rule, you can see which products experience strong demand, and for how long this demand stays in place. It is possible (when selling products cheaply) to boost their rankings. However, this would fudge the data and products would not be selling as well if they were to remain at their regular price.

To explain the 10-4 rule goes like this: The four in the rule represents four thousand dollars, and it means two to three products should be making sales of around four thousand dollars per month.

Product Competition

Competition can be seen as the direct antithesis of demand, and when there is high demand for products, there is lots of competition. There is a delicate balance which must be understood before you enter a market. If the balance swings toward a supplier, there will be too much competition for the demand. This is where the market is saturated, and prices become slashed to shift product. As a result, profit margins fall to unhealthy levels.

On the contrary, where there is high demand and little competition, you will find that this is where there is serious money to be made from your products. With this in mind, you need to find the place in your niche where you can work with lower than average competition, and this way, everyone can share the profits within the niche.

You can validate your competition on Amazon by performing a simple rule, and then find if the niche is desirable to enter. What you do is take three by a hundred, three hundred. Let me explain. What this means is you need three products to be on the first page which have less than 100 reviews, and you will also want an average of lower than 300 reviews on the first page.

The reason for this is: you want your product listing to be showing on the first page of Amazon (compared to being a few pages in) after a search has been conducted. As with many things in search, people will use items listed on the first page, and not venture further down the list of results.

When you have products which are competing against ones which have less than 100 reviews, it means you can reach that number in a short time and, in effect, leapfrog your customers and rank higher in the Amazon search. Eventually, this would lead you to receive more sales. You need to be aware though, it is of little use competing with anyone whose product has thousands of reviews, because this is an indication their sales position is too strong, and it would be challenging for you to enter the market with any amount of success.

You can see this in markets which contain sportswear, and the items are branded, and it isn't too hard to understand there is no way you can compete with this at the same price and quality. It is for reasons such as this that you'll need to drill down further into niches, and then you can create a market for products which are not holding any significant players.

This rule is flexible, and how you use it is at your discretion. However, around 300 is the general rule to give a good indication the product you're researching is in high demand, while at the same time not having a significant brand to contend with.

It is unfortunate that the higher the amount of competition, the less profit you can make, but keep in mind, areas which have high profit and little competition typically don't last that long. As you are researching your niche, other resellers are doing the same, so any niches which are wide open and ripe for entering won't last long before competition creeps into them. Keep this in mind.

When you are conducting your research, you should take this as motivation to exploit these areas in as quick a time as is possible, and take full advantage of the profitable areas while they are still there for the taking. You can also differentiate the competition as a means of boosting your potential in taking a much higher percentage of the market share. You can do this through development and innovation of your products, and this; we will go into in much broader detail later in the title.

Product Profit

Profitability is the third part of validating a product and is essential for any Amazon business to continue, and to make sure there is a healthy return on investment. The last thing anyone wants is: to invest a heap of cash and effort in bringing products to market, only to find that they are not as profitable as first hoped. When this happens, the worst case scenario is that there will be a loss, and a best case is you can get back any money you have invested... hopefully.

This is one crucial element which shouldn't be left to chance, so, due diligence and research are essential in this area before you commit to supplying products on Amazon. With this in mind, Amazon has created an official calculator which you can make use of on their website. As it's been designed by them, it is perfectly poised to let you know the exact amount of money you can make from each sale that you create by using Amazon. To begin, you would open Jungle Scout. For this quick example, we will use dining and kitchen. The price range which we will investigate is $14 to $50, between 1 thru 2500. Here, we will sort by pricing. One of the first things you'll notice will be around half a million per month, and at this stage, you should open up the item listing and check the average price for that specific keyword or for the particular item it relates to.

At this point, you should check a few prices, because it is possible that some prices have been overinflated or they have been underpriced. Once you have hold of this information, insert it into the data section and then head to the wholesale site which you have decided to use. This could be either:

- Alibaba
- Salehoo
- Oberlo

These are examples.

Use these (or any others from which you have chosen), then you will search for the exact same items on these sites, and make sure that the data is an exact match. Once you search for an average price, you might find some products are coming with accessories, so these should be avoided as the information won't be an exact match, and any calculation you make will not be correct.

When you have found the average price of the exact product on these sites, you enter this into Amazon's calculator, and it will return the result of what you stand to make after all fees have been paid. Amazon's calculator will show (in detail) the costs. However, you are able to customize this to fall in line with how you plan on running your business.

Areas you need to consider are:

- Warehousing
- Shipping from your supplier
- Transportation to and from Amazon
- Advertising

Ideally, if you can make a substantial profit straight away, that is best. By using their calculator with all your costs inputted, you can receive an estimate of the net profit you could make with each sale.

As a note, any products under $10 aren't worth selling on Amazon, mostly due to the imposed fees and shipping costs which will quickly eat away at the tiny profit you might make.

When you use the calculator, you will see which of the products offer a potentially high-profit margin, along with ones which are best to leave alone, as they come with a high amount of risk. If you find your overall revenue is three times that of your purchase price, you stand to make a decent amount of profit with your products after all the fees and costs have been taken into account. When you come to examine profit, make sure to consider any other factors you're using when you are attempting to validate your product, as these will play a crucial part in how your products are going to perform.

In addition to all this, you could think that products which have a lower than average profit margin are risky to undertake, however, if you can see there are masses of demand, it could be a product which people are continually looking for. With this in mind, a product of this type could sell more volume than products which have higher profit margins, yet a lower demand.

Note: research plenty of items before you arrive at your final decision, especially when it comes to your profitability. You will have lots that you need to consider. You might come to find a product isn't selling well on Amazon, yet it has high potential so it might have a good reason behind it.

Feed Your Passion

Have you ever noticed some of the world's wealthiest people continue working well into their golden years when they could be enjoying the fruits of their labors? We know they don't need the money, and retirement isn't an issue to them. They do it because they love what they do, and they continue to do so as long as they can, because of their passion.

You'll find that if you do something purely for the money, any passion will quickly wane as there is no pleasure factor in what you are doing, or hoping to achieve. Material gains which take a lot of effort are never enough to satisfy anyone. That's a whole other book, so I'll let you discern your opinion on that topic.

It's often overlooked, but passion is one of the most crucial aspects of creating a successful Amazon business. If you're not enjoying what you're doing, you won't overcome any of the challenges you'll meet head-on. You stand a much higher chance of success if you have a passion for your product, and are possibly a user of it, yourself. This can present new ways in which to improve it, and what you can do when something goes wrong, and this you'll find is really useful when you get to your customer service aspect.

Finding this passion isn't the most natural thing to do, and for some people, it takes years before they come to discover what it is they love. Rather than waiting for all these years, you can ask yourself two questions which will help you determine what your ultimate products will be.

"What interests and hobbies do you enjoy the most?"

And the second question is:

"If you made no money, what sort of product would you launch?"

These two questions find what you have a passion for, and with regard to the second question, it takes money out of the equation as a motivator and will leave behind the natural emotion to your products. It will also open up the bigger picture in revealing what your real motivation is, in terms of launching a product. Yes, a product that you can improve and provide; one that's better than the competitors.

A profitable niche can be around for a while, but as soon as you find a competitor begins offering a comparable product which is an improvement over yours, you might have seen there is no will or incentive to carry on. In a best-case scenario, if you have no passion, you'll see yourself starting from scratch again. So passion can help to concrete your business.

Long-Term Customer Value

Although this isn't something of much consideration to new sellers on Amazon, it is one of the most crucial aspects, and one of the more overlooked areas in business.

Once you've started looking for products to market, you shouldn't only be looking at making a short-term profit. Instead, you should be looking at the long-term for your products which will sell, and you can build a well-known brand around this concept. When this happens, you can scale your business to heights you never considered, and continually build what you've created, compared to having a product which sells loads for only a few months. If this is the way your business runs, it isn't efficient. You will also find, this is the time you hit that plateau, and your sales never increase past a certain level.

It is ideal to search for a niche which you can introduce 3 to 5 profitable products; from which you can build your brand of loyalty. All of these products don't have to make enormous amounts of profit, as the point is; this group of products is all about building your brand image for the business you have created. From this group, you might have two standout products which bring in around 80% of your profit. Nonetheless, the idea here is that once you've launched your first products and built up an email list of loyal customers, they will be keen for your next product launch/es.

For reference, it has been shown that it is around seven times easier to sell to an existing customer than selling to a new one, and this is the reason you can leverage an existing customer base above your competition when you release a new product within the same niche. To go along with this, when you release a product which is somewhat related to your others, you can use the same marketing techniques which you already have in place from the release of your other products.

To enforce this, we'll take a look at an example. If we were looking to supply splatter guards inside a kitchen niche, we should take a look at what other products these buyers have been purchasing or viewing. This can open up avenues of where to explore next, and you might notice there are abundant products which go along with splatter guards for use in the kitchen. You can choose from pan sets, chopping boards, knives, and many more useful kitchen implements.

Now, for the purposes of this example, where a customer has purchased a splatter guard, and they were on the lookout for another item, if they were presented with this item under your brand, they'd be more inclined to purchase the same brand. Usually, they want to maintain consistency of the product line because they like the brand. And, if they purchased from you before, they'll be more likely to do this again.

Overall focus should be on the business as a whole, and brand ideas compared to single items which will lead nowhere. This will open up avenues of thought of how you can group these products into building your brand. The number of products you supply doesn't need to be five, but it can be a good base on which to start, and from here you can leverage your customers and meet their needs.

Mistakes You Should Avoid

No one is perfect when they are new to any business. Actually, there are plenty of factors you need to consider, and a good few can easily be overlooked. Any new seller should learn from the mistakes of past sellers who have been through it before and come out the other end with a solution to the problem. Here, we'll take a look at some mistakes sellers make which are common ones that can easily be avoided by being aware of them.

Although typical, these mistakes can have an adverse effect on your business, and it's crucial you try your hardest not to fall into the same trap and make the same mistakes. With foresight, there is no reason to make these mistakes and end up wasting your time and resources.

Products Which are Oversized

Amazon stipulates product sizes that sellers should use as a maximum. Anything larger than this and extra storage charges will be due. Always check these size preferences on the Amazon site before stocking up. You can obtain all the item dimensions from their website, or by typing into Google "oversized products on Amazon." This also gives the charges which would be due if your item fell outside of the guidelines.

FBA fulfillment goes in-depth into all of what you should do, and what happens when you don't regard your product sizes. This can be a simple thing which is overlooked, and a product which ends up too big or too heavy will have extra charges, and these could quickly eat into any profits that you make.

Gated Categories

There are specific products which require additional checking, qualifications, and reviews before they can be fulfilled by Amazon. A product can't merely come from any supplier, and it is a best practice to contact Amazon ahead of schedule, just to make sure your supplier is a trusted one. A prime example is men's watches which are sold under the jewelry section. For this, there are additional requirements you need to comply with before selling in that particular category.

With this, it might appear to be negative, however, it can go a long way to providing protection against competition. Although you need to fulfill these extra requirements, it means they also do; now any reseller can't approach a niche and simply begin selling, not when it is gated.

Product Patents

This can cause sellers significant headaches when they are selling products on Amazon. It might be the case that their product is selling well and the business is growing. After a while, a notice is received which states the product they are selling is patented in the USA. This could lead to the product being withdrawn and the listing removed from Amazon. At this point, income will stop, and the reseller is left with unsold stock, and their storage charges will mount up.

So, to make sure you never fall for this, another Google search can be completed, this time through google.com/patents. What you are presented with is a valuable resource which you can view. As a consideration, if you are serious about your Amazon business and are at the point of investing a few thousand dollars, it might be beneficial to hire the services of a patent lawyer who can do these searches on your behalf. The cost for this could be a few hundred dollars leading up to the thousands; however, if you are looking to invest more than this, it is worth the cost, rather than seeing your business come to a standstill.

If your product is one in which you are doing the importing, it is wise to perform your own searches. Trademarks are another thing to consider during any patent searches. These are much the same as patents and can have the same effect on your business. These can easily be searched for using USPTO. Here, you can search brand names and slogans which might appear to be similar to yours, and so infringing on their rights.

Supplier Sourcing

Later, we will be going through the sourcing of a supplier. However, it is still an area that some sellers have difficulty doing. The entire process of dealing with a supplier should never be hard or overly stressful.

As an example, if you intend to sell printed pet items ready for Christmas and spend plenty of time sourcing suppliers; it can be a major red flag when none of them offer to print the collars that you asked to be printed. So, do a test first to be sure they are reliable. Check out their reviews, call them. Make sure they have a fantastic reputation.

There are more than enough suppliers around who sell the right products, allowing you to change and adapt to times like these at Christmas.

As soon as you hit some slight resistance, you shouldn't consider giving in. Instead, it should mean you are attempting to push your business onward and upward, rather than hitting a brick wall on every corner you take. The only instance where these products should be considered is: if they are highly profitable and the research you've conducted supports this. And so, it might be something worth pursuing. One thing to keep in the back of your mind is; that every day you are not selling the high levels of volume you expected is another day you're losing your revenue, which shouldn't be taken lightly. This is especially true on a fast-paced platform like Amazon.

Chapter 2 Why Choose Amazon to Sell Your Product?

More "Warehouse" Space

For large-scale sellers that want to work from home, the issue of warehouse space becomes an apparent thorn in their side. You simply cannot stock hundreds of items when your living space doesn't allow for it, and even if it does, it may make living there a bit uncomfortable. With FBA, this is no longer a huge concern since you will be able to ship all of your items to them in large packages, and they will store the items for you until sales are made. This means that your home isn't cluttered.

Access to International Marketplace

Amazon offers an international marketplace for you to ship to, and when you ship with Amazon FBA you get access to that marketplace without having to worry about varying shipping costs. Instead, Amazon takes care of that for you! Whether you want to ship to Canada, the United States, Mexico, or anywhere within North America. This increases your product reach and gives you even more opportunity to sell, with a higher number of potential buyers who may be interested in your products.

Amazon Oversees Customer Service and Returns

When you ship with Amazon FBA, Amazon takes over the responsibility for seeing to your customer service and returns associated with your products and shipments. This means that all you really have to do is pick products, manage production and manage your product listings. Everything else associated with the product and shipments is managed by Amazon.

A Prime Logo

All Amazon FBA merchants are provided with the exclusive Amazon Prime logo on their listings. This means that Amazon Prime members who are shopping for your products will know right away that they get access to all of their sweet membership-exclusive opportunities with your product listings. It is just like having a business-exclusive membership without having to oversee the membership program or processes!

Speedy Growth Opportunities

Since Amazon FBA oversees a great deal of the work involved with managing your products and shipping, it takes a lot of work off of you. That means that you can simply focus on choosing products and having them produced and sent to an Amazon FBA warehouse for Amazon to do the rest. Without you having to worry about so much of the business processes, you can focus more on the development of your business and getting the word out there! That means you can grow your business quickly and with minimal effort on your own behalf!

Easy, Cost Effective Business Model

When you are running a brick and mortar business, you have to worry about a significant amount of overhead. When you are running a regular online business, you still have a great deal of overhead when you factor in inventory storage and shipping costs. However, when you have an Amazon FBA business, your cost reduces significantly. Instead of paying for each individual shipment, and to store all of your products, you get to pay a single fee for all of this.

Inventory Storage and Shipping Services

As you have likely already gathered, the biggest benefit to Amazon FBA is that you have your storage covered and your shipping services covered. You do not have to worry about storing your products or ensuring that they are stored safely and appropriately. You do not have to worry about paying for larger storage lockers whenever your inventory levels grow, or paying extra for storage space you are not using on months when you have less inventory. You also don't have to worry about paying the enormous tab that comes with running a shipment business.

Less Manual Labor

Perhaps more importantly, the task of selling products, packaging products, and shipping products is very, very time-consuming. This is especially true for those working alone. To combat this, the solution is a service like FBA. When an item is sold, they take your products, package them in Amazon packaging, and ship them to the customer for you. This saved time and workload means you can focus more on expanding the business and less on packing boxes and making trips to the post office or other carriers.

Fast and Free Shipping

One of the great perks of Fulfillment by Amazon is that items packaged and shipped by Amazon are going to qualify for their free shipping promotions. Currently, this promotion requires that customers purchase at least $49 of qualifying products. This often leads to additional sales. What that means for a seller is that those that handle their own shipping individually will often be passed up by the buyer attempting to purchase an add-on item to bump up the order total to allow for free shipping.

Sit Back and Relax

Another great perk of taking advantage of FBA is that you really don't need to be working at all to be earning money on the products you have already had shipped to the fulfillment center. In a traditional ecommerce setup where the seller is also the shipper, the seller cannot take long periods of time away from work since they cannot avoid the need to package and ship items. It doesn't matter if you're on vacation, sleep too late in the day to go to the post office, or if you prefer to spend your time at the bowling alley instead. As you're sitting around enjoying a cold beverage and a good meal, Amazon is selling and shipping your products on your behalf. For those that wish to setup multiple income streams or are still working a "real job," this means that you're effectively still earning so long as there are still products at the Amazon warehouse that are selling. Doesn't that sound nice?

Fast and Timely Delivery

Delivery time is one factor that will sometimes make or break a sale. Customers buy items online and they want these to reach them in the shortest amount of time. With Amazon FBA, your items will have the benefit of faster shipping times. This faster delivery time is attributed to your items being eligible for Amazon Prime; it gives your items a free two-day delivery feature. On top of that, it will also make your items eligible for 24/7 customer service and delivery tracking.

Since the items are shipped from Amazon fulfillment centers, they process and ship quicker. This is way faster than having the item come from the seller directly. You can leverage on Amazon's proven track-record of quality customer service so you can be rest assured that shoppers can depend on helpful assistance.

Taking Advantage of Amazon's Reputation and Brand

This is the core of the entire concept of Fulfillment by Amazon. You as a third-party seller are basically leveraging Amazon's technology, process, reputation, and customer base to increase your business. Amazon has established itself as a household brand that denotes excellent customer service and ease of shopping online. Similar to franchising, Amazon FBA puts your business in line with the Amazon brand and lets you borrow Amazon's outstanding reputation.

This is definitely the best benefit that you can get out of Amazon FBA, especially if you are just running a small start-up business.

Simplicity

The interface that Amazon uses is favored for its simplicity and reputation. If you compare this to any other popular e-commerce website, you will notice that Amazon's platform is far superior, efficient, and well-suited for all professional sellers. You won't need to deal with different platforms like PayPal. You can easily eliminate the hassle of shipping the products yourself and managing your listings and your fees. You don't even have to shoot photographs of the products yourself. Amazon makes life simpler for a vendor.

Good Pricing

Amazon helps to get the best prices that you possibly can for your products. This is because of Amazon's Average Selling Price (ASP), which is higher for most items, even more so for all those products sold through FBA (Fulfillment by Amazon). A really good thing about the customer base on Amazon is that most of the customers are looking for ease of shopping and multiple options, and not just for products that are low priced.

Visibility

Every seller starts out as a small seller, and will still be a part of the entire system. Amazon offers much better visibility to a small seller than any of the other platforms. Amazon makes use of rotating search results, which is a great way for new sellers to get some exposure. It also provides the option of buying sponsored links to increase traffic.

Easy Order Fulfillment

On most of the retail platforms available online, it is always the seller's responsibility to make sure that the products are shipped to the customers within the given time in an appropriate manner. This increases the seller's workload, and the seller will need to contact their logistic partners or do it on their own. With Amazon, though, you needn't worry about all this. Amazon does this work for you.

Listing Fees

If you've worked in retail before, you might have an idea as to how stringent the margins are. This is the reason why sellers look for ways to reduce their listing fees. At Amazon, you needn't worry about paying listing fees on most of the items, and even when you have to, the cost is less when compared to the other e-retail platforms. This decreases your upfront costs and ensures the flexibility of your inventory.

Growth Prospects

When it comes to e-retailing, Amazon is the industry leader. Amazon's business is snowballing and will continue to do so. If you are looking for maximum exposure and action, then Amazon is a good choice for you.

Overhead Costs

Every seller wants to reduce his overhead costs. Amazon helps to do this in different ways. You can save on listing fees, uploading the photographs of your products, communication time, and even the maintenance costs. The cost of overhead on Amazon is quite low.

Stability

Unlike the other e-retail platforms, Amazon is stable in the way it works and the interface that it provides. Some platforms are much too dynamic, with ever-changing marketplace rules, demographics, fees and features. It can be quite overwhelming when a platform changes frequently.

Integration

There are some who look for flexibility and some who don't. If you are amongst the latter — someone who doesn't like going through the hassle of choosing their listing formats, interacting with the payment provider, market research provider, and fulfillment partner of choice, selecting the necessary tools, and navigating between these systems — then Amazon is a great choice. All of this is provided within a single interface, and it can be controlled with a single account.

Chapter 3 Identifying Products to Sell

When it comes to picking the right product niche and products for your business, it can be daunting as you realize the importance that this part of your business carries. You might fear that you will make the wrong decision and that you will struggle to generate any success in your business due to a poor choice made at this point. While this can certainly happen, there are plenty of strategies that you can use to help you calculate exactly what niche you should be selling in, and what products you should be selling as a part of that niche. Through using these calculations, you will be able to feel confident that the product niche and products that you choose are going to be profitable and popular enough to help you generate success. While nothing is guaranteed, if you follow these exact steps to verify and validate your product niche and products before committing in any one direction going forward, you will have the greatest odds in your favor.

Once you have gone ahead and chosen what niche you want to fill, the next thing you need to do is determine what you want to sell. Deciding what you sell is extremely important as it will influence the type of marketing you will want to try further down the line and also determine where you can go to source the things you want to sell. In general, you want items that are specific enough to not already have thousands of online stores already filling the niche, while at the same time broad enough to still see traffic from general Google searches. The right mix can be tricky, but you'll know it when you find it.

Consider the demand: One of the first things you will want to consider is whether you have the knowledge about your chosen niche that is currently being underserved by the online community. For example, if you really enjoy knitting and know that alpaca wool yarn is the best, then consider selling it if it is relatively hard to find currently. Everyone is part of a niche if you try hard enough, take the time to think about the items you buy regularly that are either hard to find or wear out extremely quickly, it can help to write the ideas down as you think of them, so you don't need to work through the entire process with each, ruining your brainstorming flow.

Any retail business, including ones in the e-commerce industry, is only as strong as the products are. When it comes to generating success in your Amazon FBA business, you need to know how to choose the right products for you to sell to your customers so you can earn a strong profit and grow your business consistently over time. At this point, you have a clear understanding of the importance of identifying your competitive edge and you are already consciously and intentionally begun to develop this skillset. Now, you are going to use this understanding to find a product niche that works for you, and to find products that are going to work for your business.

Identifying Your Product Niche

Regarding identifying your product niche, you want to start by considering what industries you are most passionate about or interested in learning about. Many people underestimate the value of picking a niche that actually interests you, but true marketing masters know that this is the key to find a niche that you are going to be able to grow in. When you are passionate about, or at least interested in a certain subject, you are more likely to invest in learning about it and actually understand what it is that you are learning about. With marketing, this means that you are going to be far more intuitive about what types of trends are ideal for you to partake in, what products are going to succeed in your industry, and how you can grow your business effectively.

After you have identified about 3-5 passions or interests that you could pursue as a business venture, you want to start brainstorming all of the possible products and product lines that you could offer in each niche. Write those potential products or product lines down under each possible niche. In addition to writing down possible product lines, consider areas that you could branch out into as your business grew, too. For example, let us say you wanted to offer graphic t-shirts for women in a product line as your primary product line or the one that you would be starting in. Possible extensions of this could be to add male graphic t-shirts, child graphic t-shirts, and even graphic t-shirts for dogs. Alternatively, you could venture into offering graphic canvas bags, totes, and other female-oriented accessories if you wanted to maintain a female niche.

Getting a clear idea of what you could offer and how you could extend your offers is important, as this is your earliest opportunity to validate that your possible chosen niche would not only be strong in the beginning, but would also have plenty of room for growth. Make sure that you take the time to really consider how these products would fit into your possible niche and whether or not they would make logical sense with your business. It is important that you are honest and concise when you validate possible product niches in order to feel confident that the route you have chosen is going to be a strong one. Now is not the time to be idealistic, but instead to be realistic, as you are going to be placing a lot of weight into this decision and you want to make sure that you minimize the risk as much as possible by validating it as honestly as possible right away.

Next, you need to start narrowing down your possible product niches into ones that are as specific as possible. While you do not want to niche down too hard to the point where you have almost nothing left to offer, you do want to niche down to the point where what you are offering is clear and easily groups together. For example, rather than saying "Gardening supplies" which is too broad or "gardening rakes" which is too specific, you might offer "designer flower pots" as a niche. This way, there are plenty of different product lines that you can incorporate, ranging from modern and sleek to flowery and feminine, yet it is still a clear niche that you are serving.

At this point, you can identify whether or not a niche is ideal based on your level of passion in that niche, the room for growth that it has, and the way that you might be able to narrow it down into a more specific category. All that is left to do is validate your niche with the outside world to ensure that the niche you pick is one that will actually interest other people, which will ensure that you are likely to earn sales from it. Nothing would be more disappointing than validating a niche with yourself, only to launch it to the public and find that it is something that not too many people are interested in. When it comes to validating your niche, you can do so by researching your chosen niche on platforms like Google Trends. You can also do basic research on social media for your chosen niche by searching up hashtags or keywords relating to your niche and seeing just how popular those terms are. Ideally, you want a niche that has 2-5 million people interested in it so that you have plenty of room for growth. If there is any more than that, you might be attempting to tap into a niche that is far too broad for you to make any level of success in. If you pick one that has a smaller audience, you are not going to have enough people to market to and you will find yourself marketing to no one.

At this point, since you are already researching, it is also a good idea to pay attention to the average price of products in your industry. Knowing this knowledge now will help you get an idea for what price points people are willing to buy the product at, which will help you determine if you are going to have a large enough profit margin to succeed with when you begin to source products for your business.

Discovering Trending and Profitable Products

Now that you have identified your niche, you need to start discovering products that you can sell in your niche that are going to sell quickly and earn you a strong profit along the way! With reference to selling products, there are a few things that you want to be on the lookout for as you choose which products to sell. These particular points are going to ensure that your product makes you the most money in the quickest period, making your business more successful.

When it comes to products that you will be selling online, you want to pick products that are trending, products that are easy to market, and products that are going to have a high-profit margin. You also want to pick products that are going to sell out quickly, as this means that you will not have to spend so much money on storage fees for the products that you are selling. The more that you can stock trending products that sell quickly, the more you are going to earn and the more momentum your store will grow with, which will result in you earning a huge income from your investment.

To begin identifying all of these highly profitable products, you want to start by doing some general product searches. General product searches involve you simply searching your niche on platforms like Amazon, Etsy, and eBay so that you can begin to see what types of products are most common in your chosen niche. Ideally, you want to look for products that retail between $10 to $50, as these are the price points where impulse buys happen, which means that people are going to be likely to make quick purchases on your products. If you price any lower, people will not see it as being worth the investment, and if you invest it any higher people will need to think it over, which will mean it takes them longer to buy the products. In both cases, you are going to be waiting for sales, which will cost you more money and result in you having to work harder to make the sales.

As you do your general search, seek to write down 30-50 products that fall in this price range, including variables and alternatives that people are selling. The more products that you can note down, the better, as this will give you a strong list to pick through when you begin to decide what products you are actually going to sell in your store.

Next, you want to use a tool like Merchant Words or Jungle Scout, which is going to help you identify how strong the market is for products that you are planning on selling. These platforms help you see the exact analytics relating to supply and demand, ensuring that you are getting into a product where the supply exceeds the demand so that you can feel confident that you are going to have people to sell to. Items that are in demand are more likely to sell both at a higher volume, and at a higher speed, which results in you earning a higher profit and in a shorter period. This step should help you narrow your list down by knocking out any products that are not in high enough demand. Especially early on, you do not want to be investing in products that you are going to have to store for lengthy periods because you have chosen something that is not earning cash fast. Instead, you want to pick products that are likely to sell quickly so that you can build momentum and get your business out there, while also quickly earning back the investment that you put into your business.

With what is remaining on your list, you want to turn to Amazon's Best Seller Rankings and begin to identify whether or not your products are ranking well on Amazon itself. Ideally, you want to check out the first three to five products that are on Amazon's Best Seller Ranking's list to see which ones are going to be the most profitable for you in your niche. You can search for different categories that are related to your niche to get each of these products, which will help you validate all of the products that you have chosen to consider for your own business.

The last thing that you need to do when you are searching for products that you want to sell on Amazon FBA is looking at the actual FBA fees. Each type of product is going to have different fees due to it having a different shape, size, weight, storage requirement, and handling requirement than other products. Even products from the same niche will have different needs that will need to be accounted for in the fees, so always consider this before officially investing in the new product. This way, you can identify how much of your profits are going to be sunk into Amazon fees, which will help you determine whether it is worth it or not. For some products, the fees might eat up too much of your profit, leaving the product not worth it for you to truly invest in.

At this point, you should be left with a handful of products that are going to be ideal for you to sell in your store. Do not worry about how many you have identified to sell, unless you have had a hard time finding good products as this may indicate that you have picked too specific of a niche or one that is not strong enough for you to sell in. However, if you find that you have 20-45 products or more on a list of possible purchases, this is a good thing. This proves that there is a strong variety of great products for you to sell and that you will have plenty to grow out into later on.

Validate Your Products through Hands-On Research

Just like with your product niche, you are also going to need to validate your products through actual humans. Understand that just because your niche and product popularity prove positive does not mean that you are going to know how to immediately access the people who are going to be most likely to actually buy your product. If you are not tapping directly into those consumers, you are going to have a hard time getting people to buy from you.

Validating your products through hands-on research allows you to get a feel for where your possible consumers are spending time online and how you can get ahold of them. This way, if you do begin selling that particular product you know exactly where to go to market your product and earn as many sales as possible right off the bat.

The best way to begin validating your audience is by going onto social media platforms and looking up your particular niche on social media. Better yet, search keywords related to your chosen product and get a feel for how many people are talking about that product or using that product in their everyday lives. Ideally, you should see hundreds of thousands of people using those products on each platform that you choose to visit to prove that there is a strong audience for you to market to right away.

As you validate your products this way, make sure that you take note of which keywords and hashtags are turning you up with the best results for where you can find your audience online. Although keeping notes on this information will not be relevant to you right now, it will help you later on when it comes time to market your products, as you will already know where to look to find the people who are most likely to buy them. When you are ready to step into your launch, already having part of the research completed will make the launch process easier for you to do.

Chapter 4 Sourcing Products

Sourcing your products is going to be one of the main aspects of making sure all your time and effort pays off. There is a lot that goes into this process. Not only do you have to leverage the cost you'll pay and the amount you can charge, but you'll have to determine just how much demand there will be for the product. The market research and purchasing may become a large part of your work. The good news is that there are a large amount of ways you can procure new products to sell.

Of course, the number one rule in commerce, and thus ecommerce, is to buy your products for much less than you are going to sell them for. For ecommerce, and especially Amazon, a safe bet is to attempt buying products for 1/3rd the cost you intend to sell them for. While there may be some more meat on the bones than this, this price ensures that your time is well spent and your profits are going to be ample. Additionally, should the price drop for any reason, there's less chance of taking a loss on the product. This is of a course a rule of thumb, and in some instances, you may find reason to believe it's okay to make less profit on a product, but it's usually safer to stick within this range.

As you start off with your work to procure the products you wish to sell, it is a great idea to go ahead and download the Amazon Seller App on your smartphone. This app can help you in many situations to quickly determine if a product is going to viable to sell. If you're sourcing products in person, you can quickly scan these items to determine the prices they are selling for on Amazon, how much demand the product has through the sales ranking, and a number of other small details. You can learn what other FBA sellers are doing with the same product as well. As a good example, if the product is selling well but there are no FBA sellers for it, then you should have no problem raising your price a little bit because Prime members will often pay a bit more to have items shipped from Amazon within their two-day free shipping structure.

The sales ranking of any given product can give you a good idea of how much demand a product has. You can find this number on any product page. A rare item may be selling for a high price on Amazon, but if the sales ranking is well above 100,000, it may be a difficult to sell item to sell through this platform. On the other side of the coin, any items that have a sales ranking of 10,000 or lower is going to be fairly easy to sell in a relatively short amount of time. With items that have a high sales rank, you run the risk of the product sitting around in the Amazon warehouse and incurring long-term storage fees. These are not the ideal products to sell on Amazon, as your profit margin can shrink tremendously and sales are never guaranteed.

Given these basic guidelines to consider, let's move into the many ways that we can source products to start our FBA business and grow it from there. Here are some of the most obvious ways to source your products.

Sell Your Own Stuff

Selling your own stuff is not really a business plan in itself, but if you're just starting out and want to raise some funds, declutter your home, and learn the process of working with Amazon Fulfillment services, then it is an easy place to start. You can use the Amazon Seller App to scan items around your home that you no longer need or want.

Scan things such as:

Media (movies, music, books)

Things in original packaging

- Anything with any type of barcode

For those items that don't have a barcode, they may still be available on Amazon, but you'll generally have to find them manually. Sometimes these are quite worth selling still, so it may be worth the extra effort, especially if you no longer want the items anyway.

At the end of sourcing the products within your own home, you may be surprised to see just how much money there is sitting around your closets, book shelves, and movie and music collections. Of course, don't start rummaging through your family's belongings and selling things without first getting their permission! After this experiment, you'll need to start looking into the other routes for sourcing your products.

Retail Arbitrage

Arbitrage, whether in retail stores or online stores, is the process of purchasing items at retail locations with the intention of reselling them online. There are many methods of arbitrage, but let's begin with retail arbitrage.

The clearance section of your local department stores, drug stores, and other retail locations can sometimes be a goldmine for turning a profit. At first thought, this may seem unlikely since these items are clearly products that have not sold well within a store. However, the truth of the matter is that often sales for these products are dependent on the region, or sometimes even as specifically as the city or town. Often, these items are out of stock in other areas and the demand for them online is still thriving. So taking the time to pull out your Amazon Seller App and scanning through the items in a clearance section can be a quick way to pull in some profit.

We repeat this a lot, but the ideal items will sell for three times the amount you must pay for them. In the best case scenario, they will also already be listed on Amazon to reduce the amount of work on your end come time for listing. If you do find an item you believe will sell well on Amazon for other reasons, you may want to create a new product page, but only take this risk when you have a reason to believe there are profits to be made and the prices you are paying are low. You can use something like eBay to see what the prices are like elsewhere online. Google Shopping search can also be useful.

Often, mom and pop's stores may have a clearance section as well, and if you work with the proprietor of the property, they may be willing to give you a better deal if you're willing to take a larger bulk of their unwanted product. Additionally, going to outlet and liquidation stores are an excellent source for products, and for those businesses that are having an out of business sale, there is a lot of leveraging that can be had by offering to take a larger amount of their stock off their hands. They're looking to clear out, so take advantage of anything like this that is happening around you.

Retail arbitrage is an excellent way to get started in ecommerce after selling off your own goods because it doesn't usually require the amount of bulk purchasing required for wholesale, which means a lower cost in initial investment. Granted, a wholesale item that sells well may pull in more profit, but the initial investment is likely to be much greater.

It may seem like this wouldn't work either, but sometimes products that are available at normal retail prices in a local market will sell for much higher online. This can happen because items are not well available in certain areas and a number of other reasons. Sometimes items are exclusive to a specific region, and those that want the items from other areas are forced to pay extra for them online. This gives you the chance to make a profit even on items that are priced at full retail. This can be every type of item, even things like food products that are able to be shipped safely without the threat of being spoiled. The most obvious places to start are the major department stores like Walmart, Target, Kmart's, etc. From there, going to smaller retailers is also a good idea.

The process of arbitrage is pretty simple, but let's go over a quick example anyway. If you go to a Target and see that they have a good deal on hand drills, you can use your Amazon Seller App to scan this item and evaluate the price that it is selling for on Amazon. If the price in store is 1/3rd the cost on Amazon, and the sales ranking is 100,000 or lower, then it is probably going to be a pretty sure bet that you can earn a profit. Buy as many as you can!

Taking this a step further, with products that are bundled together, such as tool sets, it may be worth taking the time to consider if you can make a profit by splitting up the bundle deal. Say there is a 100-pc tool set, and there are essentially a set of wrenches, a set of screw drivers, and a power drill with bits. This can become three products you can sell, especially if they are already available in these arrangements on Amazon. If they are not available in these sets on Amazon, you might consider taking the time to create a new product page and writing a compelling product description.

Online arbitrage is also an option. Once and awhile, especially on sales days, there are going to be online deals through major retail websites and even smaller retailers that will allow you to purchase products at a low price. If you're willing to wait, you should then be able to resell the product later once the sale is over and there are less of these products on the market. Online arbitrage is a little more saturated than using your local markets, though. You better believe you're not the only reseller out there trying to get great deals online and from the comfort of your home. Ultimately, you are probably going to have better luck getting off the couch and into the store, but that doesn't mean you shouldn't keep an eye out for great online sales too.

It takes some time, but as you begin scanning in earnest at different locations, you will start to see that there are patterns in the types of items that are going to help you earn a profit. It will become easier to gravitate towards items that will bring in a profit in the future. At first, you may be scanning a lot and not finding a ton of profit, but this is something that you will instinctively become better at over time.

Thrift Stores

Outside of retail environments, you can also look in thrift stores for some items worth selling. Your trusty Amazon Seller App is an excellent way to determine the value on items and if they are indeed worth purchasing for the purpose of resell. When hunting in a thrift store, the obvious items to begin looking at are media, such as books, CDs, vinyl records, and movies. You can expand on this by looking at video games and consoles, and then from there, it may also be worthwhile to look at anything that is still in retail packaging. New and unwrapped items are the best to pick up, but if you're alright with selling used goods, that's fine too. Thrift stores sometimes also have collectibles, musical instruments, and other home goods that are worth selling as well, but you must make sure to do your research.

The great thing about thrift stores is that they are constantly restocking as new donations and products are coming in, which means you can easily continue to visit these places, make relationships with the staff, and try to leverage that relationship to get dibs on certain types of items. Those major thrift store chains, such as Goodwill and Salvation Army, often have auctions as well that can bring in a large amount of product for a relatively low price depending on who else is willing to spend money on new product that day.

On top of frequent restocking and auctions, thrift stores are also great because they typically have a calendar of sales times. While sales may be more competitive than checking in at early hours during the week, they can lead to great discounts that allow for greater profits should you find items that are appropriate for sale on FBA.

Much like working in the retail spaces for your arbitrage, you will start to learn how to scan with your eyes for the types of products you have a good history of selling. As you learn what sells and what doesn't, the process becomes quicker and more efficient. That doesn't mean you shouldn't be scanning random items, but sometimes you'll just know something isn't worth picking up, and that will eventually become a huge time saver.

Yard Sales

Yard sales are like pop-up thrift stores, and often they can mean even better deals than any other method of sourcing items locally. Often, people are having yard sales because they're about to move or they want to get rid of a lot of their stuff without the stress of trying to sell it off piece by piece. This can be a huge advantage if you're willing to get up early and hit yard sales hard every weekend. You'll want to put together a plan of action, often the night before with some revisions in the morning, using listings in your local classifieds and Craigslist to find yard sales that will have the type of items (and hopefully prices) that you are seeking. You will be looking for a lot of the same stuff at yard sales as you might find in thrift stores. While there are probably far less new and packaged items available, those used items that you are comfortable selling should be in abundance. Every once and awhile you'll strike yard sale gold and make a huge profit on a relatively low investment.

Just keep in mind that you are going from yard sale to yard sale with the intention of making a profit. It can be tempting to start shopping for yourself when prices are so low, but if the item cannot make you a profit, you should really try to avoid buying too much for the sake of owning it unless you truly feel like it is something you want. For this reason, I try not to bring along the significant other! Of course, if you are prone to shopping for yourself, it's better to shop at a discount than paying retail.

As a bonus, one thing I've found great success at when sourcing during yard sales is asking the owner of the home if they have anything else to sell. I let them know what types of things I like to buy, and it's not uncommon that they'll have something they didn't set out to sell but are willing to let go! Being upfront like this may be difficult for some people, but taking the extra step of simply talking to people is going to help you make relationships that can pay off later. You may be surprised what simply asking can do for your business! Likewise, when a single seller has a lot of products I believe I can turn over for a profit, I try to work out a better deal for taking so much off their hands. Sometimes this works, and sometimes it doesn't.

Craigslist and Facebook Buy/Sell/Trade Groups

Moving into the online sphere, there are several ways to source products locally. The most common are going to be Craigslist and Facebook groups that allow for buy/sell/trade threads.

These aren't too unlike yard sales except that some people are resellers just like you, and many people are trying to get more money out of their products than they would be if they were having a yard sale. Still, you can make offers, and if you're adamant about browsing these sales groups, you're almost bound to hit a home run at some point.

This probably works better in larger cities just due to the amount of items, but smaller cities do allow for less competition sometimes. Additionally, you can use these groups and Craigslist to post ads asking if anyone is willing to sell the types of items you are seeking out. You will get the occasional angry poster that calls you "reseller scum," but don't let this bother you. Once you're counting your hard earned income, these people simply don't matter. Don't engage. Your reputation in the area should be a positive one if you want to foster relationships with people that might help you out later.

Auctions

Going to an auction is a gamble in and of itself. Sometimes there will be far too many people bidding on products, making the prices too high for any serious amount of profit, and sometimes there won't be many great products. A lot of auctions are also going to be half-blind when items are sold in large lots. A good example of this is storage locker auctions. Often you are expected to purchase the entire contents of a storage locker with only a chance to glance into it for a few minutes. This means you have to quickly evaluate if there is anything worth selling, and then you have to hope that if you do see some big ticket item, nobody else saw it! There is risk involved, but sometimes you will find gold. It's sort-of like diving for oysters with the hopes that one of them has a valuable pearl inside. There's a lot of risk, but the rewards can be very generous when you do finally find that pearl. Put simply, auctions are pretty much hit or miss, especially for the newcomer that isn't sure about what is valuable and isn't just at a glance.

There are also online auctions with sites like eBay, Shopgoodwill, UBid, and a number of smaller operations. Purchasing a single item at auction through these means is not generally going to be worth the headache, but if you take the time to browse bulk and wholesale lots, you can sometimes find great deals with products that, once sold piece by piece, will bring in a decent profit. This method is highly saturated, though, so it can be difficult.

Wholesale and Private Label

Wholesale is the process of buying products in bulk from a wholesaler or manufacturer. Typically, you would be purchasing from a wholesaler that purchases in even larger unit numbers from a manufacturer. The greatest thing about wholesale is that you will have a large amount of product at a relatively low cost per unit. The downside is that you also have to be able to sell the large amount of product, so choosing your products wisely can be a bit tricky. Additionally, wholesalers can sometimes be a little picky about who they work with. However, if you're good at product selection, wholesale is an easy way to begin selling in great quantities, find new products from home, and expand your business quickly.

Private label selling is wholesale with an added facet. Rather than purchasing a branded product, you would purchase a product and apply your own branding to it. This can allow you to buy cheaper products, but it also means that you will have to create a brand, put marketing into your brand, and then sell this brand by creating high-quality images, videos, and product descriptions. This method can be great, but it takes a lot of effort in comparison to other methods.

Because wholesale and private label product sourcing contains a lot of additional work, we will be covering these in their own respective chapters. For now, it suffices to say that if you can purchase items at a lower cost per unit and sell at a much higher price point without sitting on the inventory indefinitely, there is a huge amount of profit to be made through these methods. Honestly put, any significant amount of growth for your ecommerce business through Amazon FBA is eventually going to rely on these methods.

Producing Your Own Products

The risk involvement with creating, branding, marketing, and manufacturing your own products is a huge task to undertake. Before you even consider this, you truly need to be sure to perfect the product concept and find a method for manufacturing that will allow for sales at prices that customers are willing to pay.

The investment here is often so large that it can bankrupt newcomers, and it is almost smarter to try this only after perfecting other methods. However, if the only reason you're taking on FBA is to get your own product online and for sale in the Amazon market, then you may need to venture out and find investors or other forms of capital to keep things afloat while you work out all the logistics and build your customer base. The great thing about finding investors, or at least running test trials with many potential customers, is that feedback will help you determine if the product is worthwhile to pursue and if there are any ways you might be able to improve on the product and your branding.

If you can manufacturer the product yourself, it is possible to manufacture smaller quantities to reduce the risk of loss, but if you are to make a great amount of profits eventually, you'll need to generate a larger market for the product and determine methods to reduce manufacturing costs.

Mixed Bags

It is alright to use multiple methods to source your products. This may not be something you wish to continue with as you find success with one method, but as a beginner, it can be a great way to learn what is working for your personal business aspirations and what isn't. I personally started with retail arbitrage and continued with it even as I stepped into wholesale. Eventually, I kept the wholesale business going as I started a few private label products. Retail arbitrage wasn't as profitable in the end, and my time was better spent sourcing new wholesale items and releasing a new private label product once and awhile.

Ultimately, sourcing products has become the work I handle most of the time. Amazon does so much of the other processes for me that it seems like my whole job now is just sourcing new products and determining how they should perform on the market.

Chapter 5 Private Labeling with Amazon

Private labeling differs from retail arbitrage; it is the process of buying from a supplier and reselling these items under your own private brand. Retail arbitrage is good for starting out, but you may find yourself desiring more. Arbitrage can be limiting because of the amount of time you must spend, often physically, in transporting yourself from store to store and checking out pricing. With private labeling, you spend less time on the hunt for new inventory. Private labeling is for serious sellers only; this is the big league.

Private labeling requires that you launch your own product line. It is not recommended to jump into private labeling cold: you will need to build up the product line first. You would have a hard time making any sales from scratch, because you would not have any traffic to work with to generate sales. You need good reviews and a solid sales base to move your listings up in the rankings in order to make any sales.

Unlike retail arbitrage, which requires daily searching for a source of income, private labeling can ease the process significantly because you no longer have to spend all of that time searching for products in person. Furthermore, your supply can always increase in quantity if it sells well in a way that is impossible with retail arbitrage.

Find a Product to Sell

Just like with retail arbitrage, you will need to devote time to locating the perfect product. This is all about finding your niche. You need to find a product that is in-demand, but with a market that is not over-saturated with competitors. This is a lesson that can be applied to your search for arbitrage goods as well, but becomes even more important in the quantities of inventory that you will be handling with a private label. The perfect place to do this is the best-seller rankings. Amazon does this for the buyer's benefit, but it is easy to see how this can be used to the advantage of the seller.

Best-seller rankings do the hard work for you; it is an informal version of market research. It tells you what the customers are already buying, instead of forcing you to run the risk of testing a product only to see that it doesn't sell. Since you already know what is selling well, you are saving yourself money and energy by using it as a resource.

Depending on what you'd like to sell, check the top 11 best–sellers for that category. If you have no preference, just look through all of the categories. There are characteristics that lend themselves naturally to great selling options: things that rank well, do not weigh a lot, and are not typically associated with a brand.

Low-weight items are ideal because your shipping costs are lower. But brand name items? Remember, you are selling your own brand. It is not possible for you to sell Adidas shoes, for example, because those products are protected under patents and cannot be sold under your private label.

The purpose of private labeling is to create your own brand, under your name. This is why you should be selecting products that are easy to sell under your moniker. Cooking products or office supplies are good examples, provided they are made with lightweight materials.

Who else is selling it?

After finding a product you're interested in, you should look into how the other guys are doing. You are selling the same product as other people in the business, so you need to study them and learn their strengths and weaknesses to be able to refine your own strategy.

In the following hypothetical example, we'll be talking about an apple corer. What else do you need to know about apple corers, besides that they sell well, in order to be a successful seller? You'll need to see how the other guys are doing it. Search for your product in Amazon's search engine.

Get systematic about it: take notes on the first few listings that come up to compare pricing, the number of reviews, and information about the appearance of the listing itself. A quality listing is evident; you yourself should be aware of the elements of an attractive, professional and informative listing, so scout out the ones you are competing against for the same qualities you would expect of yourself.

When you take a look at your notes, there are things you should be looking for. It should take you a while to find a product that fits these categories. Don't be surprised if a few hours go by. This kind of research is time-consuming, but it does pay off in the long run. The time you spend searching is time you will have saved by using FBA instead of doing the delivery and customer service on your own.

You want a price that is high enough to earn you reasonable profit, but low enough to be within the average consumer's range of affordability: the lowest you would want to see is $8, and the highest $45. The other things you are looking for have to do with making the competition easier for you to scale. A low number of reviews is something to aim for, because it means you will need fewer reviews to come up in the search results. In a similar vein, look for products in which most of the best-sellers rank at less than 1,000. The less stiff the competition, the better. Poor quality or just average-looking listings are a further aspiration for the same reason.

So, let's say you've found that apple corers meet the all the requirements of this category and move forward.

Contact and Negotiate with a Supplier

Now you're looking for someone who can supply you with apple corers. The most cost-effective options are international suppliers; it is rare to get anything comparably inexpensive that is manufactured in the US. Alibaba is the database of choice for most FBA sellers; it is an international market place with thousands of listings for the products you are interested in selling.

Search for your product on Alibaba and find the product you are looking for. Be wise and do your research on the suppliers.

In private labeling, you are looking for a product that sells at a 3x multiplier for what you originally paid for it. If you buy something for a dollar, you should be able to sell it for at least 3 dollars. When you find a product that is profitable, ranks well, and fits the guidelines as dictated by Amazon regulations, you should be ready to reach out to the supplier.

When reading the listings, you are looking for information about what is necessary to place an order. Most suppliers have what is called a minimum order quantity (MOQ), which is how many units of the item you will need to purchase. They may also include information on the lead time, which is the amount of time it takes for them to deliver the product to you. It is not guaranteed that they allow for private labeling, so be sure to check that as well.

Even with this information readily available in the listing, you will need to contact the supplier personally. This is actually to your advantage as a buyer, because before you get started, you'll want to order a test batch so you can examine the quality of the product for yourself. Negotiate with the suppliers on the price of these test orders; smart manufacturers are eager to make new business connections, and so they will be more willing to give you a decent price on this test order. It is possible to negotiate with a supplier and reduce their MOQ to 300 or 200 units, which eases the burden on you to sell them off if you are less than impressed with the product itself.

Establish your own brand

While you are searching for the perfect supplier and product, you should be crafting your private label brand. This seems intimidating; after all, you may not have any marketing experience at all, and are suddenly expected to design your own campaign.

Thankfully, there are professionals out there willing to take on the task of doing the design work for you. You do not need to go it alone. Sites such as Fiverr and Upwork put you in contact with design professionals who will take care of the branding for you.

Some sites function so that you are the one to reach out to the designers with your project, whereas others have designers bid on your project proposal. The service you want to use depends on how much work and funding you want to put into design.

Superior design is what will set your product apart from others who are selling the same product. Work on a snappy name and streamlined design that entices buyers. In online shopping, this is one of your most powerful selling points.

When the design is finished, get the files to your supplier so they can carry out the order you've made.

Crafting your listing

While you are waiting for your order to come in, spend time refining the product listing. You should follow the same guidelines established above for products gained through retail arbitrage. Be sure to include a vivid product description; often, sellers don't put any effort at all into writing a description, but their products still sell well. Imagine the potential of your product when paired with an excellent description.

The first sale

Your first sale is always the most difficult to make. Without a credible reputation and trusted base of customers, you have little to work with when marketing your product. Word-of-mouth cannot be overrated as a technique; building your base is essential. This works with private labeling in the same way it can work with retail arbitrage, and is covered more thoroughly in the marketing section of this guide. There are techniques you can employ on your own page, services you can use internally with Amazon and external methods as well. The time that you do not spend searching for inventory can now be used to enhance your marketing skills.

Private labeling and earnings

Private labeling requires some initial investments funds, unlike retail arbitrage. The profits you stand to make, however, are often considerably more significant. With products that do exceptionally well, by ranking in the top 100 of their category, sellers can reap thousands in revenue on a daily basis. Items that rank in the top 500 have the potential of earning you a few hundred dollars a day. Even products in lesser rankings can result in a steady flow of side income.

There is no right or wrong amount to spend getting your product off the ground. You may only wish to spend a few hundred, or you might want to go big with a few thousand. If you are confident in your profit margin, the opportunities await you.

Chapter 6 Marketing

Amazon functions essentially as a search engine, and it is your job as a seller to improve your sales so your products show up earlier in the results. There are many strategies available to sellers for improving visibility, and you will have to experiment to find the ones that work for you.

For example, you can offer multiple shipping options on your product by editing your Shipping Settings. This is helpful, for example, if you are selling a product that often requires replacing. With this option, buyers will consistently be signed up to receive your product. This obligates you to keep a steady stock of the product so as not to disappoint your buyers and risk bad reviews.

Your Sales Page

Customers interface with your business through a sales page. Your sales page is the first thing customers interact with in your business, so you should make sure it is professional in appearance and accurately represents the quality of the products you are selling

Think carefully about the name you select to represent your business to others – be sure it is legible and professional-sounding.

Use broad keyword in descriptions for your items so they are more likely to come up in a search, but be careful not to cram the product title with too many descriptors – buyers are wary of spam and can recognize a ploy. One tool you can use for figuring out the best keywords for your products is the Amazon Keyword Tool, which utilizes Amazon's Autocomplete search tool to show the most popular keywords used on Amazon. When people type in a word on Amazon, its engines use real words searched by its buyers to suggest search terms for completion. If you are using keywords that show up in the Autocomplete results, your product is more likely to come up in the buyer's search. Keyword Tool Dominator is a service you can use to emulate the results of the Autocomplete service employed by Amazon.

Do not underestimate the value of quality bullet point descriptions. Customers use the descriptions to make decisions between products. Many of the products you sell may be similar in price and appearance to other products from different vendors. Your item descriptions are your chance to shine. The more helpful they are, the better trust you build with potential buyers. They are not, however, the place to make false promises. Be sure the information you provide in the item descriptions is vivid yet factual, honest, and truthful.

Appearance is everything. You won't be relying on your cellphone camera to take picture of your products. Some sellers outsource the task of editing photos to make them professional grade.

Reviews Strategy and Getting Feedback from Buyers

Good reviews are essential to successfully running your business. Unfortunately, 90% of Amazon buyers do not leave reviews after purchasing a product. It is important to reach out to people to get good reviews – you must build customer trust in order to expand your reach. The easiest way to do this is to provide incentives for customers to leave reviews for your products. In your position as a seller, you are able to offer your customers a special promotional code for when they are buying your products.

Offer them a discount, sometimes even a free product, in exchange for leaving a review. This does require that you put some of your money on the line, but in the context of your overall operating costs, it is highly worth it. This can help you makes sales and get reviews – the kinds of activities which in turn lead to higher listings and even more business. By lowering the buyer's perceived sense of risk with a low price, they will feel more inclined to take the chance on a new company.

A quick online search will show any number of coupon companies seeking to offer verified coupons for Amazon products. You can submit your promo codes through these sites for your products and watch your activity flourish from there.

Amazon Advertisement Pay-Per-Click

There are internal ways to advertise through Amazon that you should be aware of as a seller to make the most of your business. The primary way that people make purchases on Amazon is through their searches. Most searches are what we call "long-tail searches," meaning that people tend to search three words or more to get the best and most accurate results. Considering how many products are for sale on Amazon, this makes sense. Millions of searches are made on Amazon each month.

They know exactly what they want. Their searches are thus very powerful. When a buyer searches for something on Amazon's search engine, the most relevant products to their search are brought up. There are two kinds of results displayed when a customer makes a search: organic results and paid results. Organic results are items from sellers with good ratings and reviews. Paid results are displayed even before the organic results.

To make the most of paid results, you have to know the basics. It is not just submitting your listing; rather, you must understand the keywords that work behind it.

Your first Campaign

Amazon makes it easy to create a campaign internally. You will use Amazon Services to make your product into a Sponsored product. You manage advertisement using the Advertising section located in Seller Central. Ads are organized into campaigns so you can measure the effectiveness of your advertising.

Start by creating a new campaign. Choose an easy name you can alter in the future for different campaigns. The name remains visible only to you, so it needs to make sense to you. You will be asked to input further values about your campaign. When it comes to the budget, it is a personal preference, but many sellers recommend beginning at $50-$80 a day. This number indicates the maximum of what you would be spending per day, rather than the actual price of the campaign. It is unusual to reach the maximum cost anyway, and as a beginner, you can spread your net wide. Afterward, you will be able to adjust to a more exact value.

You may be wondering how much you should spend on advertising. Like with many options you will be faced with as the owner of a small business, this answer is dependent upon personal preference. Based on the margin available to you and what you see as a worthwhile investment in the long term, how effective your previous attempts at advertising have panned out, all of these factors contribute to your decision. If you're making money, though, and turning a profit, there is no wrong

Chapter 7 Amazon Seller Central Account

First off, I'd like you to understand that your Amazon Seller Central is going to be the main account where you'll be handling most of the operations that comes with selling on Amazon. This includes tasks such as creating a brand new product listing on Amazon, setting unit prices, running advertising campaigns and many more! So creating an Amazon seller account is very easy. Trust me, if you're able to fully digest and understand all the information provided in this book, then I believe that you should be able to create an Amazon seller account with ease. Now, what you'll do is to simply fill every information that Amazon requires and your account should be ready in no time! But, before you create your very own Amazon seller account, here are a few things to keep in mind.

The first thing is, Amazon charges a monthly membership fee of thirty nine dollars and ninety nine cents. And in my honest opinion, $39 a month is relatively cheap considering the gazillions of cash you could make with this business model! Another thing to keep in mind is, your Amazon seller central account also comes with a metric called account health.

So basically, the account health represents the health of your Amazon seller central account. Now, what determines the health of your account will depend upon the relationship between you and your customers. For example, if you're trying to sell a product like hair dryer and it's receiving a lot of complaints from customers, then that will badly affect the health of your Amazon seller account. And the reason why you want to avoid this is because if you have a bad account health, your account could be at risk of deactivation. Now, understand that Amazon is a very customer centric company. Which means that for you as an Amazon seller, the key is to focus on serving the best quality products in the market! Because see, if you're selling amazing quality products that customers really love, then Amazon will reward you by displaying your products to even more consumers! Which results to even more cash in your pockets!

On the other hand though, if the products you're selling are receiving too much complaints or returns from customers, then Amazon wouldn't like that. And as I've mentioned, your account could be at risk of deactivation and that is the last thing you'd want! So once again, make sure to keep track of your Amazon seller account health and focus on serving good quality products.

That is everything you'll need to know about setting up your own Amazon seller central account. If you need more in-depth information to help you with your decision, make sure to check out Amazon's official website.

Chapter 8 Understanding Seller Central and FBA Fees

To help with the sourcing of items and the listing process, it's a good idea to glean some understanding of the way the fee structures involved work. We mentioned that rule of three (where you should only buy a product if it can be sold for three times the cost), and these fees have a lot to do with that requirement.

While our main focus is selling with Fulfillment by Amazon, understanding the fees for sales that you fulfil yourself will help to understand the additional fees involved with Amazon fulfillment as well. Let's begin there.

Fulfilling Orders Yourself

When packaging and shipping an item to a buyer yourself, there are two major fees involved. First, there is the "referral fee." In most categories, the referral fee is going to be a static 15% of the total sale. However, this fee is sometimes lower for certain categories, such as home computer and photography gear.

The other fee involved is the "variable closing cost" fee. This fee is $1.35 for any media, such as books, video games, or music items. For other items, the fee is generally only $0.45 cents plus $0.05 cents per pound in weight.

These fees are based on the sales price, and it does not include any shipping costs. As an example, consider what happens when you sell a textbook sold for $25.

$25 for the item

+ $3.99 shipping credit

- $3.75 "15% referral fee"

- $1.35 "variable closing cost"

= $23.89 deposited into your Amazon Seller Central Account.

When selling without Fulfillment by Amazon, any shipping labels purchased from Amazon will be taken directly out of your current balance. Should the shipping be less than the shipping credit, you get to keep the change. Should the shipping be higher, then you have to eat those additional costs. Keep in mind that you will also be paying for any shipping materials used, ink for your printer, printer paper or sticker labels, etc.

Fees While Using Fulfillment by Amazon

Moving forward, let's consider how fees work with Fulfillment by Amazon. I explain the fees without just so you can compare. Much like the standard method of packaging and fulfilling your orders yourself, the referral fee still applies despite using Amazon's fulfillment services. However, the shipping credits you would receive are no longer applicable. For small, cheaply priced, cheap-to-ship items, that may mean less revenue.

Keep in mind that FBA isn't a free service either. On top of the usual referral fee, the fee structures involved with FBA depend largely on your choices and the items you happen to stock.

With the "Individual" plan (free), fees include pick and pack, weight handling, and storage.

Storage fees fluctuate throughout the year, and for this reason, it's wise to consider what you're willing to keep stored in the warehouses and for how long. Additionally, larger items may be considered "oversized" and incur an increased storage fee.

The "pick and pack fee" is that $0.99 cent cost per item we spoke of earlier. Again, if you're selling more than 40 items per month, it's time to upgrade to the professional Seller Central account, as these fees are completely removed with the professional account. This is the only fee that changes with the professional account over the individual account, but a dollar per sale can be a huge difference.

While it's true that the fees involved with FBA takes away additional cost, a high-volume seller is going to make up the difference by having more time to work on sourcing new products. In most cases, the benefits of having Amazon fulfil your orders is such a time saver that you will ultimately save money as well (even if it doesn't seem that way when you look at your Amazon reports).

The Quick Solution

By now, you're probably groaning at the idea of calculating all of these fees and trying to determine if an item is even worth selling, especially if you made the mistake of purchasing it for more than one-third the amount you can sell it at. The good news is that SaleCalc exists. SaleCalc is a simple website that allows you to type in your product cost, desired selling point, and a host of other details that determine roughly what the fees and profits for each item will be.

SaleCalc.com

Make sure to bookmark the website http://salecalc.com. This website will save you a ton of time. They do a solid job of keeping everything updated, but be sure to check that it has been updated recently or the information you receive may be slightly off. They also provide fee services for a number of other online marketplaces should you need them.

Amazon Revenue Calculator

Recently, Amazon also rolled out a revenues calculator, and it is more powerful and more useful than SaleCalc when your only source of sales is Amazon.

Take a look at it by navigating to https://sellercentral.amazon.com/hz/fba/profitabilitycalculator/index?lang=en_US, and you'll quickly see how useful it can be.

Almost There...

Understanding the fees helps to justify the low cost you must procure items for, but it also enables you to understand which items are going to be worthwhile for selling. Take the time to learn the costs involved with storage for the current season, and determine if keeping all of your items in the warehouse for seasons where they're less likely to sell is worth it.

Now that you understand where to find items and how to get a rough idea of the fees involved, it's time to consider the listing process.

Chapter 9 Listing Products on Amazon Seller Central

Now that you have a nice little collection of items to sell, it's time to begin listing products for sale and getting them prepped for shipment to Amazon's warehouses, also known as fulfillment centers. It is ideal to handle these listings on a computer rather than trying to handle them all on a smartphone. Not only are you going to need to print stuff later (much easier on a PC/MAC than a smartphone), but the entire process is just a lot easier this way.

Step 1. Evaluate Products and Pricing

Log into your Amazon Seller Central account, and on the menu, find where it says "Inventory." Place your cursor over this, and from the menu options displayed, select "Add a Product."

This will bring us to a page asking to identify the items. If the item has a barcode, there are two options. Either type in the barcode or use the scanner (optional gear mentioned earlier) and simply scan the barcode. The scanner will really save a lot of time and help avoid errors in typing out the numbers.

Most of the time, the item is probably already available on Amazon for sale. Make sure it is the correct item, size, color, and every other detail. Most of the time this won't be a huge concern, but when it is, listing an item incorrectly usually means returns and/or refunds. Click on the product to see the details.

Under the description, there will be offers for the products. This includes both new and used offers; click whichever one best represents the item being listed. Do not list used items as new.

The following page will show the prices that other sellers are offering the product for, and on this page are also short descriptions of the products and their condition. When selling through Fulfillment by Amazon, the major competition is other Fulfillment by Amazon sellers. While other sellers may be competition still, they receive none of the perks of being shipped and handled by Amazon, and often people will purchase an FBA item over a random seller item, especially Prime members enjoying the quick and free shipping.

Taking a look at other FBA sellers and their prices for the product, we can learn how best to price the item. In most scenarios, if the product is of the same quality, it is best to at least match the lowest price available. This helps sales in two ways. First, the item appears near the top of the list in relation to other FBA sellers. Second, the "Buy Box" on product pages are almost always from FBA sellers, and this increases the chances of becoming the seller whose item is sold when someone doesn't evaluate offers and takes the quickest route of purchase. Keep in mind that a professional seller account is required for this perk.

To make this process a bit easier, certain search options are available. With these search restrictions, it is possible to view only the Prime and free shipping items, which weeds out all the extra sellers who aren't direct competition. There will be a clear marking next to a seller's name that says, "Fulfillment by Amazon."

That said, sometimes a product is worth listing a bit higher to make the profit required from it. If it can be listed confidently at a higher price and the seller is patient, this can ultimately bring in better profits and return on investment. On the flip side, avoid underselling other FBA sellers. Anytime people start to price items lower and lower, a price war is likely to ensue, which translates to everyone losing money. Don't fall into that trap. Price MATCH, don't try to undercut!

Going back to the Seller Central page, which should have remained open in a separate tab or window, there will be a "Sell Yours" link next to the product. Click on this to begin listing the product on the following page. The following steps will cover the required fields on this page.

Step 2. Condition Notes

The condition notes are about the only content that most sellers ever create. Even if you're not a great writer, this should be taken seriously. Far too many sellers simply copy and paste the same condition notes for everything. While that may save time, it can also lead to lower sales and more returns/refunds.

Writing honest and complete descriptions for each item helps your business stand out amongst the competition.

With any opened media items, test them and include a note that they are tested and working. For new items, mention that they are brand new in packaging. You can reiterate obvious facts like the free two-day shipping offered by Amazon, and explain the methods used to ensure the item remains in great condition.

Do NOT skimp on these condition notes. For those buyers that don't simply click the "Buy" button, these notes, the prices, and the feedback score you have are usually large parts of the decision to purchase from one seller over another, especially since prices are likely to be close to one another.

Step 3. Pricing and Shipping Options

At this stage, you should have already determined the best way to price the item. If you haven't, return to Step 1. Add in the price.

Scroll down to the bottom of the page, and in the shipping options, select the one that says, "I want Amazon to provide customer service for my items if they sell." This is how you begin the FBA process. Click "Save and Continue."

Step 4. Create a Shipping Plan

Since you have chosen to have Amazon handle customer service, the next page contains a prompt to create a new shipping plan. Choose "individual products" for the packing type. The follow page will list the product and ask you to enter the quantity of the product you intend to ship to an Amazon fulfillment center. Click on "Save."

Now, it's time to repeat the above steps until all the items you wish to send to Amazon are listed. While doing so, make sure to place all of the products within the same shipping plan (the one you just created) rather than creating a new one for each. The more products to ship at the same time, the better, as this will keep shipping costs down.

When the list is finally complete, click "Continue" on the screen that lists your products allocated within the shipping plan.

Step 5. Information on Prepping Items

The next page will ask for your address. Simply enter this and continue.

Following this, Amazon will provide a list of requirements for how items are prepped and packaged. Common requirements include packaging items in poly bags, putting items in their own boxes, or bubble wrapping items for extra protection. Not following these requirements can cause problems, so never skip this step. It is advised to make notes on this or screen shot the page to review later, as we typically handle this step later in the process.

The item is ready to be listed, but it won't be listed until after Amazon receives it. The next steps are getting everything labeled, packaged, and shipped to Amazon for fulfillment.

Chapter 10 Launching Products with Amazon

With everything in place and your products arriving at Amazon's warehouse, it is time for you to launch your products! Launching products on Amazon is actually incredibly simple, but it does take some practice to memorize each of the steps and have a big impact on each launch. As well, you will find that each launch grows as you go because you are better at it each time, and you already have some credibility established around your brand and your reputation. The momentum between your own knowledge and this recognition will help each launch do better than the last, so long as you grow with the momentum.

In this chapter, we are going to go through a simple launch sequence so that you know exactly what you need to be doing in order to succeed with your brand. As you launch your first products, follow this sequence exactly so that you are able to get everything done. Make a note of anything you feel you could do differently to accentuate your strengths and do better, though, so that you can create your own launch sequence that perfectly fits your business and keeps you growing.

Optimizing Your Listings

The first thing you need to do to launch your product on Amazon is to optimize your listing. Once your listing is branded as per the instructions in all you have to do is upload Search Engine Optimization (SEO) features into your listing. Since Amazon works like a search engine, just like Google search does, using SEO is important. This will help your listings show up toward the top of the page, meaning you are more likely to get viewed over the people who fall later than you in the listing rankings.

The best way to SEO your product page is to use relevant search terms in your title and your product description, without going overboard or being spammy about it. Amazon actually has a clause built into their algorithm that prevents people from ranking well if they put too many keywords in their listing. Amazon assumes that these listings are spam and then ranks them incredibly low, preventing them from ever getting found by anyone who is using Amazon to shop. The key is to use keywords sparingly, and in a way that actually makes sense in the flow of your listing.

A great way to spot rich keywords that you could use for your listing is to use a keyword search tool such as Keyword.io or Google's built-in keyword app. Both of these will give you the opportunity to search for keywords that are relevant to your industry so that you can use the best keywords on your listing. Each keyword tool will have its own way of ranking the quality of keywords, so make sure that you follow this ranking to find keywords that are going to be supportive in helping you get found. Typically, these ranking tools will help you avoid keywords that are saturated or ones that are not used enough to really be worth the effort of fitting them into your description.

It is also important that you do not overuse a single keyword in your description. Using a keyword any more than 1-2% of your total description can result in you being marked as spam and your posts not being shown. Find ways to use relevant keywords without overusing them by choosing alternative words, too, so that you can stay optimized in the search parameters.

Outlining Your Launch Strategy

Once your product listings are all set up and optimized, and your store is ready to go, you can outline your launch strategy. It is crucial that you do not start a launch plan until after your entire shop is set up and ready to go, as doing so could result in you not having everything ready come your chosen launch date. Pushing back launches to accommodate tech glitches or malfunctions is incredibly unprofessional and can massively destroy the momentum of your launch, so avoid that by preparing everything first.

With everything prepared, you can go ahead and create a schedule that will outline your strategy. Ideally, your schedule should include the date that you want your shop ready by, the date that you will start organic advertising, the dates that you will start paid advertising (and what types of paid advertising will be started when) and the dates that you will monitor your growth for important metrics in how you can improve momentum. Having all of this outlined in your schedule in advance will ensure that you know exactly what needs to be done on every day leading up to the official launch of your product so that you can stay on track and continue building momentum.

As you will quickly learn, momentum is the backbone of any strong launch, so having a strong flow of momentum building up around your products and business is essential. You want to build up momentum around your launch, as well as use that building momentum from each product to carry into your next product launch so that you can get ahead each time.

Note that when you launch your first products, you are also going to be launching your store for the first time. For that reason, you should use all of these strategies for the items that you think are going to be most popular, and for your branded store in general. This way, you are promoting both your store and brand itself and the products that you are going to have for sale. This will build momentum and recognition around both your brand and your products, making for a much more successful launch right from the jump. In future launches, you will not have to do as much work around promoting your brand to really get your name out there.

Chapter 11 How to Grow with Amazon FBA through Profit Cycle?

From the time you started selling on Amazon, you may notice the increasing number of items listed on Amazon marketplace over time. This indicates that sellers are continuously arriving to compete and more active Amazon sellers are growing their businesses.

I believe that FBA is a factor of such growth. And the growth happens due to a repeating process of restocking the bestsellers, getting away of the unsalable items and scouting of new products.

To have a constant growth in your Amazon FBA business, your existing inventory should be evaluated and assessed in a strategic manner based on data. But be also ready to answer some questions because you need to assess your FBA operations.

First, let me discuss the most important concerns that a seller should focus on.

1 - Where's the Profit?

Basically, your profit depends on the products you sell and your sources. And so, it is important to identify which are the most profitable brands to sell with Amazon FBA. Review your sales data to check which of your product listings are generating profits on your portfolio.

If you haven't heard of the 80/20 rule especially in running a business, let me share it with you because it will guide you through the first step of the FBA profit cycle.

The 80/20 rule is named as the Pareto Principle which explains that 80% of the outputs are produced from 20% of the inputs. The principle can be applied in your Amazon FBA selling business when identifying the most profitable SKUs and suppliers from your list. Do this to cover the 20% of your inputs and when these products sell on Amazon, expect the 80% output to give you good results.

You should be able to identify which of the *SKUs you sell are generating more profit for you.

* Stock Keeping Unit (SKU) is a product you sell that has a distinct characteristic in its brand, variant, and size or packaging. No same SKU is considered to be the same because each SKU is distinguished from other items.

Additionally, other SKUs from your list that do not sell well should be liquidated so you can divert the investment to the most profitable products.

2 - How to Scout New Products?

Since you have found the brands and suppliers that give the highest profit, you should maintain your focus in scouting for more new products to the list that belong to the same brands and suppliers. In this sense, you are expanding your business through adding new profitable products and restocking the profitable SKUs.

I want to reiterate that stale inventory should be managed very well. Make sure to liquidate them regularly until such time that only the profitable items are listed.

3. How to make the Right Price?

There are various <u>repricing   tools</u> (http://www.amazon.com/dp/B00SF16CLM) that are available to Amazon sellers that you should use to ensure a real-time repricing of your products. The profitability of your products will depend on the repricing strategies you do that should be aligned with your business strategy.

Though you have the competitive advantage against the non-FBA sellers, I advise you not to compete with Fulfilled By Merchant prices because you may end up in an unprofitable price war.

4. How to have a Continued Growth?

Every sale you earn will indicate the result of the actions you took by practicing the 3 steps above. And so, it is necessary that you review product sales regularly. Make sure to restock the products that are creating sales since those are the products that are making you most of the profits.

When these concerns are addressed accordingly, it creates an FBA profit cycle. Repeat the process of identifying the most profitable SKUs, scouting new products and strategizing reprice of products and then review your sales.

Do all the steps all over again so you'll succeed with Amazon FBA. The proper way to do it is to list the right product with the right price and restock the product on time.

You probably still have questions on how you can profit or how can a profit cycle earn you highest profits ever with Amazon FBA.

It's necessary that these strategies should be practiced to earn big profits in Amazon FBA through a continuous cycle.

Here's the 4-step process which I have been very excited to share with you. Through this cycle, you'll be able to create more income with Amazon FBA.

Step 1: Identify the Most Profitable Brands and Suppliers

Have you thought of your bestseller items? But have you ever thought of the products that are profitable? If ever you know the profitable SKUs, do you already have a time table in reordering each item so there would be no out-of-stock? Do you have stale inventories and have you considered how much FBA fees are spent for its storage? These are the most critical questions that you should address as you start a profit cycle.

There is a common mistake that sellers do when it comes to optimizing the FBA selling business. It's not merely managing the bestselling products. It's also the constant identification of the most profitable brands and suppliers and the monitoring of potential stale inventories through time.

Thus, assessing each SKU is necessary.

Here's a checklist that can guide you to evaluate your brands and suppliers.

1 - Determine the sellout rate.

> You need to monitor how many units are sold and if you are profiting from it, assess if it is enough to continue listing the SKU.

2 - Determine the profit margin.

> In selling a business, profit margin relies on the business strategy. Usually, sellers go for higher profit margin, and I can say that it is preferable. But then again, it depends on your strategy because there are some sellers who make low margins with high volume business.

3 - Observe the price trends.

> Price competition is normally disadvantageous to your business. Whenever competition leads to a price war, you have to be extra watchful on pricing your items. The items that are driven below your lowest acceptable price are definitely not worth investing and restocking.

4 - Decide on reorder quantity.

> Determining how many units to reorder is a crucial decision to make especially when each SKU differs on reorder quantity.

There are data that you need to review to be able to get your Reorder Quantity (RQ). Here's the list of data you have to consider:

- Lead-Time (LT) - How many days will you expect to receive the products after placing your order?
- Basic Stock (BS) - How many days of inventory are kept in a normal period?
- Safety Stock (SS) - How many days of inventory are kept in case of emergency?
- Sales per Day (SPD) - What is the average number of items sold per day?

After determining the above data, use the formula below as a guide:

$RQ = [LT + BS + SS] \times SPD$

5 - Prepare your Purchase Order.

Each profitable SKU will start making money with the right number of units to reorder. Prepare your purchase order according to the suggested formula I discussed in #4.

With this basic framework, you can now evaluate your existing FBA inventory. Remember that profiting from selling with Amazon FBA does not end in evaluating the existing inventory. Evaluating products are essential because it is very rare that a product will sell at the same rate within several months. And so, a constant scouting and testing of new FBA products should be done as well. You can't tell when a competitor will come out with a lower price or possibly Amazon will sell the same item as yours. In these instances, you have to be prepared with new products on your list.

Now, it's time to assess if you have stale inventory because it can be a silent killer to your FBA business. Are you aware that if ever you have stale inventory, it's actually a loss of money in terms of fees and opportunities?

Stale inventory is disadvantageous to your business because:

- You'll be charged with semi-annual fees by Amazon depending on cubic volume.
- Your capital will be tied up wherein you can't use it to invest in new products or for other operational costs.
- Items that are seasonal, trending and perishable will only incur fees if no action to dispose or liquidate is taken.

Whenever you see some stale inventory on your list, try to check your options. You may either sell them at a loss or communicate with the supplier to return. However, you will be charged with return fees by Amazon if you opt to return the product to your supplier.

Step 2: Scout New Products

Initially, when you scout new products it doesn't require going too far from what you already have. Save your time in scouting by checking your existing most profitable brands and suppliers.

Listing of new brands is one of the biggest challenges of a seller, and so it is advisable that you start with the existing networks to optimize the relationships. Try to look into some items that your supplier carries and determine if you can sell them. Definitely, seeking other opportunities in your existing suppliers can make your business grow.

Here is a guide on how to evaluate new products to sell on Amazon.

To Do #1: Check if Amazon is a seller of the item that you wish to sell.

You can proceed to evaluate the item if Amazon is not a seller.

To Do #2: Review the Sales rank of the item.

In choosing new products, it is recommended to check the top level category rank of the item on Amazon. If the rank is below 5,000, then you can consider adding the product and continue the evaluation process.

To Do #3: Determine the presence of other FBA sellers.

This will give you an idea of the competition level of a particular product. If there are few or no other FBA sellers, then proceed to the next "To Do" step. Still, current competition should not prevent you from pursuing a product because more FBA sellers only show a demand for the product.

To Do #4: Assess if the product is profitable to list on Amazon FBA.

You do profit calculation whenever you scout a product.

Use your current profit calculation formula if you have any. You can also use the Amazon FBA Revenue Calculator (https://sellercentral.amazon.com/gp/fba/revenue-calculator/index.html/ref=xx_xx_cont_xx?ie=UTF8&lang=en_US) that can provide you the fulfillment and real-time costs comparisons between your own fulfillment and Amazon FBA offers.

Here's a sample calculation that you may use:

> *Profit = [Buy Box Price - (Wholesale Cost + FBA Fee + Amazon Fee + Commission % + Shipping cost)] x Quantity to Order*

To Do #5: Evaluate if the profit is adequate for your business.

You may set your product profitability requirements before deciding to sell and base your decision on the size of your business. If the profitability of the item is adequate for the business, then make a purchase order of this new product and start selling it with Amazon FBA. Otherwise, do not add the item and just look into other products to evaluate.

Believe it or not! Scouting and listing the best brands and suppliers that are identified to have the highest profits can turn up your sales volume and earn you more income.

Step 3: Strategize the Right Price of the Products

Now that you have evaluated a new product to sell on Amazon FBA, the next step is to ensure that the selling price will earn you high profits. To do so, you need to have the right strategy to price it right.

At this stage, you should aim to take control of getting the Buy Box. There can be a lot of challenges in winning the Buy Box, but more opportunities to profit will come when you reprice strategically.

If you haven't used any repricer tool or software, there are various tools available to Amazon sellers such as RepriceIt, ScanPower, Sellery and *Teikametrics*. Repricer tool can make repricing an easy task, but you should think about your repricing strategies thoroughly so your sales will increase and your business will grow.

You should be watchful in using repricer tools and strategizing the right price of your products.

Here's what other sellers are mistakenly doing and thinking which does not help them in making good strategies to earn more profit:

- Sellers are pricing a product for competitive advantages.
- Sellers consider all repricers as the same.
- When price rules and seller's strategy don't match.

Most of the sellers struggle in winning the Buy Box because of its subtle and unusual changes over time. Some sellers reprice the items with higher price whenever a competitor has no stocks or there is no other seller of the item. There are also instances when a seller increases or lowers the price depending on who fulfills the orders, whether by Amazon or by Merchant.

Having the competitive advantage over other sellers should not drive a seller to reprice a product because price rules against an FBA seller would not apply to another FBA seller. The common mistake of sellers is repricing a product to have the advantage and compete with other sellers just to win the Buy Box. But, repricing only requires understanding the behavior of Amazon's Buy Box.

Step 4: Review Results, Restock Products and Repeat the Steps

The most crucial step in the profit cycle is to ensure continued growth in selling with Amazon FBA.

At this stage, you should review how your products perform and watch out when Amazon would not allow a listing of a certain product or your supplier would not want you to list the product on Amazon. If you do not act offensively on how Amazon and other sellers behave, you'll end up frustrated when sales are cut.

Every seller recognizes the intense competition in Amazon, isn't it? In fact, there is no guarantee that your bestseller item today could remain a bestseller the next few days. And so, it is recommended to keep an eye on every item that sells, makes a profit, and the inventory that may generate extra storage fees.

Upon sales review of each item, make sure to restock the profitable products and keep scouting products first from the existing brands and suppliers. Act on the stale inventory and repeat the process from Step 1. Your business will grow when you do all these tasks consistently.

Chapter 12 Fulfillment by Amazon

What is Fulfillment by Amazon?

Fulfillment by Amazon, or FBA, is the official fulfillment service that Amazon offers. There are plenty of well-established fulfillment companies that you can make use of to store and ship your products. Via FBA, Amazon attempts to validate and monitor the products they are selling. It shows an active interest towards what the customers are buying and where they are getting the products.

FBA isn't a new initiative, and if you are used to selling products online, you might have heard of it. It is a fantastic service offered by Amazon and is quite popular in the seller community. However, if you haven't heard of FBA yet, then read on to learn more.

The FBA program was unveiled by Amazon a few years ago, and since then sellers all over the world have been making the most of this service. By exploring the service to its full potential, you can improve your profit margin. It not only is useful for sellers, but it is quite beneficial to the customers as well. The items offered in this program fall under different promotional offers offered by Amazon, like Free Super Saver Shipping and Amazon Prime.

As a seller in the market, it is important that you know who your competitors are, the profits they are making, and the areas in which you are lagging behind. FBA is an excellent service, and it can help you to increase your profits, provided you know how to use it. Understanding how FBA works and how you can use it for getting ahead of your competitors is important for your growth.

How Amazon describes its service

By using Fulfillment by Amazon, you can directly send your product inventory to Amazon's FBA storage unit. Your inventory will be stored in a constantly monitored and secured facility with a climate-controlled environment. Whenever a customer places an order for your product, the packaging team at Amazon will meticulously select, pack, and ship the product to the customer.

Amazon is a leading e-commerce company, and it receives millions of orders every year. The team at Amazon strives to provide sellers with top-notch service and maintain customer trust and satisfaction. To meet these expectations, Amazon developed different innovations in the field of product processing and fulfillment operations. This transported Amazon into a web-to-warehouse, in-a-day delivery organization with comprehensive shipping carrier integration. Amazon's technology keeps improving so that they will be able to serve all interested parties in a better manner.

There is no scientific formula to start selling on Amazon using FBA. Try experimenting with different things, do plenty of research, talk to other sellers and be patient. Yes, trial and error are the best way to go about doing business on Amazon. In this chapter, you will learn about selling through Amazon's FBA program. So, let's get started!

Were you under the impression that Amazon was just for books? In 1994, Jeff Bezos founded this e-commerce website in his garage in Bellevue, Washington. When customers started purchasing books from this website, Jeff was amazed that he was able to sell books to buyers located all over the country. That was when Bezos decided to create a company that offered more than just books. By the beginning of 1998, there were CDs, computer software, DVDs, electronic gadgets, video games, toys and even household items available for sale on Amazon.

By 2000, Amazon had over $1 billion in sales. Several large retailers, including Target, Old Navy, and even Kohl's, agreed to sell their merchandise on Amazon. These large retailers helped Amazon to expand its product offerings and allowed it to add new categories of products as well, paving the way for several small sellers to start selling on the platform. There are more than 30 product categories on Amazon and more than 36 million products (exclusive of books)

There is plenty of potential that Amazon offers a seller, and it allows the seller to connect with a large number of buyers seeking different products. If you are interested in adding FBA to your business mix, then you can reach out to a wider audience. Amazon is not restricted to books any more. With the right set of tools and knowledge, you can earn a handsome profit.

It is important to understand the Amazon customer, and Amazon's customers are quite different from those on other platforms (e.g., eBay). A customer on Amazon is willing to pay more for a product than an eBay customer. They don't mind, in fact, paying for intangibles like fast shipping or an online shopping experience devoid of all hassles. Also, the Free Super Saving Shipping option on Amazon allows customers to qualify for free shipping when the cart total exceeds $25, which implies that an Amazon customer is likely to spend more while shopping. In addition, all those customers who have the Prime membership are entitled to free shipment within two days. On Amazon, there is no room for bargaining or haggling. The price at which the item is listed is the price at which it will be sold, unless there are discounts or sales going on.

Why choose Fulfillment by Amazon?

As a seller, you need to understand the different ways in which you can optimize your business. There are a couple of benefits that FBA has for a seller, and they are discussed in this section. *Triple-win:* FBA is often described as a triple-win scenario, as it is beneficial to the seller, the customer and the organization, all at once. Below are the three benefits, or "wins," that can be achieved by using FBA.

Higher prices, better profit margins, and larger payouts: These three aspects might seem quite different. However, FBA is the thread that binds them all together. Higher prices help to increase the seller's profit margin, and with better profits, the distributors will be able to earn larger payouts as well. Sellers often hesitate to set higher prices for their products, but with FBA, they don't have to think much about this aspect of their business. Most of the products that are listed under FBA are covered under Free Super Saver Shipping and Amazon Prime. So a seller can increase their price, and they will still have an advantage over their competitors. The listed price is inclusive of shipping charges as well.

The shipping charges for non-FBA products are higher than those charged for FBA products. An FBA product can be sold at a higher price because shipping is under the care of Amazon. For example, think of a situation where a non-FBA or an independent seller is offering a product priced at $25 (inclusive of shipping charges) and an FBA seller is offering the same product priced at $25 without shipping charges (since Amazon takes care of shipping). Also, Amazon highlights an FBA product as its beneficiary; it displays the product as its offering.

You don't have to worry about packaging: As an FBA seller, the work you have to do is less compared to other sellers, and this is a critical advantage offered by FBA. FBA products can be shipped any time of the day or night, even during the weekends or the holiday season. The shipping of these products isn't affected by the availability of the seller. All the seller has to do is package the product and send it to the FBA warehouse. That's about it; the seller doesn't have to do anything else. All the product management can be done through the Internet on Amazon with exclusive add-on features like monitoring of inventory levels and adjustment of the selling price. As a seller, you won't have to stack boxes, envelopes or other packing equipment. All you have to do is ship a carton of your products to the FBA inventory at Amazon, which shouldn't be a cumbersome task.

Customer satisfaction: According to Amazon statistical data worldwide, around 40-50% of Amazon customers do not prefer buying products on sale through a third-party merchant. It can be inferred from this data that most of the customers not only trust—but even prefer—to buy from FBA sellers. Amazon is considered a good option for purchasing items because the products ship faster, and in cases of discrepancies, the Amazon customer service responds positively (it includes a valued return policy). You, as a seller, can attract a greater number of customers who are willing to pay that extra dollar for Amazon's fulfillment service. Any seller will naturally want to seize this opportunity, as the total price paid by the customer is higher. The customer's need to receive the item earlier, and with reliable customer service, can be used as a key business opportunity.

Small sellers no more

With the advent of FBA into the selling business, the added benefits of being associated with large-scale sellers have dissolved. Beginner sellers who aren't very experienced with the business, can, through FBA, experience and receive the same outputs as the well-established sellers.

When you're a small-scale seller, your garage or backyard is probably all the packaging space you have for all your products. You can't devote all your time for the listing, delivery and tracking of your orders. During the holiday season, you could even run out of cartons or tape. The initial orders are fun, and you are ready to pump out another ten to twenty orders. But with an increase in demand for your product, you will fall behind on orders. That leads to canceled orders, which will hurt your image as a start-up business.

This issue can be solved with FBA, as the scalability from small-scale to large-scale is very insignificant. Your business can grow as big as you want, and it won't involve needing access to a gold vault. The storage space and time limitations you suffer can be eliminated with FBA, as Amazon treats your company just like the other established sellers, offering you the same inventory storage and other benefits. All of these services have restrictions. If you have products in bulk, you could deliver the whole shipment in a day to the FBA inventory and conveniently sell them all over the week. If you can regulate your inventory population, you could be selling thousands of your products right from your backyard.

You sell, and they ship. Amazon has created one of the most advanced fulfillment networks in the world, and your business can now benefit from their expertise. With FBA, you stock your products at Amazon's fulfillment centers, and they directly pack, distribute, and offer service for these products. Other benefits

Exclusive discounts:

Most customers who shop on Amazon wait eagerly for offers and discounts. The Free Super Saver Shipping and Amazon Prime are FBA exclusive discounts on Amazon. These discounts are delivered with free shipping.

Better pricing:

The total price of your product in the FBA listing on Amazon is exclusive of the shipping cost. Hence during the sorting, your product will appear at a much lower price, attracting more customers with a competitive price.

Reliability:

Your FBA product will display the words "Fulfillment by Amazon" in bold with its logo, which indicates to the customers that the product can be trusted as there is high-level monitoring of packing and delivery. There is also better post-order customer service and a return policy, all under Amazon's care.

Anytime access:

Through FBA, you can manage your inventory anytime, anywhere via an app on your smartphone. You can manage your space while getting the damaged products repaired and then returned to the inventory at the Amazon fulfillment centers.

Functioning of FBA

When using FBA, you only send your inventory over to an Amazon Fulfillment Center, and the people over at Amazon take care of your inventory from there onwards. They handle all the back-end operations. They store the stock, fulfill the orders, and handle customer support and returns. This makes the fulfillment of your orders more consistent and reliable. You can choose to store as much or as little as you can afford. Here are the steps to register for FBA:

- Open your web browser and go to www.amazon.com/fba. Then click on "Get Started."
- Since you already have an Amazon Seller Central account, just select "Add FBA to your account."
- Log into your Amazon Seller Central account from here and go to the Inventory tab.
- Then click on "Manage Inventory." From here, you can choose which products you want to list for FBA. Select the checkbox next to each product you want to list.
- Now go to the Actions dropdown menu, and click on "Change to Fulfilled by Amazon."

- Click on "Convert" on the page that follows.

When you have completed this, your next step is to ship your stock to an Amazon Fulfillment Center. For this, follow these instructions:

- Log into your Seller Central account and go to the Inventory tab.
- Go to "Manage Inventory" and select the check boxes against the items you want to send to Amazon Fulfillment Centers.
- Go to the Actions menu and click on "Send/Replenish Inventory."
- You will be prompted to provide a shipping address.
- Next, you will be asked how you will ship the products: individual items or case-packed.

Note: Take a look at the Dangerous Units, Hazardous Materials, and EBA Prohibited Products page before doing this, just so you're sure everything is legal.

At this point, you need to review the labeling requirements of your products. The receiving systems at Amazon are barcode-dependent. Every unit you send to them needs to have a barcode that can be scanned. You can do this in three ways:

- You can print and apply labels manually to each unit.
- Use FBA Label Service. Amazon will label your products for you.

- Sign up for Sticker-less Commingled Inventory if your products are eligible for it.

When you are preparing to print your product labels, follow these recommendations from Amazon:

- Avoid inkjet printers. They are more prone to fading and smearing. Use a laser or thermal printer instead.
- Make sure your printer is capable of handling a resolution of 300 DPI or more.
- Use the proper print media.
- Clean and replace the printer heads periodically.
- Scan your label yourself from time to time to test them.

After entering the number of units you want to ship for each product, click on "Print Item Labels." A PDF file will be created that contains printable labels, which you can use later. You have to print these labels on white label stock that has removable adhesive. This helps in easy scanning and clean removal. If there is an original barcode or multiple barcodes on your product or its package, make sure you have covered them well. Only your Amazon-provided product label should be visible.

If your products need some prepping when they arrive at the fulfillment center, it will slow down the shipping process. You can avoid this by using Amazon's FBA Prep Services, or you can send them fully prepped and ready to ship.

Each box that is sent to Amazon should have a unique shipping label. That is the only way to identify it at the fulfillment center. Follow these guidelines to print shipping labels from the shipment creation workflow:

- Place the labels in the middle of the box, or at least somewhere they won't be cut off. Avoid placing them on corners or box seams.
- Each box has to have a unique shipping label.
- Pallets need to have five labels each. One label goes on the top and the other four go on the sides.

After properly fixing the labels to your products, you have to schedule a time on the Amazon website for their pickup, and then mark it as "shipped" in the Shipment Summary. In your Shipping Queue, you can track the status of your shipment. You should allow at least 24 hours for the status to be updated to "Delivered."

Once the status has been updated, contact your carrier to confirm delivery. If the status shows "Checked-in," it means that at least a part of the shipment has reached the fulfillment center. Once the center starts scanning the barcodes on your units, the status changes to "Receiving." It usually takes six days at most for all of your shipment to be received and scanned. After this, the dimensions of your products are recorded and they are stored, ready to ship.

Amazon uses an advanced web-to-warehouse picking system, which is fast and sorts through the warehouse inventory quickly. When a customer purchases your product, FBA ships your merchandise to them according to their preferred method of service. The customer can track their order through the website and can contact them in case of any issues.

Getting paid with FBA

You can check the status of orders placed with you from the "Manage Orders" page in your Seller Central account. It will either show "Pending" or "Payment Complete." You can also check if you have received the payment by going to the "Reports" tab and looking for the order transaction.

Chapter 13 Using Platforms to Sell Products Through Amazon FBA

When you look at your business plan, you will need to also research the workings of Amazon, eBay, Etsy, Craigslist, etc. As part of your business plan, you will build in strategies as to how to make a great profit with healthy margins. You will need to research and study each site, to include factors such as fees for the purchase, processing, shipping, taxes and other fees for both the platform as well as Amazon. Once you set your dollar amount, you will design a profit margin formula to get there which will also include steps and strategies such as types of items, photos and item descriptions. All of these variables affect your prices.

Reselling and selling are a serious business. If you give it proper attention it will not just succeed but it can grow. As you will see with Private Label e-commerce, you also can scale up your business.

eBay

The site eBay.com is one of the primary Fulfillment by Amazon (FBA) Multi-Channel Fulfillment "platforms." Again, this allows you to work through Amazon to ship and sell and store goods on your behalf.

For now, this applies only to domestic inventory, but you do still have the option to ship things on your own as well, if needed. Listings on eBay have somewhat more limitations than if you were using Amazon directly. You should always read eBay's policies when setting up your account.

Selling from Amazon-to-eBay is interesting. A buyer most often does not care that an item came from Amazon necessarily. In most cases seeing an Amazon box is a good thing. However, many people also don't look at their packaging. We will cover this area later however.

Storage and shipping rates are usually quite good for the FBA Multi-Channel Fulfillment. Low shipping costs can be set up as leverage for selling more than the competition on eBay. You do not get any Amazon commissions as you would if you are working directly through Amazon unfortunately however. This is one downside. Rates will be provided in easy tables however. Price fluctuations between Amazon and eBay can affect your buying source materials, or even selling your items. Price fluctuations are unavailable though and it could affect your profits. This is something that may be difficult to keep up with but there are solutions for this problem that will be covered later.

Each multi-channel FBA requires different techniques and strategies.

Craigslist

Craigslist is usually a very easy way to buy and resell online. Local deals are a different target market. Most other sites are either domestic or international buyers.

When using Craigslist for sourcing goods, choose to view the listings with pictures. Also, you should try out different variations on words when ordering and word stems (i.e. fence, fences, fencing, and wire fences). You can also try different state and regional listings. Adjacent states are also places where you can source new items.

Craigslist is intended to be used by locals. If you see something, most often you can go and see it before you buy it. That does not have to be the case, but that tends to be how it is arranged. If you want to purchase new or vintage items that you would like to see for yourself, this may be a good way to go. You potentially could set up shipping for products you sell yourself on the site however. Read the rules before you post.

When you first get on the site and do keyword searches, you can highlight what you see as your favorites using the star feature in Craigslist, and go back to them later. Compare similar items then go in for the buy if you are still interested. Yet act fast as things on Craigslist do not usually last long, especially if they are of a really good quality and value.

Create a personal connection if you are looking to buy something, especially if it is unique, large, or special in some way. Making a connection through a non-generic email sometimes will be a deciding factor. A seller may not want to part with a beloved or appreciated item that will go to just anyone. If you say you are interested, do follow up and show up if you agree to meet. Craigslist has its own dynamics which differs from sites like eBay and Amazon.

Etsy

Many sellers and buyers also go to Etsy.com. Etsy provides specialty, hand crafted, one of a kind, or limited productions of many different items. Each Etsy seller has their own virtual store.

Take a look through at the type of products that sell on Etsy. You will gather much information on the markets, types of shoppers and sellers and the unique niches that it serves.

With Etsy (like other sites) pictures are important. Perhaps with Etsy, the pictures are even more relevant, given that most of what is there can be considered to be art in some form. You won't see what you may see often on sites like Amazon where a generic photo is used for the same product across sellers.

The item descriptions are also important as are good descriptions that pop. The descriptions should not be vague. The items on Etsy are generally not what you would find on a retail or department store site therefore they need to have great selling points. Personalized descriptions also help draw buyers. You should differentiate your items from the rest in the best way that you possibly can.

Chapter 14 Increasing Sales with Marketing

Pay-per-click

Pay-per-click or PPC strategies are misunderstood, underutilized, and if done well, will lead you to increased sales. Once you have your items sourced, stocked, and listed, you want to market them for sales. Pay-per-click advertising, better known as simply PPC, works by converting your advertising into sales.

When shopping, and typing in key words for products, Amazon will pull up pictures and descriptions of both paid search results and organic searches. The organic search results appear to a shopper under the paid ads. They pop up because of search words and key words that you will set when listing as well as use in your Pay-per-click. On the top and/or right side are the paid-ads. Few people notice the difference. You should understand the difference in terms of your marketing.

By using pay-per-click, you target market your product better. By using a pay-per-click campaign, you are using a focused approach to identifying your customers and honing in on what they are looking for (which is your product!). You only pay for the ads as shoppers click on and open them. Data is also gathered from your own campaign and available to you for study and use.

Focus on Your Rankings

First things first, you should always focus on your rankings when it comes to growing your Amazon FBA business. You want to focus on your product rankings and your seller ranking as both of these are going to help you get in front of your audience in a bigger way.

With Amazon FBA, there is an email sent out after products are purchased which encourages people to leave a review for your products. You are not going to need to do anything to encourage these. The same goes for your seller ranking as people can rank both you and your store. Due to the nature of Amazon FBA, any reviews that complain about shipping or product management will not go toward your overall ranking as these are the responsibility of Amazon, not you.

What you can do to really contribute to your rankings improving is ensure that you are always offering the highest quality products possible and that your product descriptions are accurate so that people get exactly what they order. The more accurate and high quality you can make your shop and products, the more you are going to earn high-quality reviews that improve your rankings and help you sell more.

Do What You Know

When it comes to selling on Amazon FBA, you are already likely wandering in a world that you do not yet know much about. For that reason, it is a good idea to do what you know by sticking with your strengths and selling products that you understand. Doing so can ensure that you are not adding more stress to the learning process which will help make the learning process go even smoother.

The best way to grow your business is to do what you know and teach yourself the most important basics first. This way, everything you are learning and everything you are doing are familiar, and you have an easier time doing it well which will only help your store grow larger and with greater integrity.

Always Track Your Numbers

When people do not pay attention to their numbers, you can tell. Businesses fail when people are not watching the numbers because they do not have a clear idea of what is and what is not working. At the end of the day, all of the advice in the world will not give you a more accurate view of what you need to do to grow your business when compared to the actual numbers that you are receiving. Pay attention to them and use them accordingly as this is your only way to track your momentum and guarantee your growth.

Grow Your Online Presence

If you really want to scale your business, you are going to have to run some form of an online presence. At the end of the day, Amazon is not going to turn as many eyes toward your store as you can until you have some of the best possible rankings all around. Even then, relying on Amazon is not necessarily the best way for you to really guarantee your growth.

You can grow your presence on Instagram, Facebook, Twitter, YouTube, and even Pinterest as a way to get your name out there. Growing your own blog is another great way to establish your brand and drive more traffic to your website so that you can improve your chances of getting found.

Use Paid Advertising

Paid advertising is an incredibly valuable way to grow your online presence. Although it does cost more this way, it will support you with getting seen by an audience that you may not necessarily see otherwise. As well, it automatically improves your ranking results by putting you right at the top of the listings rather than you having to rely on organic SEO (Search Engine Optimization) alone to rank higher.

Add More Products to Your Store

If you want to scale up your business, one obvious way might be to add more products to your store. Having more products available for your customers to purchase means that you are more likely to have an increase in your sales because you are offering things that your audience actually wants to have more of.

When you are adding more products to your store, make sure that you are adding products that your customers actually want to buy. As well, make sure that every single product you sell makes sense to your brand and fits into your industry. This way, you are confident that your brand stays organized and relevant, and that it remains stocked with products that your customers are more likely to be interested in.

Conclusion

In this book, we have given you amazing information in terms of growing your very own Amazon FBA business. As you can tell after reading this book, you will be in much better hands in terms of growing your business the right way.

You now have the right knowledge and tools to grow your business without any worries. You are ready to start making some money now. We taught you all of that and more, and helped you start to get your business rolling. This book is geared towards people who are just starting out their Amazon FBA business; however, there are still some amazing techniques you could use to grow your already advanced business. In this book, we also showed you how to get more sales using some social media techniques.

It is very important that you understand this concept as it will help you to grow your business tremendously. We have covered some amazing topics, so once you have understood a topic, apply it. One more thing- if you don't understand some concepts, then we would advise you to take your time and come back to it. Make sure you fully understand the knowledge in this book before you move on.

Make Money with Blogging

The Ultimate guide to make profitable blog with Proven Strategies to Make Money Online While You Work from Home. Change your mindset to join the new rich.

Table of Contents

Description

Blogging is one of the best ways to build an online presence that can be monetized. If you haven't noticed by now, a blog is crucial to maximizing profits across almost every method of creating passive income. Whether it's a way to share your affiliate links, or a place to promote your online course and grow your email list, a well-design blog is a huge asset to any online business. Maintaining a blog does have the potential to be time consuming, but you can outsource almost every aspect of the process to freelancers, from choosing a name and building a website to creating the blog's content. Your blog is a great place to connect with your audience by offering them valuable information for free and establishing yourself as an expert within your niche.

When you're creating content, it needs to be informative, entertaining, and real. Your blog may be centered around sharing valuable information, but it shouldn't read like a boring lecture. Be personable and write the same way you'd speak in a conversation (or have your freelancer write that way) so your readers feel more deeply connected to your content. These kinds of posts are more likely to inspire readers to share them on social media or send them to their friends.

Share perspectives on recent events or trends within your niche, studies that are relevant to your subject matter, "Top

10" style lists, and how-to guides. You can, and certainly should also incorporate the products you sell, paid promotions, affiliate links, etc., but you want to come across as though you're sharing a product with a friend- something that will benefit their lives, and not like you're a salesperson trying to turn a profit. The large amount of valuable free information you provide will make your readers more likely to want to buy you products when you do share them.

Building this type of relationship with your audience allows them to appreciate the value you bring to their lives and trust your suggestions. You should also be sure to always inform your audience if you stand to profit from any actions they take on your website, whether it be clicking on ads or buying products from a link. Again, the more your audience trusts you, the more loyal a customer base you'll have.

This guide will focus on the following:

- Blog Types
- Picking Your Topic
- Which Blogging Platform Should I Use?
- Desired Qualities
- Topping The Charts
- Tips For Creating Posts
- Marketing Your Blog

- The Complete Marketing Plan
- How To Keep Your Traffic Coming Back
- What Is The Difference Between Adsets And Ads?
- Monetization
- Affiliate Marketing
- Monetized Through Products
- Other Monetization Methods
- Measuring Blog Success
- Income Streams... AND MORE!!!

Introduction

A blog is not really an article... now and then there is a distinction. A blog is a discussion amongst you and the peruser; it is more personal, yet it ought to be educational, moreover. An article is a snippet of data. It is composed by a proficient person who is viewed as a specialist by what he or she posts.

In any case, there is a parallel amongst blogs and articles... actually they can be a similar thing.

Most entrepreneurs will post to their blog and exclude personal data since they are utilizing the blog to improve their business as opposed to utilizing it to associate with their loved ones. The fortunate thing about educational writing done by somebody who is a specialist on the content is that individuals will tune in (simply ensure regardless you endeavor to be utilize a personable voice to identify with your group of onlookers).

It is another marketing instrument to compose articles from a specialist position which can be presented on a couple of chose article registries. Try not to present your article on each place you can on the Internet. Ensure the indexes are legitimate and just post to 5-10 catalogs.

A couple of the catalogs I exceedingly prescribe are EzineArticles, GoArticles, Biznik. Notwithstanding perusers finding your articles on these catalogs, the articles from these locales likewise appear in seeks (on Google, Yahoo, and so forth.) when somebody is searching for your aptitude.

Article marketing is another approach to get your blog out there (as the locales require a bio) and show individuals what you bring to the table.

Social Media Marketing

Presenting a message on various social media systems is as straightforward as entering the message into the fitting window. Nevertheless, there could at present be an issue. Imagine a scenario where you don't post all the time. Are individuals going to hear you out/perused your blog when they have no clue your identity? The appropriate response, obviously, is no. You need to make a nearness on the social media locales, build up a group that trusts and tails you. You require some online companions and supporters.

This is done essentially by posting a couple of times each day (the measure of posts relies upon which social media organize you are presenting on) with things of intrigue. By doing this you will assemble a following and individuals will anticipate your messages. They may likewise visit your site to take in more about you and your business.

Tip: Even however you can utilize HootSuite to plan these posts for the week, I would at present recommend you visit the social media systems you are more required with every day and physically post data and connect with others. In case you don't, your associations will see that you are not so much systems administration with them and simply advancing your business (regardless of the possibility that the week after week posts are special).

Video and Podcast

Your blog content can be extended significantly further. Recordings and podcasts can be added to your blog as marketing devices. The group of onlookers becomes more acquainted with you better and has a superior comprehension of your advertising. At one time, I would not have even recorded these as a basic blog marketing procedures, yet in the present online world, they have both turned into a central point (particularly recordings).

Video Marketing. Notwithstanding presenting a video on your blog, you can circulate it to video catalogs.

YouTube is a standout amongst the most prevalent destinations on the web today and it has been for various years. Anybody can post a video, about anything, and put it on this virtual board. This can profit you if an individual is hunting down recordings in your subject matter or if companions need to perceive what you bring to the table.

Podcasts. Podcasts take somewhat more association, yet they can likewise be an incredible marketing apparatus. It is fundamentally an internet radio program that you have or are a visitor of. Making the podcast is as straightforward as purchasing a mouthpiece and the product required. A few people go greater and rally up their creation esteem, yet you can keep it basic.

When you make your podcast, you can transfer it to a plugin on your site and it will be consequently circulated to iTunes.

There are numerous systems that can be added to your blog marketing design, however this will give you a decent begin. When you begin a blog for your private company, ensure you spread the news about what you have composed. Advance your new blog post in social media, bookmark your post (or host a third get-together do it), present the content to fitting article catalogs, present the content to suitable article registries and genuinely consider making a video and additionally podcast from that blog post content. In case you do the greater part of this, you will be end route to an effective blog!

Blogging as an Employee

If you are an employee and one of your job responsibilities is to write blogs for the company, every blog post you write for the company is a work made for hire. Your employer owns the copyright to all the content of your work blogs, not you. You may not put any blogs in your portfolio to seek other work without your employer's permission. Doing so would infringe on your employer's exclusive rights to decide where its blogs will be reproduced and displayed.

Your employer only obtains the copyright to the exact verbiage you create for the company. You may write about the same topics in your personal blog or for your portfolio, unless your work contract prohibits this. You just can't copy what you specifically created for your employer without their permission.

If you have a Twitter handle or accounts on other social media sites that you use to promote the company and its blog, there may be a legal question regarding who owns the accounts and whether you retain the rights to your accounts and your followers when you leave the company. These are issuing you and your employer should resolve in writing before you create these accounts.

Independent Contractors

If you are a freelance blogger, companies hire you to write blogs on their behalf. Unlike people who blog as company employees, the company that hires you may not automatically own the copyright to the blog posts you create for them. The company will own the blog content you create for them if you have a written agreement that is signed before you begin the work, if the contract states that your posts are works made for hire, and if your blog posts qualify as "commissioned works". According to the Copyright Act, a commissioned work made for hire must fit into one of the following nine categories:

1. A contribution to a collective work,

2. Part of a motion picture or other audiovisual work,

3. A translation,

4. A supplementary work to a publication (i.e. forward, afterword, illustration, map, chart, table, musical arrangement, bibliography, appendixes, editorial notes),

5. A compilation,

6. An instructional text,

7. A test,

8. Answer materials for a test, or

9. An atlas.

The law regarding works made for hire was obviously created for copyrightable projects that have multiple contributors, like books and movies. There is a viable argument that blogs created by freelance writers are part of a collective work or a compilation.

If you blog as an independent contractor and you don't have a contract that was signed before you started blogging stating that your posts are works made for hire, you likely own the copyright to the content you create. The company that hired you does not own it; it just has permission to publish it on their website. If you find yourself in this situation, you own all the exclusive copyright rights regarding the reproduction, distribution, and display of your posts, and the right to make derivative works based on your content. You can register your copyright with the Copyright Office. If the company wants to use your posts in other ways, it needs your permission to do so. If the company wants to own the copyright to your work, you can make them buy it from you.

Are You an Employee or an Independent Contractor?

If a court has to decide who owns the copyright to a work, it may start by examining whether you were an employee or an independent contractor when you created the work in question. Whether you are an employee or an independent contractor may have a significant impact on who owns the copyright to your work. The court will consider how much control the person or company that hired you had over your work. It may examine many factors in deciding whether you were an employee or an independent contractor including:

- The skill level required to create the work,
- Who provided the tools and equipment to create the work,
- Where you performed your work,
- Whether the person who hired you could assign you other tasks,
- Whether you worked on an ongoing or on a project basis,
- Whether the person who hired you could control the days and hours you worked,
- Whether you were paid hourly, weekly, or on a project basis,

- Whether the person who hired you controlled your ability to hire assistants,

- Whether the company that hired you does the work that you were hired to perform as part of its business,

- Whether you received employee benefits, and

- How the company classified you in terms of taxes.

The court will consider the circumstances surrounding your employment, not just what you consider yourself to be or what the person who hired you calls you.

Licensing Your Blog Content

When you write blogs for your own company or blog, you have the ability to license your work to others. When you license your work, you retain the copyright to it, but you give someone permission to use your work for a particular purpose. For example, you may write content that others can repurpose or republish on their websites. If you create original artwork, you may license it to others to use in their projects.

The benefit of licensing is that it allows you to use the same content in multiple ways. This increases your chance of exposure, as well as your ability to make money multiple times from one literary or artistic work.

Your licenses must be specific about how the person who is licensing your work can use it. The licensing agreement should state whether the license is exclusive or non-exclusive. When you grant someone an exclusive license, only that person can use your work in a particular way. If you give someone an exclusive license to use your work, you could be prohibited from using your own work in certain ways. When you give someone a non-exclusive license, you have the ability to license the same work to other people to use in similar ways, and to use it yourself.

Be mindful when you write your licensing agreements that you specify how the other person may use your work, including whether he has the ability to sublicense your work to others, and any limits on where your work may appear. You may not be happy if you give someone permission to publish your content on any website they own if you later learn that one of the sites is a porn site. You also want to specify how long the license will last—whether the person can use your work forever or only for a limited amount of time. You should also be clear about the payment structure.

It may seem strange that you can create a literary, artistic, or audiovisual work and not be able to use it, but that's how it is sometimes. If you sell your copyright to someone or you create a work made for hire, you can't use your own work without the risk of being accused of copyright infringement. If you sell your copyright to someone else and you later regret the decision, you can ask to buy it back from whoever owns it. When you create work made for hire, particularly if you're a freelancer, make sure your contract includes a license for you to use your work in your portfolio so you can use it as a work sample to obtain other work. With this license, the other person or company retains ownership of the copyright, but you have permission to use the work in a limited way.

Chapter 1 Blog Types

So, to summarize, you have now made the decision to blog and know exactly why you want to do it. You also understand what niche you want to occupy. Now it's time to think about what type of blog will suit you

Expert Blogs

Expert blogs are set up to make money. The main goal of a niche blogger is to create content, which will be valuable for a certain set of people and are frequently used as a passive income stream. They are usually highly targeted and they have strong on-page Search Engine Optimization (SEO) which helps to bring in visitors quickly from Google. Profits and commissions can then be made from the purchases and clicks of the visitors as well as advertising fees from advertisers.

Business Blogs

A business blog is meant to have high-quality content on different areas of interest for customers to read. Business blogs can be about almost any topic, but they are always related to the core of the business that is being marketed. As such, they usually provide high-quality information in areas that they actually care about. This, in effect, draws even more visitors to their business' website, making it more of a marketing mechanism.

Professional Blogs

Professional blogs are hybrids of business blogs and niche expert blogs. Usually, the creators write about topics that they love and are knowledgeable in, with the blog itself also an essential aspect of their business. Professional bloggers make money by many different means. There are usually not many advertisements or affiliate links on their sites – instead, professional bloggers use their sites to promote their own eBooks, courses, subscriptions, consulting services, and other digital products. These businesses usually do not have an offline presence, but you will find high-quality content on these sites because this content is an important part of their business.

Personal Blogs/Journals

Many bloggers create personal journals to document their day-to-day activities. They keep their readers posted on the events happening in their lives. Many times you'll find people who post short stories or poems which either they or someone they admire have written.

The writing of web journals takes a narrative style and is more informal in nature. The authors of journals may write about a variety of topics, much like how one would write in a traditional diary. Some may have a large number of readers depending on how long they have been blogging for and the nature of the topic they blog about. Journals are not usually set up for profit but are merely a means for creative expression or to have fun. The authors usually post content frequently, often daily or every two days.

Such blogs can be interesting to those readers who enjoy being engaged in the experiences of other people. An example would be a travel blogger or those who describe how they moved to another country.

Educational Blogs

A number of Universities and other educational organizations are now posting educational blogs, posting information concerning lessons or lesson plans, allowing students to ask questions or provide input. Using this form of digital communication allows students who have missed classes, or who may need additional information, to easily find their assignments and ask questions. Educational blogs are very popular for instructors teaching online classes.

Educational blogs can be lead not only by educational institutions. If you are an expert or have experience in a particular field, you can also create a blog to train other people. Such a blog can be interesting for both those who are just eyeing this profession and for those who are already working in it.

Educational blogs usually promote training courses and can also make money by advertising these services.

Branding Blogs

Branding blogs are set up by people who want to make a name for themselves as experts in their fields before they start seeking monetary gain from the blog. As such, they usually shy away from short-term advertising, and their blogs are not usually filled with affiliate links and advertisements. Their content is usually of high quality.

In fact, any successful blog is a brand. Whatever niche for your blog you choose, your blog will differ from others only in your own voice, style, opinion, etc. Of course, this result you can not achieve in a short time. You need to work hard to develop your own style. But this is exactly what will lead you to success.

Your personal brand is determined by many factors: your values, your talents, your relationships with people. In fact, this is practically the same thing as personal contact with people in real life. You start to communicate with someone and very quickly understand whether this person is interesting to you, whether you want to communicate with him or not. With blogging, branding happens this way.

So before you start, create your own image. Write on paper who you are, what your values and abilities are. Imagine your audience and decide for yourself what values you will carry it.

Promotional Blogs
These blogs are usually written by those who are selling a new product, such as a book. You will not usually find them on a single website, but rather they will 'guest post' for several different blogs. Sometimes, these bloggers will not even have a blog site of their own. They simply exist through interviews and postings about their products on other sites.

Let's sum up

Blogging is fun and can suit nearly everyone. To start, all you need to do is type Blogging Sites into any search engine. Then just start checking them out to see what will work best for you! Knowing the type of blog to choose and actually succeeding as a blogger are two different elements. Therefore, we must explore the qualities of successful bloggers that you should try to embrace if you wish to be successful.

Chapter 2 Picking Your Topic

Before you begin writing a blog, it is important that you choose your topic. You may or may not already have a topic in mind. If you do, I strongly encourage you to continue reading this chapter anyway. Reading this chapter will help you look deeper into the basis of your topic, determine whether or not it is actually profitable, and help you refine your topic so that you pick one that will take you to the top.

When you are choosing a blog topic to generate a six-figure income, you need to consider both your interests and the profitability of the topic. You are not simply writing for pleasure, but rather you are looking to turn your blog into a business. For that reason, you need to look at it from a business perspective.

Brainstorm Topics You Enjoy

Before you begin looking into the profitability of topics, begin by brainstorming what types of things you enjoy talking about. Consider topics, but also consider niches. In general, most blogs perform best if you speak to a specific niche within an industry. So, try and consider what specific types of topics you like talking about, and which audiences you would enjoy interacting with the most.

It is important that you choose a topic that you genuinely enjoy. The idea of creating a blog that earns you six figures per year is typically built on the desire to have freedom. This should involve you considering both financial freedom, and time freedom. If you constantly feel annoyed or stressed about what you need to do for your blog, you are not going to experience time freedom. Furthermore, this will eventually lead to you not fully investing yourself in the business, and therefore you will not experience financial freedom, either.

Choosing a topic that you enjoy will assist you in feeling more confident in and excited by doing work for your blog. You will genuinely have fun when you get to research topics, write new content, and share it with your audience. This excitement will pour through in your writing and sharing, too. When people are passionate about what they write about, their audience can tell. This is usually what draws their audience in.

To make this step easy, start with at least three to five different topics that you would enjoy writing in most. That way, at least one of them should be a topic that you can easily profit from. If there is only one topic you really want to talk about, consider different angles or perspectives that you could approach it from to see if you can find unique niches around the topic. That way you can explore profitability and choose the option that is going to be the most fun to write and share about.

Research These Topics

Once you have chosen which topics would excite you the most, you want to start to research these topics. How many blogs already exist in this niche? Are there any that are performing particularly well? What can you tell about these blogs? You want to collect as much information as you can about the topic itself. Notice how many blogs are already successful, and whether or not they are making a profit. Also, notice what angle they are taking on, and how popular the topic actually is. The following three points in this chapter will point out the three things you need to consider most when you are researching a topic. By the time you research all three of these aspects, you should be left with one or two topics that are clearly superior to the others in regards to being worth the investment. If there is more than one, you get to decide which you would prefer to write in. Otherwise, stick to the one that is most likely to make you more money as this will be the best business decision.

Consider Profitability

Profitability is a major key when you are looking to blog for, you know, profit. So, you need to consider the profitability of each niche. There are many ways that you can assess a topic for profitability. This will ensure that you can really consider how much profit you can actually make. After all, we are not looking for a couple hundred dollars here and there. We are looking to consistently make six-figure annual salaries through the blog. For that reason, we need a topic that is going to be highly profitable and successful.

The first thing that you want to do when you are checking for profitability is to bring up about ten blogs that each discuss the same topic you want to talk about. These should range in popularity from some of the biggest blogs in the niche to smaller and moderate-sized blogs. Then, you want to scan these blogs and see how profitable they actually are. Who is already making a profit on this topic? Are they making a decent profit? Where is their profit coming from, as far as you can tell? You can determine this by paying attention to monetized features. The most common sources on blogs include advertisements, sponsored posts, affiliate links, and products that are created by the bloggers themselves.

You want to get an idea of where the profits are coming from and how many avenues are being addressed in this way. That way, you can get a sense of just how profitable a blog topic can actually be. Remember, you don't want to pick one where you are only going to be able to make a limited income, you want to pick one where you will be able to make massive income. So, pay attention and look to see how many ways they are profiting.

Then, pay attention to the top bloggers. Your goal is to become amongst them, so you want to see the average income range for these bloggers. Since you have a goal of how much you want to make with your blog, you want to make sure that the top earners in your chosen industry are making about as much as you want to be making, if not more. If they aren't, there is a good chance that the topic you are looking into is not profitable enough for you to invest your time into it.

Once you have gone through all of the topics you chose and have determined their profitability, now you can begin to eliminate the ones that will not earn you a significant profit. After that, you can begin to move down the list of what you need to consider to ensure a topic is worthy of your attention!

Consider Content Value

The next thing you need to focus on is content value. If you start a blog that is not going to give you plenty to talk about and with a great value attached, you are going to run dry quickly. You will not have the opportunity to make six figures from your blog because there simply won't be enough content to get you to that point. You have to make sure that the topic you are choosing to talk about is going to have plenty for you to discuss with your audience.

Go back to those ten blogs you selected to pay attention to and see what types of things they are talking about. Notice if these are topics that you would actually be interested in talking about and if they are going to be able to keep you sustained for a long time. Pay attention to see how many times they repeat similar topics, approach them from different angles, and recycle content. A blog may appear to have a lot to talk about, but upon closer inspection, you may realize that they actually do not have much new to talk about. This can result in you being run dry of topics and ultimately losing your audience. Alternatively, you may have to rebuild your audience consistently because your existing audience gets bored and moves on. If this is your goal, then choosing a topic like this is fine. If a six-figure income is your goal, then you need to choose a topic that will give you a lot to talk about.

After you have reviewed existing blogs, sit and brainstorm yourself. What topics do you think you would like to talk about? How many different topics can you come up with off the top of your head? Is it easy to draw on these ideas, or are you finding yourself struggling to come up with more? Knowing how easy it is to come up with fresh content will help you determine whether or not the topic can actually serve for a long time. Remember, you want to have plenty to talk about for a long time if you are going to grow your blog to a six-figure income earner.

Another thing you should consider is how well you know the content that you are considering writing about. While we can always research to freshen up or get more information on specific angles, writing about a topic that you know absolutely nothing about can prove to be difficult. While it does give you a chance to explore it, you will not connect well with your desired audience because they will end up clicking through to blogs that discuss the topic with greater certainty and knowingness. Choose a topic that is easy for you to talk about and that you have a strong basic understanding of at the very least. This will ensure that when you talk about the topic, you can speak with authority, and people are more likely to listen to you. If you speak too timidly or regularly recite wrong facts or information that does not make sense, people will begin to realize that you are not a reliable source and they will go elsewhere for their information.

Consider Your Audience

Finally, you must consider your audience! There are a few ways that you can factor in your audience. Since you don't actually have one already, you need to consider who your audience is going to be.

One great way is to take a look at your existing audience. Although it may not be much beyond your friends and family, consider the ones that you speak with most about this specific subject on. What is it about them that keeps you talking about this subject? How do they resemble the audience that you may eventually speak to openly on your blog? Pay attention to these factors and use them to begin generating an ideal audience.

Another thing you should consider is who the audience of your competition's blogs are. Pay attention to blogs that are similar to what yours will be and consider who they are speaking to. This will be very similar to the audience you want to speak to, so paying attention to this information and generating an understanding of who their audience is can help you when it comes to knowing who you are talking to.

Finally, consider who you want to talk to. What audience excites you the most? What is it about them that makes you eager to talk to them and share your information with them? Why are they the best people for you to speak to? How can you serve them? Get clear on the specifics between you and them. You want to consider your audience because this is how you are going to pick your final topic. Your final topic should align with an audience that you feel comfortable speaking to from a place of authority. If you don't, you are going to struggle to position yourself as an expert and acquire readers and people who are willing to listen to you.

The Final Pick

The topic you end up picking should be one that will provide you with ample opportunity to generate your desired income, that will have plenty for you to talk about, and that will speak directly to your desired audience. You should know how to approach your audience, communicate with your audience, and keep your audience. If you want to generate six-figure earnings with your blog, you do not want to choose an audience that will come and go quickly. Instead, you want to build a relationship with your audience and keep them coming back for a long time. This will ensure that you can build your audiences loyalty and, later, capitalize on that loyalty!

Chapter 3 Which Blogging Platform Should I Use?

The core essence of any blogging platform is its Content Management System (CMS). A CMS is a system that helps you to manage your content. It includes creating, editing, publishing and saving content, among others manipulations. These CMS platforms are differentiated by the following factors;

- Programming language
- License type
- Hosting type
- Pricing

Programming language

There are many programming languages. Programming language is extremely important as it will determine how easily you can access professional help should you desire to tweak or customize some CMS features.

The following are the most popular programming languages for CMS (server-side);

- PHP
- C#
- Java

- Python
- Node.js

PHP is by far the most popular CMS programming language. As such, it is easy for you to learn or get professional help should you desire to tweak or customize your blog. Most popular blog platforms including WordPress, Joomla and Drupal are written in PHP.

The second most popular CMS programming language is C#. But it comes at a very distant second to PHP. Java and Python are less popular. Node.js is a new entrant that is growing in leaps and bounds and is likely to grab a big share in future as it continues to increase in popularity. It is more likely to rival PHP in the near future. For the time being (as of publishing this guide), there are very few host providers for Node.js, C# and Java.

License type

Coming close to programming language is the license type (which is dependent on the language used). There are basically two main types of licenses:

- Open source license – Open source license allows you free access to programming codes (source codes). This is extremely important when you want to tweak or customize your blog. PHP, Java, Python, Node.js are all open source programming languages.

- Proprietary license – Unlike open source license, proprietary license is associated with closed source programs. Being closed source means that you cannot access all or some parts of the source codes. Thus, it is hard to tweak or customize the platform as desired to suit your particular needs. C# is partially proprietary and partially open source. While you can access, tweak and customize some codes, backbone codes and the engine that drives them is inaccessible.

Hosting type

Hosting simply refers to providing server space for the blog to run and connecting to an address (domain URL) for it to be accessible on the internet.

Hosting type is determined by two critical factors;

- Server OS (Operating System) – There are two major types of Server OS – Windows and Linux. So far, Linux is the most popular server OS for internet. Over 80% of websites and blogs run on Linux server. This is majorly because Linux OS is free and open source while Windows OS is paid-for and proprietary.
- The hosting party – Hosting party simply refers to the person in charge of hosting your website or blog. There

are two types of hosting parties; self-hosted and non-self-hosted. Self-hosted simply means you are responsible for hosting the blogging platform. Non-self-hosted simply means that the provider of the blogging platform hosts it on your behalf.

Pricing

There are two pricing options when it comes to blogging platforms;

- Free – A free blogging platform simply means you don't pay anything to acquire it.
- Paid-for (non-free) – Paid-for blogging platform simply means that you have to pay to acquire it.

Popular CMS

There are over 50 CMS in the market today. However, the most popular CMS are;

- WordPress
- Drupal
- Blogger
- Joomla

Recommended choice criteria

The best platform to choose should have the following key features;

- Programmed in a most widely used language – PHP is the most preferred as it is most popular and can be hosted on Linux server

- Linux hosted – Linux servers run over 80% of blogs and websites across the globe. You can easily find a host provider on Linux unlike Windows.

- Open source – PHP is the most popular open source language for blogging platforms. Node.js is competing for the second place.

- Self-hosted – Your content is your property, your investment and your wealth. You obviously need to own it! Self-hosting is the only guarantee that you own your content and thus can fully monetize it.

- Free! – Why pay when you can get it free? Surprisingly the best blogging platforms are free. WordPress, Joomla and Drupal are absolutely free.

Why self-hosted WordPress is the best CMS for you

There is no doubt that, if you consider your content as your most important asset, then, you would naturally want to self-host. Also, you would naturally desire to spend less cost on acquiring the CMS. This rules out blogger and other non-self-hosted CMS. It also rules out non-free CMS. In this case, there are very few candidates left to compete with self-hosted

WordPress CMS. Such other competitors include Drupal, Joomla, among others.

However, WordPress stands out from the crowd due to the following reasons;

- It is less bulky.
- It is easy to use.
- It has a large community of users.
- It has the largest community of developers.
- It is so easy to install.
- There are plenty of plugins that can help you optimize SEO, monetize, automate income, and many others.
- There are plenty of themes to boost the 'look and feel' of your blog.

Most host providers can install WordPress for you at no extra cost. There are several specialized WordPress host providers that you can engage to help you out on this.

Steps to building your blog

The following are important steps that will guide you in building your blog;

1. Determine your type of blog
2. Choose a domain name
3. Register your domain
4. Open a host account

5. Install your blog CMS

6. Create blog content

7. Promote your blog (so as to build audience and generate traffic)

8. Monetize your blog

9. Automate your income

Choose a domain name

Choosing your domain name is extremely important for purposes of SEO and user scanning.

The following steps will help you choose the most appropriate domain for your blog;

1. Come up with a domain name that matches your niche

2. Match the domain name with seo keywords of your niche

3. Make the domain name as short as possible (without compromising on 1 & 2 above) – this is for easy scanning and memorization by readers

4. Choose non-limiting domain extension (e.g. .com, .net, .org)

5. If domain you want is taken, slightly modify it without stripping it of core essence (1 & 2 above)

Register your domain name

Once you have a domain name, the next thing is to register your domain. The process of registering, though extremely simple (and largely automated), varies from one domain registrar to the other. In case of difficulties, you can always get assisted by your domain name registrar in the setup process.

The following are popular domain registrars where you can easily register your domain;

- Namecheap
- GoDaddy

Namecheap is the most preferred of the two options. GoDaddy used to be the best but it has descended due to its insistence of compliance with government policies that restrict internet freedom, more so, when it comes to protecting the anonymity and privacy of domain ownership.

Open a host account

Once you have registered your domain, the next step is to host your domain account. Hosting is simply providing a space for your web content and directing your domain address to it so that the web content can be available when people enter your domain address to access it.

There are thousands of hosting service providers. However, the following are the most known;

- HostGator

- <u>Bluehost</u>
- <u>Siteground</u>
- <u>Scalahosting</u>

The process of hosting varies from one host provider to another. Nonetheless, most hosting providers would be willing to guide you in setting up your website at no extra cost.

Install your blog CMS

Once you have successfully registered your domain and it has fully propagated (that is, the domain name is recognized by servers across the world) you can go ahead and install your WordPress blog.

Most hosts, like the ones mentioned above, have cPanel. cPanel is simply a dashboard with tools and resources that enables you to manage and optimize your website. The most popular of these tools is known as <u>Softaculous</u>.

<u>Softaculous</u> is a tool that enables you to install your WordPress blog without complications. It is automated. All you need is to fill in the required details in a form provided by it. These details include;

- Your blog name
- Your blog email address
- The folder in which you intend to install your blog (just provide the name of the folder). The folder must not exist as Softaculous will automatically create it.

- The place on the server where you want the folder to be created (by default, within 'public html' otherwise known as public directory). By default, Softaculous installs WordPress in the public directory. Thus, if you want to install in the public directory, leave the place for directory blank.

Once you provide these key details plus some other basic details, you simply need to click on the 'Install' button for Softaculous to automatically install the blog for you. Within 30 seconds, your blog will be up and running. You will be provided a URL address to the blog site and URL to the admin where you will log in with your admin credentials (username and password) to continue customizing your blog and adding content.

Select a great theme

Softaculous has a wide variety of themes which you can select prior to installing your blog (prior to clicking the 'Install' button). For a start, select an appropriate theme among those provided by Softaculous. You can later on easily change them when you find a better one that suits your content and layout through the admin panel.

You can find ideas on theme sources and other relevant information on WordPress from WPexplorer. Themeforest is another great place to find WordPress themes.

Create your blog content

For information on creating your blog content, please see the section titled "How to Optimize Each Blog Post".

Promote your blog

For information on how to promote your blog, see the section titled 'Other Ways to Generate Traffic'.

Monetize your blog

For information on how to monetize your blog, see section titled "How to Monetize Your Blog".

Automate your income

For more information on automating your income, please read section titled "Automate Your Income".

Chapter 4 Desired Qualities

Now that you know what blogging is, why people blog, and the types of blogs available, you are likely asking yourself, "Do I really have what it takes to be a good blogger? What are the qualities of a successful blogger?" The qualities described below are assets that all successful bloggers have in common.

Passion

To be successful in the blogging sector, you must be passionate about what you do. Whether you use blogging as a means to express your creative side or as a means to disseminate information, you need to love and be passionate about doing it if you want to be successful. It is this love and passion that will give you the drive to continue blogging, especially when you are just starting and there aren't many people visiting your blog. If you keep blogging and working at it, however, you will soon be able to generate a lot of traffic because your readers will identify with whatever you are blogging about. They may also be motivated to share your posts by empathizing with the passion you have for the topic.

Dedication

It is possible for you to be passionate about your blog and the topic that you write about but still not be dedicated to the actual writing. If you are serious about blogging, you have to show commitment and produce content on a regular basis. Even if you are able to write the most moving post, if your subscribers see that you are not posting regularly, they will stop regularly visiting until they eventually stop visiting altogether. A successful blogger has to be dedicated to the task at hand in addition to also being creative. Coming up with new content on a regular basis is not an easy task, but it can be done. It simply requires a lot of dedication and hard work.

Knowledge about your topics of interest and desire to learn more

In order to write engaging posts that are both informative and fun to read, a blogger must have extensive knowledge or experience in the specific topic at hand. No one will subscribe to a blog that they know is providing erroneous or deficient information. Therefore, a blogger should ensure that he or she is well-informed about the topic that they are writing about.

A good blogger must also be willing to learn new information about the topic they write about. No one knows everything about any particular subject, and at some point in time, a blogger is going to have to do new research so that he or she can create new content that subscribers will love.

Ability to write quality content

Even if you are the most passionate and prolific writer of all time, all of your efforts will likely go to waste if you are unable to bring the content across in an informative and engaging way that is also different and stands out from the crowd. This is the type of content that people are always willing to share, bookmark, tweet, mark as a favorite or follow, and it is bound to build you a large following in the process.

This does not mean that your content should always be light or fun. First of all, you should take care of such things as:

- Informativeness. Your content should contain the information your reader is looking for.

- Structured. Your content should be clear and consistent. If you have a lot of content, structure it, otherwise, the reader will lose interest in your blog if they cannot understand it.

- Accuracy. Whatever type of content you use – text, video or photo – it should be designed carefully and without factual errors.

Good marketing skills

A successful blogger knows how to promote their blog without coming across as annoying. There is a delicate balance between effective marketing increasing traffic to your blog, and annoying marketing that spams people's emails. Constantly asking people to read and share new posts will only put people off, and you will end up getting less traffic to your blog. A more effective way of marketing includes asking close friends to share your posts so that they gain a wider audience, or by writing guest posts for other bloggers with links to your own blog.

Thick skinned

To succeed in the world of blogging, one must learn to be resilient to criticism. There will be many instances in which people will disagree with what you write, and some will voice their opinions in the harshest and cruelest way possible. As such, you need to learn to accept opposing views, and if you need to respond, you should do so respectfully. This will show your level of professionalism, and it will gain the admiration of many of your subscribers who will respect you for your composed and mature response.

Helpfulness

Helping fellow bloggers and subscribers in the blogosphere where possible will, in turn, help you succeed in the blogging world. If you would like other individuals to share your posts, start sharing other people's posts. It is a subtle way of asking people to promote your posts as well. You should also try to help your subscribers. Respond to comments made on your blog as much as possible, and answer questions when you can. This is a great way of making your blog more interactive for everyone. Subscribers are more likely to share your posts with their friends and family when they feel that they are important to you and your blog. Make your subscribers feel needed by responding to their posts regularly and respectfully.

SEO Knowledge

Promotion is not so much a difficult activity as a time-consuming one.

If you want to be an effective blogger, you need to learn some SEO as this is what will promote your website on search engines. Even if you are not promoting your blog yourself and have found a specialist for this, basic SEO knowledge will be useful to you to set a clear task for the performer and then adequately evaluate its implementation.

I recommend you take free SEO seminars or watch YouTube lessons. Over time, you will be able to decide whether you should deal with SEO issues or not. Ultimately, it will be significantly easier to attain your blogging goals when you have more people visiting your blog after searching for a certain keyword.

Organization and time management

Blogging requires time and effort, and you need the discipline to research your topic, write high-quality posts, promote your content, and even engage your audience. All of these require time and effort, making it critical for you to plan your time wisely.

Start managing the process at the very beginning while your blog has not yet grown. Make a to-do list, ranked by priorities. Be sure to determine the frequency of each task. This will greatly facilitate your work and will help prevent you from burning out. For example, I recommend making the process of writing articles a mandatory daily task. Even if you post 2-3 posts per week, you will have enough material for the blog to work without interruption. This will give you time for maneuvers, as well as for rest and unplanned situations.

So equipped with this knowledge about the qualities of a good blogger, you should be ready to start a blog. To get started, you need to know the ingredients of a blog, which we will explore first before we delve into the more complex elements of setting it up.

Chapter 5 Topping The Charts

Part of having a successful blog is knowing how to get to the top of Google charts and other search engine charts. With so many blogs on the web right now, being the best of the best is essential. This is how you get discovered, and this is how you make money. While this may sound challenging, it is actually quite simple. The main reason why most bloggers will not actually top the charts and go big is that they lack the necessary commitment to get there. As long as you stay focused and devoted, you are certain to make the top of the charts and to get yourself far more exposure for your ideal audience.

Getting to the Top of Search Engine Results

If you want to get seen, you need to get your blog to the top of search engine results. This is not as hard as it sounds, as long as you follow a few important steps. They are as follows:

1. Write Great Quality Content
   The better your quality, the better your results. When search engines "crawl" your pages to find information and present it to their searchers, they check to make

sure that grammar and other such things are correct. They also want to make sure that what you are sharing is relevant to what the person is searching for. You can do this by writing great quality content that is popular and trending. Well-written blogs will naturally move up rankings as more visitors land on them, link to them, share them, and revisit them.

2. Use Your Writing To Optimize Your Page

Search engines cannot see how pretty your page is. The aesthetics are for your readers. What a search engine is looking for is relevancy. They want to make sure that what you are sharing is aligned with what their user is looking for. They have bots known as "crawlers" that read the first one-third of each page before moving on to read the next page. This is how they produce their results. The ones that are most relevant are at the top of the search ranking. If your first one-third includes relevant keywords and information that relates to the search, you will be more likely to rank higher. Keep these words specific, relevant, and optimized for what your reader is most likely to search. For example, if they are looking for "easy recipes" your text should say "easy recipes" at least once in the first one-third of your post.

3. Keywords In Text, Phrases, and Code

In addition to the first one-third of your page, your website, in general, should contain keywords throughout. Your titles, phrases, texts, and even the names of the documents you upload and the code you input into your website should feature keywords relevant to your niche. This increases your relevancy and makes you more likely to be shown at the top of the list.

4. Include External Links

Sharing to reputable external links is another great way to get seen by your audience by rising up the list. Search engines love seeing this on pages because this means that you are increasing your user's experience by sharing high quality, reputable content with them. You can do this by sharing the link in your posts, or by having a directory of your favorite blogs and resources on your page.

5. Share to Social Media

Sharing your content on social media tells search engines that it is more relevant. Furthermore, it increases the number of people likely to visit your page—meaning your page hit number increases. As this number rises, search engines believe your page is more popular, so it is more likely to share it over other pages that are not too popular.

What Constitutes as "Quality" Content?

You may be wondering: what constitutes the high-quality content that search engines are looking for? The answer to this is quite simple. Furthermore, it is not necessarily the direct thing that search engines are looking for. Search engines do not have a brain; therefore, they are not capable of determining what content is interesting versus what content is not. What they are actually looking for is how many people have landed on your page. The more interesting and high-quality your content is, the more likely people will visit your website. Then, as your hit counter rises, your popularity rating rises in the back-end information that search engines are looking for.

Keeping quality content on your page is more about increasing your likelihood of being shared on other pages, websites, and social media accounts. It also increases your likelihood of being revisited by the same readers. So, when you are writing, you want to write things that are interesting, fresh, and relevant. The better it is written and the more it entices your readers, the more your rankings will naturally rise as you are shared amongst others.

There are several types of blog posts that are known to be considered more interesting by readers. The following templates are great ones to follow if you need inspiration on what constitutes as interesting and high quality to your readers. Remember, grammatically correct writing that is free of spelling errors is important, too.

1. Tutorials and how-to guides
2. The latest industry-specific news and current events
3. Subjects that are considered controversial
4. Checklists (i.e., "New Baby Checklist," "New Home Checklist," "Spring Cleaning Checklist."
5. Lists (i.e., "5 Things You Need to Do Before Summer is Over."
6. Infographics
7. Case studies
8. Profiles on people relevant to your industry
9. Interviews
10. Expert advice
11. Comparisons and reviews
12. Video and audio content
13. Resources
14. Problems and solutions (i.e., "The One Thing You Need to Stop _____!")
15. What Others Are Saying (i.e., "What Gary Vee Thinks About _____ and Why I [Agree/Disagree.])
16. Behind-the-scenes content

17. Inspirational stories

18. Parody or funny posts

19. Quizzes, surveys, and polls

20. FAQs

21. Questions you should be asking (i.e., "Six Questions to Ask Before Hiring A Lawyer.")

22. Roundup posts (i.e., "The Top 10 Funniest Twitter Posts This Week" or "The Best Summer Wardrobe Pieces for 2019.")

23. Contests

24. Time-saving posts (i.e., "How to Save Time Buying Groceries.")

25. Event summaries

26. My top Takes on _____.

27. Rants

28. Beginner's guides

29. Guest bloggers

30. Myth vs. Fact posts

How Facebook Will Maximize Your Exposure

As you learned earlier in this chapter, sharing your content on social media is important. First, it shows search engines that your content is being shared, thus making it more "popular" in rankings and helping it rise to the top of the charts. Second, it helps it get seen by your target audience. This means that by sharing it with your building audience on Facebook, they are more likely to see it and click over to reading it. This behavior increases your hit counter, rising your content even further up the rankings. Another thing that happens is that it is more likely to be shared. Readers are more likely to share a post that is already made than they are to make their own post. So, having this part already done for them makes it far easier for your reader to tap "share" and show it to their own friends and family. The more it is shared, the more it rises up the ranks in search engines. Furthermore, the more it is seen by others, which means the more hit counts you get, the more likely you are to be shared again, and the higher you rise once more.

Another way that you can use Facebook is by creating a group. Building an online community is a great way to increase your outreach, thus giving you direct people to share your posts with. Furthermore, individuals in a group are more likely to engage than page followers. They are also more likely to see what you are sharing, based on the Facebook algorithm, giving them a better chance to actually see it. This means that building your community can have a great impact on helping you have a greater outreach. Lastly, Facebook groups are a community that you can pay attention to and listen inside of. As your group members begin engaging with you and each other, you can see what questions they are asking, what information they are searching for, and what they are sharing with each other. This makes it easier for you to determine what your target audience finds relevant and what you should be writing for future posts. Thus, Facebook groups are both a way to engage with and build loyalty amongst your existing readers and create relevant content to keep your current readers satisfied and attract new readers into your community.

Chapter 6 Tips For Creating Posts

In the above text, you will definitely be able to master over your blog on WordPress and can establish it without any help from someone. There are complete tools in WordPress that can be used to set up a blog with creation of new content and posts. However, here are some tips that can make you an expert blogger and you can have more enriched experience of writing and publishing your thoughts online.

- Take a look at the plugins which are popular in the bloggers. Research their efficacy and read the reviews of the bloggers on that plugin. It will keep you updated with the performance of your website as compared with others'.
- Keep your blog updated on regular basis. It keeps your audience as regular visitors on the blog on one side, on the other, Google crawls it on regular intervals which increases the worth of your blog in search engines.
- Learn to write faster blog posts so that within minimum time, you can write more. There are some plugins to serve this purpose. You can upload them to improve the writing speed.

- Multi-author blogs are more influential. It creates better impression and diversity of thoughts on blog instead of having monotonous tone of words by one author.

- Answer the comments of those who visited your blog post and left their opinion on the topic you discussed in the post. Individually addressing those visitors will bring good will to you.

- Know your audience; their demand, expectations, possible responses or reactions to a particular thought you expressed in your post. Other features you should consider while posting are age, education, culture, mindsets, occupation, gender, income bracket, geographic zone, hobbies, and interests. It will help you write better and be understood in a better way.

- Bring something unique and surprising in your blog posts. No idea or thought is absolutely unique. It is your words that will make it unique and impressive. Show your personality out of your words and make others feel the warmth and efficacy of your ideas. Words are the window towards your soul. Make this window attractive and opening new horizons of ideas and debates.

- Keep the blog content unique. Never copy and paste the idea or words of someone else. It will damage the strength of your thought in the eyes of visitors on one hand and will decrease the rank and value of your blog in search engines on the other.

- Make your share buttons smooth and active and share it on all Social Media icons regularly. It will make your blog an interactive community sharing thoughts with the like-minded people around the globe. Sharing buttons should be easy and in the right place to be shared by the readers using maximum icons including FaceBook, Twitter, LinkedIn, Pinterest, Instagram, G+, and others.

- Adopt an effective and multi-faceted approach to promote your blog. Promotion of the blog is equally necessary as the writing posts on regular basis is important. It is not an overnight process. It will take some time to be visible and popular but after getting popular, it will bring the fruits.

- Make sure everything you post on your blog is true, not misleading or hurting anyone's thoughts, culture, and creed. You will be responsible for every word and image you post on it.

- Make your blog attractive to look at. Its theme, colors, and face should be appealing to please the visitors. A beautiful but professional theme enhances the readership of your blog. Research the topic you are writing on. Proofread it before publishing.

Chapter 7 Marketing Your Blog

After publishing, your post sits there on your site. When you first launch a website, odds are you won't have a following right away. You're going to need to gather readers if you want that amazing post you just created to get some recognition. Marketing your blog is extremely important or else how will you get subscribers? You also need to have subscribers if you want your blog to make any kind of money. It would be great if you could just rely on dumb luck, but that's just not how it works. Yes, there is more work ahead, but you will have fun with it.

It should be noted that you can set up your site so that when you publish a post, it gets automatically shared on social media sites of your choosing. This feature can be very helpful. But if you use this method, make sure the shared post says what you want it to. Take the time to set it up each time you publish a post. Some people like that method better, especially after becoming more successful. There isn't a whole lot of time in the day to individually share your post on each social media site.

There are, however, several bloggers who will tell you not to automate your social media sharing. Twitter only lets you use one hundred and forty characters per post. This means your share must be short and to the point, with room for the hashtags you want to use. Facebook lets you use all the characters you want. You'll still want to keep your share shorter, but you have more wiggle room for a better description of what you are sharing. Instagram needs a picture to be shared, and Pinterest is its own beast. It may be more time-consuming to share to each site individually, but sometimes it can be well worth it.

Social Media Marketing: Social Media (you know, Facebook, Twitter, Instagram, etc.) can be a major source of subscribers. You're already on Facebook all day long (come on, you know you are), so why not use it to your advantage? Social media is a fantastic way to connect with potential readers. Yes, your first subscribers will probably be family and close friends. No, that's not as pathetic as it sounds. Subscribers are subscribers.

Twitter, Instagram, and Facebook have an advertising feature you can use to promote either your entire site or a singular post. This is not free, however, but there are reasonably priced options. Advertising on social media can be really helpful. Set up an ad and let it run for a bit. You can choose your plan options and duration of the ad on each social media site. You can get a lot of clicks and likes this way.

You shouldn't completely rely on social media, however. Paying for advertisements constantly will drain your bank account really fast, and you don't always get loyal followers this way. If you are just starting your blog, you will want to focus on organic growth. Organic reach is when people find your content without paid advertising. I know, I know, but how will you get your blog out there if you're not making advertisements?

One big thing you are going to want to learn is hashtags. Or as some of you know them, the pound sign (#). Hashtags are what everyone uses to connect different themes and ideas. Have you heard of #MotivationMonday? Search it sometime in any social media outlet, and you will find a ridiculous amount of sickeningly peppy, motivating pictures and quotes. Hashtags are how people find things they are interested in and see what others are saying about them.

Each time you publish a blog post, share it on social media. On Twitter, it's automatically public, but on Facebook, it's not. Make your posts about your blog public on Facebook, then add hashtags that relate to your target audience and the blog post itself. Still writing about cats? Each time you post a link to a cat article, hashtag it with words like #cutecats, #crazycats, #kittens, etc. Anyone who searches for cat posts will eventually come across your cat posts.

At first, it feels weird to promote yourself so much. Most of us are taught from a young age not to brag. But in the blogging business, you pretty much have to brag all the time. Not only that, but you have to do it in a way that doesn't say, "Look at me! I'm the best!" You should get it out there that this is what you do, that your niche is what you are interested in, and that people will want what you have to offer. It's okay to talk yourself up a bit but don't be condescending. You want readers to start thinking about you when they see something that involves your blog and niche. When someone sees a cat, let them be reminded that you have a great cat blog and then maybe they will go and check it out.

Another social media technique to use is to start getting involved with the community. Get on Twitter and start following people who share similar interests. Find people who share your love of books, or other bloggers in your niche. Twitter users almost always follow you back! Find groups on Facebook that may be interested in what you have to offer, and join those groups. Even if only a few people find you at first, that's okay. We all start somewhere. Remember too that every person who finds your blog and likes it will most likely tell someone else that they should check out your blog as well.

Pinterest is kind of a big deal now. It used to be so simple, but now it's grown into a trendy way to market yourself. Get to know Pinterest. Create an account just for your blog. Start boards that have to do with your niche and add your blog posts. Come up with creative board names and pin regularly. Make you're your blog name is listed on your profile so people can easily see it when they check out your profile. Write in fun descriptions when you pin and don't over promote your blog either. Pinterest can get you a lot of followers and subscribers. All you need are some great pictures and good content. Follow others and they will follow you back.

Make sure that your blog name and URL is on your profile of every social media account you have. Set that part of your information to "public" and make it as bold as you can. When people look at your profile to see who you are, make sure they see you have your own website. If they like the content you share on social media already, they are likely to follow the links to your blog as well.

Remember that blogging can feel a lot like a popularity contest, but you still need to keep the social media aspect of it. Not only will marketing on social media get you subscribers, but it builds a hefty group of followers on each platform. This will come into play later when you want to get advertisers to work with you. You are going to want to show sponsors or advertisers that people listen to what you have to say.

Create a Facebook page just for your blog and invite everyone you know to like it. Share the link to your page on other social media platforms and be sure to direct people to your page when the situation calls for it. Having a well-liked page will only benefit you when you are trying to make money blogging. Make sure that the page has great content and does not just have links to your latest blog posts. Be a person, tell jokes, and try to stay within your niche as much as possible. But people enjoy seeing that you are a normal person and it's not all about the blog for you.

You can also start up a Facebook group just for your blog or for your niche. Get people involved with your blog or the niche. If you are blogging about blogging, set up a Facebook group just for your subscribers or for other aspiring bloggers. If you blog about dogs, start up a group all about dogs, peoples' love of dogs, or useful dog owner tips. People like to get involved and feel like they are a part of something. Set up a group for this!

And please, don't be pushy with your social media promoting. Letting people know some new information about your blog or the newest post you created is great. But bombarding people with posts about your blog gets boring for followers. Do you like it when friends continuously push stuff in your face (think Lularoe or Beachbody) all the time? Post about your blog once a day, but then engage in building relationships with followers and post about other things too. Make sure people see that blogging isn't your entire life.

Email Marketing: Email marketing is probably one of the best ways to make and then keep followers. You create emails and send them out so many times a month (not every day!). First, you will need to find a site that you can use to create popups, opt-ins, and emails. ConvertKit and MailChimp are two very popular email marketing tools. MailChimp has a completely free option that works very well if you are not making money yet. ConvertKit is a paid subscription but offers a lot more for your marketing needs.

When using these tools, you will want to set up some kind of opt-in for your blog. You can create a simple "subscribe" button for your site. One of the best opt-ins is the pop-up form. This is a window that appears on your blog for viewers after they have been on a page for a certain length of time. You can choose a pop-up to come up after a visitor clicks on a link, or after they have been on a page for ten seconds. The pop-up is great because it's not something your followers will miss. It shows up right in front of them and they can opt out, but at least the option is right in front of their face. Once you have created the pop-up with your email marketing site, you can plug in the code it gives you into the widget section of your blog.

Okay, so you're ready to set up an email. One of the first emails you should get going is the "welcome" email. This email will get sent out to people who have recently subscribed to your blog. It gives your subscribers some more information about you or the blog. It could contain an incentive you offered (we will get into this soon) or ways to reach you. The welcome email will let your subscribers know what to expect from here on out and how often they will receive emails from you. Make the welcome email inviting and friendly. After all, you are welcoming a new subscriber home to your community. Let them know what they can expect from you and the blog, and that they can find you on social media too.

You should also take the time to set up templates for your emails. Create a basic design you want your emails to look like and save it so that each time you create new emails, the template is already ready and all you have to do is plug in the information. Your email blasts should contain information about the new things happening with your blog such as store news, recent posts, new offers, and ways to share! Sending emails to your followers keeps you connected to them on a more personal level. Did you know that you can even customize your email blasts to include the name of the recipients? People love that! It's as if you personally sent each follower an individual email.

Be sure to keep a close eye on your email analytics. Most email marketing companies offer this option. With it, you can see if people are opening emails, clicking on them, or unsubscribing. If you have a large number of people who aren't engaging, you have lots of work to do.

You can use these numbers to better your email marketing. Separate your subscribers into lists such as "store customers", newsletter subscribers", and "second chances". Create more enticing emails for those who don't seem to be interested. Send emails about your latest store updates (if you have a store) to the people who make purchases in your shop.

Your email lists are important. So many bloggers don't focus enough on their email marketing strategies and their blog suffers because of it. Your emails are how you connect with new and returning readers. This is where you can get more personal with your readers and share new things in your life and with the blog. Ask readers to respond to your emails and take time to read through those emails when they start responding. Show them you care and actually take the time to listen to what they have to say. You are building relationships with your email subscribers. This will prompt people to either stay with you or even invite others to join your community.

Remember to be true to your word. If you tell subscribers you will send emails once a week, you better send them once a week. Any more or less than that will drive subscribers away. They want good content that arrives when promised. If you can't keep you word on that, you won't keep subscribers.

How to Get Email Subscribers: To get new subscribers to your email list, you need to be prepared to offer others something. People need to be coaxed a little bit into giving up their email. Everyone is already asking everyone else to sign up for things. And a simple "sign up for updates" campaign isn't going to get you many subscribers. People want to be compensated for their time. What can you offer them?

Time to start thinking about what you have to offer people. Remember when we talked about being able to solve a problem for people? This is where you can really use that information. If you blog about how to make money blogging, you can offer new subscribers a free eBook on how to email marketing. If you blog about cats, offer a special email series about the best ways to train your cat. Do you blog about Bigfoot? Tell new subscribers they will get a special weekly email with top-secret Bigfoot information.

It doesn't matter what you blog about. You need to come up with ways that you can offer new subscribers some kind of special thing for signing up. If your blog has a shop, set up a discount for first-time purchasers if they subscribe to your blog. I'm not saying you have to buy loyalty, but you kind of have to bribe people to at least get them to give your blog a chance.

Comment on Other Blogs: Bloggers are typically awesome people. They understand that it is hard to get your blog off the ground. So, connect with them! Go search for other blogs in your niche and start reading their posts. Then, comment on them. Subscribe if you'd like. Start connecting with other bloggers.

When you take interest in other bloggers, they notice and begin to take an interest with you. They may eventually direct others to your blog for more on a certain subject, or even ask you to collaborate with them. Their subscribers may take notice of your comments and see that you also have knowledge on the information. People are nosy, and they will try to see who you are and what you're all about. Use that to your advantage.

Collaborating: When two bloggers come together for a post, wonderful things can happen. Be a guest post on someone's blog. Lots of bloggers want to work with others so that each blogger can gain new subscribers. You may know more on a subject than a fellow blogger, so why not work together to get you both new subscribers?

Find Communities to Interact With: This means all types of communities that relate to your blog. No, this is not the same as social media. Look, you're going to have to become somewhat of a social butterfly if you want people to follow you. Learn how to reach out to people and build relationships.

Online, you can find forums and sites devoted to whatever your niche may be. There are chat rooms and communities for everything. Yes, you will come across people who won't exactly be your cup of tea, but that's part of the business. Engage in discussions with others and communicate with them. Find out what these people are looking for in regard to your niche. Not only will you gain new subscribers, but you may also get ideas on what you can offer as an incentive for subscribing!

There are plenty of bloggers who stick to blogging from their house and don't want to get social outside of the internet, and that still works fine for them. But I would encourage you to get out into the real world a little more and see where you can promote your blog. If you're a book blogger, and you're near a library, join their book club! It provides you with a space to talk with others who are similar interests and you can promote your blog in person. If you blog about dogs, go to the dog park and start making friends with people. See what they have to say about training, what types of dogs are good for kids, etc. You can learn a lot by interacting in person with others. Have business cards made that you can hand out anytime someone asks you what you do. Give them out at your book club. It is possible that people will take it and throw it away. But it is also possible that someone will take it and look into your blog.

Try to Post Often: You won't be bugging people because they will be subscribed to your emails (unless you set your blog up differently). If you can come up with a post every day or every couple of days, that's great! Having a lot of good content will only help you. Then, when you send out emails, give subscribers a taste of what you have been writing about. Let them choose which articles they want to read, but make sure they have lots to choose from. You want your blog to be entertaining enough to keep your followers happy.

Get to Know Your Analytics: Knowing your stats for your blog traffic is a huge help and will come into play numerous times throughout your blogging career. *Google Analytics* is a go-to program for many bloggers. Signing up is free and it is worth every bit of time you invest into learning all you can about it. At its most basic, Google Analytics will give you insights into how many people visit your blog and how they are finding your blog. It would be in your best interest to take advantage of Google's free Analytics training courses, which will be offered to you when you sign up. That way, you will learn all the ways to master analytics so that you can use that information for your marketing strategies.

There are analytics add-ons you can add to your dashboard on your site so that you have access to snippets of information about blog traffic. If you see that your organic reach (the people who find your blog without paid advertisements) is very low, you know that you must find a better way of reaching others. Google will tell you where your traffic is coming from, what they are clicking the most, and much more. If you see that your post about the best gadgets of 2017 got a lot of views, but your post on fish tanks had almost no views, then you know you should probably stick to posts like the first one.

Advertising with Search Engines: If you feel like putting the money into it, you can also advertise your blog on search engines like Google or Bing. You can easily set up advertisements with these search engines and choose where the ad will show up. You can choose for your ad to show up with search results or have a display ad set up on other sites as well.

While paid advertising can get you new subscribers and potentially get your blog some notice, you aren't getting organic reach. Remember, organic reach is getting new subscribers through searches or any other method except paid advertising. More organic reach means that you will get recognized by search engines and get ranked higher in search results.

Marketing your blog is a lot of work, I won't lie. But it is very worth it. You need to get your blog out there and you need people to be interested in what you have to say. You cannot make any money if no one is visiting your blog! Even if you are making money through ads and affiliates, you can't make money with no traffic. Some marketing strategies may work better for you than others, and that is okay. You will find your own methods and combinations of marketing that work for you. Use those techniques and if something isn't working, be flexible. Change what you need to change. Good marketing strategies will greatly increase traffic and money to your site.

Chapter 8 The Complete Marketing Plan

Marketing is a low rate racket regardless of how you do it, yet blogging can appear to be the close to worthless. It appears that some days nobody is focusing on you by any stretch of the imagination. You may not be utilizing the greater part of the assets available to you or, in case you are, in the best possible way. You can't blog alone and need an arrangement set up.

Blog Writing and Posting

The title of this segment may sound self-evident (considering the title of the article), however it is the initial step. You need to compose a blog. Obviously, you can have this piece of the arrangement finished by another person (say an expert author), yet regardless of the possibility that this is the technique you pick, ensure that the content matches your message/item/benefit.

Once the blog is composed, it should be presented on your site and upgraded. Nevertheless, is this every one of that should be finished?

Previously, you may have composed the blog post and simply place it in the line and trusted that individuals would read it.

Regardless of the possibility that individuals read it, they may not react. The issue here is that you are not really marketing; you are simply writing a blog now.

Individuals who are keen on either your content or what you need to offer may discover you and read the post, yet the dominant part of individuals, who are potential clients, won't read it. The post needs a greater send off.

Blog Promotion

Social Media Communities. Social media is an awesome business instrument since it associates individuals. In spite of the fact that organizations are starting to see the advantages of utilizing this medium, perhaps you haven't yet. When you compose a blog, there is a group of individuals on Google+, Facebook, Twitter, LinkedIn, need to think about it.

In the event that you have legitimately set up your gatherings and have been following and posting intriguing goodies before, you will get your blog to a bigger group of onlookers. Other individuals in your circle will tell individuals in theirs who haven't found you yet. Start exchanges in these systems to develop associations with their individuals.

Social Media Updates. Notwithstanding beginning dialogs in social media groups, ensure you inform your social media organizes immediately of the new post. This is the way a restricted your one blog post can accumulate you an astounding measure of new business.

Tip: Some individuals will recommend that you add a plugin to your website to have the new blog present naturally sent on your social media systems. I exceptionally dishearten this. It doesn't look regular and you truly have no control of what content is posted. I propose you either go to every social system and post about your new blog post or bounce onto HootSuite (or some other social media administration apparatus) and have it sent from that point.

Chapter 9 How To Keep Your Traffic Coming Back

Repurpose Old Content

One of the most important things you need to learn how to do as a blog owner is to repurpose your old content. Sometimes, even the most creative bloggers can have a hard time coming up with absolutely new material 100% of the time. The good news is that nobody expects you to do this and in fact, it's even counterintuitive. Your readers keep coming back because they like what you have to say. There is no need to reinvent the wheel.

Make sure that you keep a pulse on your content and understand what has performed well and what hasn't. This is why having access to a program like Google Analytics is extremely important. Dig into your analytics and figure out which of your blog posts have performed extremely well and try to figure out why. Do you do best with topical subjects? Or is it your evergreen content that keeps people coming back?

"Evergreen content" is content that will stand the test of time and likely never go out of date. For example, an excellent recipe for your grandmother's chocolate cake is definitely evergreen content. Chocolate cake is not going to become outdated. On the other hand, a post about the very first Google

Panda update is definitely topical and will become outdated. Anything regarding the apocalypse back in 2012 is also topical and is now considered outdated.

Content that is evergreen is very easily repurposed, as the information in it is still good. If you have a particular blog post that went viral and is evergreen, there's no reason not to recycle it. In terms of posts that are more topical, you may not be able to recycle the actual content of that blog, but you can take cues from the topic and the angle you took on it to help you create content that is along the same lines.

For example, an excellent way to repurpose "how to" topics in your blog is by taking a series of blog posts and turning them into a guide or eBook. If you had a lot of posts about Twitter advertising that did extremely well, consider taking all of those posts and compiling them into a book. You can then use the book on Amazon or use it as a freebie to entice people to sign up for your email marketing list.

Another excellent way to repurpose evergreen content is to turn it into an infographic. People love infographics; they are very easy and likely to be shared if they are done well. Of course, creating good infographics often requires a considerable amount of artistic skill.

Also, remember that you can repurpose your content to use directly on social media as well. For example, if you have a collection of interesting statistics, those make for fantastic twitter posts. Statistics are short, and often entertaining. Using statistics from a blog post to create a twitter post will help you increase your social media leverage.

Another creative way to recycle good blog post is to consider starting a podcast channel. Many people prefer to listen to their blog post rather than actually read them. In this case, you can literally just read your blog post and not have to rewrite it at all. You may be surprised at the amount of attention you will get if you start a podcast channel. Again, people who sign up for your podcast may be inclined to sign up for your blog.

If you do a lot of work with PowerPoint presentations, those can easily be changed into SlideShare or YouTube posts. If you conduct webinars, those can also be converted into YouTube posts as well.

There are many clever and assorted ways to make use of your old content to keep on using excellent material that shouldn't be left out of the limelight simply because some time has passed! Bringing forward the content that brought your readers to your blog in the first place is an excellent idea to keep your blog fresh, interesting, and timeless.

Engage with Your Audience

We have spoken extensively about the importance of networking with other bloggers in your vertical. However, if you want to keep your audience coming back for more time and time again, it is important to keep the conversation going with them as well. Remember that in the days of social media and instant communication, readers expect that their blog offers are going to take their concerns and considerations into account. They want to have a "live" experience with you, not have you be an unreachable author on a pedestal.

One of the most important things you can do is be around to answer questions on your blog. Again, this is a good way to make use of your analytics. Study the times of day when your blog gets the most traffic. This is a good time for you to post and then be around to interact with comments in real time if necessary. Anybody who comments on your blog should get a courteous and friendly response. Even if your response is merely "thanks!" this can make a world of difference.

Also, be open to friendly critique or suggestions. Especially if you are running your blog as a one-person operation, it will not be unusual for you to sometimes make typos or other small mistakes. If a commenter on your blog posts out grammatical or factual errors, make sure to thank them for their eagle eyes and then adjust your blog post accordingly with credit. People are more likely to come back to your blog and keep engaging with you if you create an environment of open conversation.

Social media is also extremely important in this. Many people who interact with you on social media will be your readers, not other bloggers. If one of your readers mentioned you in their social media, make sure to take the time to give them a shout

out. On some social media platforms, you can even private message people. This is a great way to personally thank individuals for interacting with your content and turn them into loyal readers.

Another way to encourage people to interact with your content is to offer contests or other fun activities. Many high-ranking brands use this to great aplomb, particularly on picture-heavy social media sites like Instagram. If people are participating in your contests with pictures, you can feature those pictures on your main social media platform, the more fun and interactive your brand persona is on social media, the more likely it is that people are going to follow you back and eventually find their way to your blog.

Another wonderful way to interact with your audience is to simply ask them what they want. In your blog, you can occasionally set up polls or other interactive devices to learn more about what your audience specifically wants to read about. People love to be asked their opinions; take advantage of this.

If you are a blogger who proves responsive, informative, and entertaining, people are going to keep coming back again and again. Remember that your content isn't just about the information that you spread, it is also about the person who is providing the content.

Chapter 10 What Is The Difference Between Adsets And Ads?

After you have figured out the goals, decide on the overall ad set you want to use and get it ready. An ad set is a series of ads that meet the objectives you want. You can get as many ad sets produced as you want but they should all meet the overall goals you have for getting more people to visit your site. There are a few things you can do when getting such a set ready:

1. Create a name for your ad set.
   Give your set any name you wish. Make sure the name is distinct and that you can tell it from any other campaigns you want to run.

2. Determine your audience.
   Decide on the specific audience you want to target within your group. The audience can include one of many groups including the following:

   - People within a certain location; you have the option to add as many locations as you want.

   - People in a particular age range; these include people as young as 18 or those in the 65 and older group.

- People who speak specific languages; this could work if you are targeting a certain region where many languages are spoken.

- Those of a certain gender; you can choose to target both men and women or just one group.

- Anyone with certain interests; Facebook lets you enter keywords that relate to particular interests.

The worst thing you could ever do when marketing yourself is to be generic. You cannot assume that everyone in the world will be interested in your work. Work toward targeting the audience that will actually be interested in your content. The overall reach might be small, but you will not target the people who probably don't have an interest in your work and only those who will notice.

3. Use the detailed targeting feature for very specific groups.
   Detailed targeting allows you to search Facebook to find detailed and exact groups where you could market your wares. This would be choosing to work with people based on extremely particular demographics, their interests, or any opinions they might express while on Facebook.

4. Add the specific connections you want to follow.
   People who express certain connections to your site can get access to your ads. You can add connections where

people will be more likely to see your ads based on things like the following:

- What pages they have been on

- Whether people have liked your page

- Any interactions someone has made with your page in the past

- Events relating to your business as listed on your page

The connections you choose are important to help you decide what is available.

Determine Where the Ads Will Be Placed

Now that you know what you want to do with your campaign, you will decide the exposure of your advertisements. The following steps will help you to get your ads out to the right spots. These are all to be found on the Placements section of the Ads Manager:

1. Go to the Placements section of your site and list where your work will go.

    You can decide where on Facebook or on any other site owned by Facebook your ads will appear on. Make sure you carefully analyze what is available.

2. Review the individual parts of Facebook where you can get your ads placed.

Choose to add your posts onto feeds, instant articles, in-stream videos, or suggested video listings, among others. You could also ask to have your ad appear around a certain keyword. This is provided you decide on the correct keyword(s) for your ads. The Ads Manager system will let you determine which specific feeds or features you want your ad to appear. Put a decent value on your ad so it will be more likely to show up. Your ad might not even appear if it is too cheap. This point will be discussed after the finances for your marketing campaign is determined.

3. Determine where on Instagram you want to get your ads placed.

Facebook has a sizable share in Instagram, another social media platform that you will read about later in this guide. You can choose to add your advertisements onto Instagram by getting your ads onto a person's particular feed. It is optional to get your Facebook ads listed on Instagram, but this could work when you consider how popular Instagram has become recently.

4. Decide on which devices to have your ads appear.

You can get your ads to appear on all devices, or you can just ask to get your ads to appear on Smartphones and tablets and not on larger desktop or laptop browsers. For the results, it is best to have your ads appear on all devices. You might want to use a mobile-only approach if you are adamant on selling something like a mobile app or if you are targeting people who are visiting a certain location and are far from their regular computers. The Ads Manager section here will let you choose the devices you want your ads placed.

5. Let your ads appear automatically in different places. Although you could let Facebook automatically place your ads at certain spots, this is not always the right strategy to use. Facebook has an algorithm that determines where your ads would perform the best. That does not mean it will go as planned every time. Look at the placement menu to see what options are available and make a decision where you feel your ads would perform their best. Be willing to experiment now and again with different ad locations.

How to Write Facebooks Ads that Sell?

Assuming that you have a website, or somewhere else for this community to go (if not, creating that would be the first step), the first step is to set up a space for blogs on that site. Starting a blog section on your website is probably one of the simplest ways to begin creating communities with your prospects.

The next step is to create those 10 pieces of content described above, preferably in your voice. Actually outline the question and answer as if you were having a conversation with a potential customer, not only providing a solution but also explaining why you do it that way, what variables you take into consideration, and anything else the customer would need to know about the topic. You might want to hire a VA who specializes in editing this kind of thing to edit it down.

Next, create a Facebook page. If you're selling products that fit the same demographic, try to create a page that's inspiring to that demographic. For example, for women, that concept could be living your best life with your family, and you can create a Facebook page revolving around that inspirational idea, catering to that demographic. It can be called by the brand name, if the brand name alludes to what you do; if not, maybe choose something that's in keeping with the theme of the page. Then start posting your blog onto that Facebook page so that you're sending traffic to your websites. Install a Facebook pixel on your website (it's not difficult, and you can find instructions on Google) to track your traffic.

The reason that I believe that blogs are so important is that they've proven themselves to be an incredible resource. We track our clients' data, and when purchases come in, we can track them back to where they originated. Over the last 75 or so clients that we've worked with, we've found that in general, there have been 5 audiences that proved to be the most successful, and which need to be built continuously:

- The first (and most profitable) audience is website traffic, and the easiest way to build that is with your blog.

- Video viewers. In order to keep these people engaged, you need to regularly create videos on Facebook.

- The email list. Two or three years ago, uploading this with the Facebook ad tool would have yielded the highest sales. Today, however, we're seeing that blog visitors and video viewers are both purchasing more than the audience from the corresponding email list.

- Page engagers – people who are engaging with your page, which needs specific memes to be targeted to the appropriate audience.

- Your Facebook fans. A lot of Facebook specialists debate whether or not it's worth growing the number of likes on your page or the number of fans. I'm a firm believer, because I've seen that it can be monetized. I've had clients say, "Well, we've heard that likes are only for vanity," to which I reply that if I couldn't monetize them, I wouldn't recommend it. However, since I *can* monetize them, I want to grow them. I treat them like another mail list – I want to make sure that each fan routinely gets some of our posts and some of our blogs to keep them warm, just like an email list.

So, to sum up: write up those 10 blogs, upload them to your website in a blog section, and then start running them to your likely traffic, specifically the traffic that's most likely to purchase your product long term. Once they've gone to the blog and read it, they'll get pixeled; you can then retarget that pixel traffic for a purchase.

What is Retargeting and How to Set it Up?

Facebook offers a remarkable chance of setting ads to reach more than 500 million dynamic clients in a single place. It doesn't get more streamlined than this. You can without much of a stretch select your target gathering of people by pinpointing the age, area, and interests you might want to speak to. You can likewise test basic picture and content-based ads to perceive what works best and respond in like manner.

When you claim a shop, advertising will be a little unique when utilizing pay per click. The huge advantage is as that you can target a particular area as I expressed previously. When you are a business with a shop and a website that offers products, at that point you can advertise to places outside of your area if you wish. This is an extraordinary way to investigate and find new customers. On the off chance that your business does not work in a specific area then different principles apply.

First, let's talk about users with a physical shop. Users who work in a particular area would profit best by targeting people in a specific radius of their business. I recommend you make a rundown of how you're going to target your customers. I will use a pet shop for instance business. A pet shop in York PA with no website would begin their targeting list by targeting the York PA Area, or potentially a couple encompasses districts. Next thing on Facebook we need to investigate the age and sexual orientation. Contingent upon your product, these options will be set quickly. For our pet shop purposes, we will Focus on people who are between the ages of 30-50. Next category will be particular intrigue. Since we are a pet shop, lets target #Animal Planet. Attempt to be innovative when your targeting. Facebook additionally offers a Broad Category area where you can be more particular about your targeting options. The following is an example of what our targeting would resemble.

Instagram Ads

Instagram is a visual social media mobile app, where the user's profile is composed of photos and videos, and the feed shows all the photos and videos posted by the people who the user follows (ordered by an algorithm, instead of chronologically like it used to be). Instagram also has a temporary content component: the Instagram Stories, but it has evolved so much during the last few years.

Instagram has been around for almost a decade, but it has become especially popular during the past couple of years (although in the beginning, it gained an incredible amount of one million users in just three months of existence, and all organically!). And rightly so: if you recall, the human brain processes images way faster than text. Visual is easy and that is what people want when they log in to their social media.

In 2012, Instagram was bought by Mark Zuckerberg, the founder of Facebook, so the two platforms can easily be connected and managed side by side, which will definitely make your job easier, but I will get into that later.

Today, Instagram is the number one photography app, that is used by all kinds of people: from the individual who just wants to take amateur photos of his or her daily life, to the professional photographer who only posts high quality visuals. It is available for both Android and iOS, so you do not need a specific device to create your profile; and you can also access it on your computer, although the functionalities are limited (it is more of a solution for desperate times, like if you ever lose or break your phone).

Chapter 11 Monetization

One of the most frequently asked questions I get is "how do you make money blogging?". The answer is that there are a lot of ways to do so. Different options lend themselves to different kinds of blogs, subjects, and types of content, so there's no one-size-fits-all model for monetization.

Display Ads – Display ads are the most basic form of advertising on blogs. These are the banner ads and text ads you usually see on the sidebars of websites and search results on search engines like Google. There are lots of different kinds of display ad networks you can choose to work with, from Google AdSense to blog-specific networks and industry-specific networks. If you don't know where to start, Google AdSense has the widest variety of advertisers, and is a good one to pick.

Display advertising is easy to set up and has essentially no barrier to entry—you can usually start putting display ads on your blog as soon as you set it up. As such, it's easy and quick to experiment with.

Display advertising works on a Cost Per Click (CPC) or Cost Per Thousand Page Impressions (CPM) basis, meaning that you either earn money every time someone clicks on an ad on your blog or every time an ad has appeared a thousand times. The ad networks will usually serve an optimized combination of the two types of ads on your blog, so you don't have to choose which one you want unless you have a specific reason to.

In some industries, the rate you earn per click or per thousand page impressions is high, and in some low, but in general bloggers don't make much from this kind of advertising. This is primarily because in order to make a lot of money from display advertising, you have to have a lot of traffic and a good number of ads displayed very prominently on your blog. Displaying ads prominently tends to turn off your readers, who might see them as spammy, so as a blogger you have to strike the right balance between displaying the ads prominently enough that you make money, but not so prominently that your audience deserts you for being too commercial.

If you are interested in testing out display ads, do a quick Google search to find out what the average CPCs and CPMs are for the topics you blog about. This will give you an idea of how much you might earn from display ads.

Affiliate Marketing – Affiliate links are unique links to merchant websites that you put on your blog. If someone clicks on them and makes a purchase (or takes a required action), you earn a commission. Commissions can be in the form of a flat fee or a percentage of the sale, and like display advertising, commission rates can vary from high to low.

If you want to test out affiliate links on your blog, there are a lot of different third party agencies that act as middlemen between merchants and publishers (as a blogger, you are a publisher). There are also some companies that run their own affiliate programs. You can sign up with one or more of them, apply to work with relevant merchants, and once approved, get unique links to those merchants' websites. Once you have earned a certain amount of commissions, you get paid.

Popular affiliate networks include Awin, affilinet, and, Tradedoubler, but they vary by country, so make sure you sign up with the ones that have merchants in your country (or the country where your readers are).

Affiliate links make some bloggers a lot of money, and other bloggers very little. The key to making them work for you is twofold. First, you will have the most success if you write dedicated blog posts about specific products and get your readers to purchase them. Second, you will have more luck if you focus on products that are relatively affordable and can be purchased on impulse. For example, inexpensive fashion items do very well for bloggers that use affiliate links. Many people buy affordable clothing and accessories right after reading a blog post about them. On the other hand, travel products like flights tend to not do well, as they are usually high-value and it takes a long time for a person to make a decision about buying them (you probably wouldn't book a long-haul flight to Hong Kong right after reading a blog post about how great a particular airline's seats are even if you're completely sold on the idea).

As such, think about your industry and what kinds of products you could successfully market to your readers through your blog posts. If there aren't any that would be easy to promote, you may want to think about other types of advertising.

In any case, if you're using affiliate links on your blog, it's a good idea to disclose to your readers that you will earn a commission if they buy something through the links. It's ethical and transparent, and your readers will appreciate your honesty. Most bloggers put a sentence in italics at the bottom of the blog post disclosing that they've used affiliate links and thanking their readers for supporting the blog through their purchases. This is a legal requirement in some countries, so make sure you know the rules before you start.

Sponsored Content – Offering sponsored posts is another popular way for bloggers to make money from their blogs. Many bloggers offer relevant brands opportunities to pay them to write content about a product or service and publish it on their blog. Rates for this vary depending on how much traffic you get and how established your blog is, but it can get very lucrative as your audience grows. The same goes for sponsored social media posts, which work the same way.

Reviews – Product and service reviews are another way bloggers make money. While some reviews are done on the basis of receiving a free product in exchange for writing a review, others are done on a fee basis. The rule of thumb is usually that the more traffic and authority you have, the more likely you will be able to charge a fee for doing reviews.

Partnerships and Sponsorships – Partnerships and sponsorships come in a variety of forms and are growing in popularity as both blogging and influencer marketing get more established. From brand ambassadorships to sponsorships, there is no limit to the type of partnerships that can be formed. For example, I have been sponsored to use a life-logging app for three months, and I have been a brand ambassador for a hotel group for six months. I have also done sponsorships exclusively on my Instagram account, and paid partnerships that involve both my blog and my social media channels.

As with some of the other high-level monetization strategies, partnerships and sponsorships tend to happen as you get more established. Still, it's worth thinking about how you can partner with brands so that you're ready if any approach you early on.

There are a lot of agencies that aim to bridge the gap between bloggers and brands, so you can sign up with one or more of them if you want to use a middleman. Most bloggers don't rely exclusively on agencies or agents to bring them partnerships, but it can be an easy way to get partnerships coming to you.

Blogging is still relatively new, too, so if you have an idea for a partnership, you should approach a company about it. Many companies want to work with bloggers but aren't sure how, so going to them with your idea can be something they welcome.

Chapter 12 Affiliate Marketing

You can't stick affiliate links everywhere and expect money to magically start rolling in. No matter what the "experts" say, it is not a get-rich-quick scheme.

To consistently earn money from affiliate marketing, you must build trust with your audience. It takes time, but it pays off in the long-run.

Since affiliate marketing is a low-cost, low-risk opportunity, many bloggers start here when creating a monetization strategy.

How To Become an Affiliate

Unless you are an affiliate with an affiliate link, you aren't going to earn money recommending or reviewing products. If you just stick a standard link to an item on Amazon, or any other company, people can click on it and buy it all day long and you won't see a dime.

You must first become an affiliate for the items or services you want to promote. Often companies or brands run their own affiliate programs. You sign up for these directly on their website. If this is the case, you fill out an online form to apply to become an affiliate. The company will contact you directly to let you know when or if you are approved.

Other companies outsource their affiliate programs to affiliate networks. In this scenario, you join the network and become approved to promote many products. ShareASale is one example. You click on the "Affiliate Sign Up" button on their homepage and create your account. Once approved, you follow a similar process to apply for the different brands. They represent companies like:

- PicMonkey
- Cricut
- Zazzle
- FreshBooks
- Green Kids Crafts

With companies in several different industries, most bloggers find at least a couple of brands that are a good match for their audience.

If you're struggling to find suitable affiliate programs, think about what products or companies you personally use and love. Then type "Name of company + Affiliate program" into Google. Many companies have affiliate programs available, so it's a good idea to check.

Understand the Affiliate Agreement

When you become an affiliate for a company, make sure you read the fine print. Before you promote a product through affiliate marketing, make sure you know what the benefit is.

Sometimes you receive a percentage of the sale. Other companies have a flat-rate referral program.

Since companies want to make sure the sale goes through and the product isn't returned, there's often a delay in payment. Some affiliate companies pay out after thirty days, some after seventy-five days or even longer. This information should all be available for you. Become familiar with it.

You also need to be aware of any restrictions or expectations. For instance, Amazon requires you to have their disclosure statement on your blog (see chapter seven).

Terms and conditions get updated occasionally. When they do, read them and look for any major changes. You always need to know what restrictions are in place.

Companies like it when their affiliates are successful, because it means they are selling more. To help you promote their products, many provide you with a variety of tools. In addition to your unique affiliate link, you may find:

- Banners
- Social media images
- Special coupon codes
- Ideas for promotion
- Video instruction to help you earn more as an affiliate

Take time to explore your affiliate dashboard (or portal) and see what is available. If you don't know what you have, you can't use it.

Provide Value To Your Audience

You must earn your audience's trust before they start making purchases you recommend. Part of earning their trust means always providing value.

Don't promote products you don't believe in just because there's a nice affiliate reward. Readers will see through this and quickly walk away.

The following are four tips for always providing value for your readers.

Tip #1: Match Your Niche

Are you a fashion blogger? Affiliate links to beauty products, spa services, and idea books for makeup make sense. They fit nicely with your niche and wouldn't seem out of place to your reader.

An affiliate link to a new computer? That connection isn't as obvious. While there may be certain situations where it's appropriate (like if you're posting a behind-the-scenes glimpse at how you blog), your readers won't connect the dots as easily. It will look like you're just in it for the money.

Pick products your ideal reader will benefit from.

Tip #2: Don't Just Link Drop

Stuffing your posts full of affiliate links isn't a good strategy. It overwhelms your reader and cheapens their experience on your blog. Instead, have a purpose behind every link you include.

Are you talking about how you use a specific product each day? Go ahead and include the link. Are you comparing two products? Link to both of them.

For every affiliate link you use, make sure it ties into the content and makes sense.

Tip #3: Be Honest

No one wants to read a gushing, over-the-top review. There are pros and cons to everything, so many people don't trust that perfect reviews are genuine. Honestly talk about the product. Share what you love, what you like, and what you wish were different. Or share who might really benefit from this product and who probably won't.

This honesty helps your readers learn to value your opinion. It helps them learn to trust you. And if you gain their trust, you will earn a lot more from the products you recommend.

Tip #4: Know Your Readers

If you want to succeed as an affiliate marketer, you must know your audience. Understand their pain points. Then find products to solve them.

Also, know their budget. If you only recommend big ticket items because that's how you earn the most, you might miss spending from frugal readers.

Back in chapter one, I covered creating your reader avatar. If you haven't done it yet, find time to do it now. You must know who you are selling to, or you won't sell anything.

Promote On Social Media

You can include affiliate links in your blog posts, but that's not the only way to promote them. If you disclose, you can share your affiliate links on your social media channels. This includes both your business pages and your personal ones.

Just remember, no one likes the annoying salesperson. Don't let your feeds get bogged down with affiliate links. Instead, include this type of link in your rotation to keep a variety going.

Here are two ideas for wording that don't sound super salesy, and still offer some personal insight or value:

My kids love playing with Jenga blocks while I work. They've been building towers, making letters, and creating tunnels for their toy cars. While they play, I get some quiet minutes to knock out a blog post. Win-win! See if your kids love it as much as mine do [insert affiliate link, and disclose by stating this is an affiliate link or by using #afflink].

Throw a picture in to make it even more personable.

Are you thinking of starting a freelance writing career? This course by Gina Horkey was the best investment I made in my business! What do you have to lose? [Insert your affiliate link and disclose.]

Make sure your content matches the platform. If you're trying to use an affiliate link on Pinterest, make a pin that your readers will click on. On Twitter, use relevant hashtags. On Facebook, tag the company or brand.

And always, always, always disclose that it's an affiliate link.

Promote To Your Email List

You can include affiliate links in the emails you send your subscribers. Well, usually. There are exceptions.

Including Amazon affiliate links in your email violates their terms of service. This includes sending out your blog post via RSS feed to your readers. If your readers can click on an affiliate link from your email and wind up on Amazon, you are in violation and risk losing your account.

Other companies may have similar policies. The fine print is important. Ignorance is no excuse. Take time to learn how you can promote your links.

As long as email marketing is permitted, you can include a properly disclosed link or two in your regularly scheduled newsletters.

Just don't let affiliate links take over your emails. No one wants to read that, and your unsubscribe rate will spike.

Promote Using Video

Another idea is to create a video review of the product and include your affiliate link in the comments.

Are you doing a Facebook Live? If you talk about a product in it, include your link in the comments there, too. Remember to disclose.

Video content is shared more frequently; it's a great way to bring more viewers to your content.

Promote Within Your Products

Are you creating an eBook or a course? If an affiliate product is a good match, include the link.

Of course, you must check the terms and conditions again. This wouldn't work for Amazon links. That's because you can't include Amazon links anywhere but on social media and on your website.

Including links in your products will work for many other affiliate programs. As before, read the fine print so you know what's allowed.

And you can always link to a resource page on your blog, which then provides the Amazon affiliate links for your readers. This is a workaround that many bloggers use.

Even if you aren't creating a product, a resource page is another way to promote affiliate links on your blog.

Go Back Through Your Old Content

If you wrote any blog posts before you were an affiliate, go back through them. Read your old posts and look for opportunities to update them with your affiliate links.

Perhaps you need to add another paragraph to tie it in. Or add another section to the post.

It's worth taking the time to do, especially on your top-performing posts. Find out which posts are bringing you the most traffic and monetize them.

You really can earn money promoting other people's products. It's a monetization strategy you can start quickly. And it makes a great first step in monetizing your blog.

You can do this. And the feeling when that first deposit makes its way into your account is amazing.

Action Steps

1. Decide whether you want to use affiliate links to monetize your blog or not.

2. Pick 5 to 10 companies to become an affiliate for, and research their affiliate programs (you can add more over time, but this is a good number to start with).

3. Apply to become an affiliate for these companies.

4. Make sure your blog has a disclosure page

5. Weave an affiliate link into your next blog post.

6. Create a social media update about an affiliate product and include the link (remember to disclose).

7. Go back through your old content and look for ways to include affiliate links.

Chapter 13 Monetized Through Products

The final most popular and high paying way that you can monetize your blog is through creating some form of products or services for your clients. The popular products and services are typically an evergreen course, a PDF, an eBook, and other things that can be placed on the site. These are typically based specifically on your expertise and are designed to add "more value" than your blog itself. That way, if people like what they read, they can purchase more and learn more. As a result, you get paid.

When You Can Start Selling Your Own Products

Technically, you can start creating and selling your own products right away. However, you will likely notice that you don't make a significant return right away. Until your audience begins to grow, you may not make too many sales in the beginning. That is okay, however. Remain dedicated and continue creating. The more you get to know your audience, the more you can tailor your products to serve their needs.

Some blogs begin selling basic content, such as eBooks or pre-recorded specialized webinars right away. As a result, they can make a fairly decent income really close to the time they launch their blog. If you want to do your best to start monetizing instantly, you can begin creating and selling smaller products such as this. This will help you make more money sooner, as well as gain further analytics on your audience and what they are interested in.

Creating Your Own Products

Creating products to sell on your blog is easy. First, you have to consider your area of expertise and your industry. Then, you have to consider what your audience is most likely to buy. Once you have, you can start creating anything that you think your audience would consume.

If you are unsure, go back and revisit the other high performing blogs in your niche. Look to see what they are selling, and use that as inspiration to help you. Essentially, you want to take an already-popular form of product and customize it to suit your audience, filled with your unique information and expertise.

The majority of products that you would sell through your blog take very minimal investment and can result in you earning a high amount of profit. Typically, you simply have to put together your best information and package it in a way that is easy for your readers to purchase.

In addition to books, services, and courses, you can also sell actual products. Many blogs have made branded products such as cups, t-shirts, hoodies, hats, and other products that they sell on their blog. If they have a particularly popular catch phrase or motto, they will put these onto the products and sell them. Alternatively, they may sell products that are relevant to their niche. For example, if you wrote a crafting and DIY blog, you may create a page on your website where you sell your own creations to your readers.

Chapter 14 Create your Own Digital Products

Creating a digital product may take some time, I'm aware of that, and you will need a sales strategy to get the results that you expect. However, at the beginning of this book, I warned you that you have to commit to your monetization objective and be constant and responsible.

Through your mailing list, you have a good sales percentage guaranteed. You only have to use the same principles to create products as you proceeded to start your blog. Design and create products with your audience in mind; relate to your readers by delivering high-value content products. Show them the benefits, help them become aware of what they need and you'll be motivating them to buy what you have to sell.

These are some digital products that will allow for a good and effective monetization:

Digital books

Creating eBooks is an effective way to monetize. You just have to write, focusing on the subject matter that your audience has shown interest in.

If you write a digital book that will offer solutions to your readers and you have managed to click with them before by delivering high-quality content, then you most certainly have established your authority in that field.

Your book can be hosted on platforms such as Amazon or you can sell it directly on your blog, relying on plugins that will enable the adding of payment gateways and downloading options.

The sale of your eBook can start a new email campaign since every reader who has bought your book will be willing to get news of similar products that you might offer.

Online courses

These are digital products that allow for a healthy profit. When you design an online course, creating one is the same as selling one, in the sense that you invest once and automate it for selling.

You can create online courses to be delivered in deliverable files or using a video format. The lessons/modules are delivered via email with an automation platform. You can choose one from the platforms mentioned in chapter 4.

Online courses represent a passive income with good potential. You can create an online course about any of the topics you deal with on your blog. The course should be attractive, solve a problem and represent a benefit for your ideal readers.

You can adjust the cost of your course to the purchasing power of your audience but take into account that people are more willing to spend a higher amount of money on courses than on eBooks.

People pay up to USD30 for a book but are willing to pay between USD 50 and USD200 for a course, depending on its level.

What you need to sell your online course is:

- An audience who trusts you.
- Understand your audience to know what to offer to them.
- Marketing skills to position your course
- Automation tools

The good news is that if you manage to create an effective course and present it to your emailing contacts the right way, you'll get a satisfactory income.

As this is one of the most efficient ways to monetize, I'll show you the "road" to create one:

- Pick a subject matter.
- Analyze other courses that are similar to the one that you intend to create.
- Create a technical file to present your course.

Such a file is created under the following guidelines:

Pick an attractive title. Go back to the principles that I shared in chapter 2 about creating attractive titles for blog posts.

Then, describe the content of your course in two paragraphs. Being brief is important here as readers need a wide picture of the course; it must be enough information to motivate them to buy it.

Next, you have to determine who your course is addressed to. Within your market niche, there will surely be one type of reader that is more likely to buy your course. Narrow down your audience and clarify on your file who this course is for. This will allow readers to determine whether they have the same features as the intended audience for your course.

It's also important to have a table of contents; an outline showing how the course is structured and what topics will be covered. This will create more specific expectations.

The next step is to define a date for your course. It's true that your course will be automated, but if you want it to be more effective and get meaningful conversion rates, then you need to build some expectation by launching an email marketing campaign that specifies the time and date of the course.

It's also important to define a methodology for the course; how the classes will be delivered or sent to the buyers. A clear methodology on your file will help them understand if the course dynamics are right for them; they'll feel motivated to buy if the methodology is clear and suit their needs. For example, you can establish that since it's an online course, they can access it at any time and from any location.

Next step, if you're delivering the course, then you need to explain why you're qualified to do it and specify your credentials.

Lastly, the costs and payment methods must be absolutely clear.

Exclusive areas on your blog (Memberships)

Memberships are another effective way to monetize. They consist of protecting or hiding certain areas or posts of your blog where you can offer exclusive content with higher-than-ordinary value. You can offer a monthly subscription for this exclusive area as well. This is a good strategy if you have proved to your audience just how valuable your posts are. Only then will they be willing to pay to know what exclusive content you have developed for them.

For your membership area to be effective, communicate the benefits of being a member of your blog with your audience via email marketing. You need to tell them what they'll find in the exclusive area and what they'll accomplish with the knowledge that they acquire through it.

This is a common strategy among digital newspapers, and also among blogs. So, don't stay behind and create your exclusive membership area for paying subscribers.

By offering this option, you'll be securing a strong monthly income.

Group or one-on-one coaching

Coaching is a trendy service. This is because users are aware of the need for knowledge in their specific areas. So, they are willing to pay qualified mentors for consulting.

The idea behind this service is to offer help in very specific areas, to lead them from where they are to where they want and should be.

Users hire the services of a coach to receive a clearer step by step guidance. You can segment your coaching program and offer different packages: VIP, semi-VIP or general.

You can also sell sessions, defining them as 90-minute coaching sessions, for example.

These sessions can be held in groups, work teams might be interested in these. Or you can sell one on one sessions which are a more personalized version.

Coaching doesn't necessarily have to be offline; it can be online and virtual so that your users can choose the most comfortable time for them and follow your coaching session from wherever they are.

This is a good option, but I recommend to start with one on one coaching. As you gather more experience, you can move on to the group sessions.

Mastermind

It's a kind of membership, but it's even more exclusive than a restricted area within your blog.

Memberships allow for the increase of monthly income by adding new members. In the case of mastermind, you don't aim at monthly growth, but to maintain a select group of customers.

A mastermind is a group of people, no less than 3 and no more than 6, with complementary knowledge on certain topics.

You can monetize this way by selling sessions to old customers or readers on your list. You can have several Mastermind groups to increase your income, but the number of members in each group can't exceed the number specified before.

Podcasts

You can make money if you include a podcast session on your blog. A podcast is an audio file distributed through RSS distribution system and whoever wants to have access to the podcasts, must subscribe.

There are very good subscription programs like SoundCloud or iTunes, which allow you to download audio files to better enjoy them. But you don't need to limit yourselves to audio as you can create videos as well.

As I said, podcasts are a very effective monetization option nowadays. You can even get a sponsor and thus make an income through that sponsor and through the sales of your podcasts on your blog.

There are podcasters who make a living through that system. All you have to do is start. Remember that if you already have an audience that trusts you, then you'll make significant sales off your podcast by offering exclusive benefits.

There are some other services worth considering like conferences and workshops, consulting via Skype or email, group Webinars (online seminars). Since you have an immense world of monetization options in your hands, you should grab each opportunity with zeal. Don't let anything come between you and your monetization dream!

I'd like to congratulate you on having completed all the necessary steps for monetization. Keep learning, for digital marketing and monetization through virtual media is a multi-faceted subject. I'm willing to share with you all that I know about it in the future. So, stay tuned to my channels and my networks because I won't rest until I can actually help you monetize.

Save this eBook, keep it at hand because you will have to go back to it many times until you know each step by heart.

Your blog is a goldmine. Now that we have reached the end of this eBook, I'm sure you know I'm not exaggerating one bit when I say that.

You have endless ways of generating money if you follow the right principles. Now more than ever, there's an exponentially larger number of bloggers who join the exclusive club of effective monetizers every day.

In this eBook, I have outlined the road to reach the monetization goal, a safe road that will help you reach the desired destination. Just remember that it all depends on your willingness to follow each and every step that I've outlined.

Monetization is most certainly possible. You can make a living out of your online enterprise; your blog. So, start working on the aspects that I've described.

I know many of the principles that you have found here might be in direct contradiction with a lot of your preconceived ideas about blogging, but trust me: put my ideas to the test and let me know how they worked.

As I said in the beginning, everything is based on my own experience, so I can promise you that you'll get good results if you follow the steps as I did.

Right now, you're probably wondering, "Russell, that's all very nice, but how long will it actually take me to monetize?"

I have the answer: "That's up to you."

I'll give you a tip, however: the bloggers who manage to monetize quickly take between four and six months to make a profit. The slower ones can take a year or more.

It's your call. You decide if you devote time to your blog and work regularly to get conversions or if you work on your blog when you have nothing better to do.

I'm not saying you should quit your job or stop living and glue yourself to your blog. It could be great for you if you did that, but let me tell you that if you work with dedication, there will eventually come a time when you'll be able to be a full-time blogger and digital producer without having the need for a job elsewhere.

Remember that you need a paid blog hosting; forget about free versions, that's the first step towards commitment. Your blog must be optimized to target your ideal readers, so stick to your segmentation for every strategy and content creation session.

Make sure your blog is well positioned, your content is rich and that you are driving traffic to your blog. The most important thing: acquire your reader's data to create your mailing list and come up with an email marketing strategy.

Forget about magical formulas. You need to have the right mindset, and that's what I'll talk about in the following lines.

To succeed in the blog monetization business, you need the right mindset and see your blog as what it is: a goldmine.

You have a mission and you need to embrace it: your mission is to help your readers with your knowledge. Embrace that and it'll help you write passionately on the subject matter that you specialize in.

This sets the difference between a mediocre blogger and a successful one; the former posts just to kill time while the latter does it to connect, share, help and contribute to their audience.

So, cultivate the right mindset; only then will you see positive results. Then nothing will stop you and you'll be determined not just to share but to receive what you deserve in exchange.

The monetization mindset is being aware that through blogging, you have the chance to make an exchange. So, don't refuse to receive what you deserve in exchange for your expertise.

With the right mindset, you'll be unstoppable! It will allow you to stay on the right track and meet your goals. Remember that trust and reputation are essential to monetizing your blog. So, don't let opportunities to build trust and reputation slip you by. Become an authority in your niche market and that will earn you their trust and a good reputation.

Remember that writing an eBook is the best way to establish yourself as an authority figure within your niche market. Our minds are trained to associate books with knowledge. So, if you manage to publish on platforms that your ideal readers have access to, like Amazon, your reputation as an authority figure will gradually increase and you'll earn your reader's trust.

How to Sell These Products

Selling the products on your blog is actually simple. First, you want to make a page for your product(s) on your blog. Then, you want to make a post that directs people to this product or service. Refrain from making the post too salesy. Instead, make it informative. Next, you want to talk about it on your social media platforms. Do not make it the highlight of what you talk about, but rather infuse it anywhere that it fits organically. As well, you can share it intentionally a few times per week. You can also pay for ad space to sell your products.

You do not want to bombard your audience with your sales. Otherwise, they are going to feel like you are not a blog but rather a salesperson. Instead, you want to talk about your products or services about 20% of the time and provide other content around 80% of the time. This will ensure that you are easily managing the balance and that you are not overwhelming your audience with salesy posts. Remember, they came to you because you provide value. You cannot change that now and begin only providing value if they pay you. Continue being true to the blog you have always been, but add this additional element for those who want to receive more of what you offer. If you are genuine and loyal to your followers, the majority of them will be genuine and loyal back. This can result in massive profits over time. In fact, many bloggers make several six figures through their products and services that they offer alongside their blog.

How You Get Paid

Receiving payment from your blog through your products or services will typically depend on what platform you are using. Generally speaking, you will get paid anytime someone purchases your product or service. How that payment is issued to you, however, will depend. If your platform is connected to a specific platform, like PayPal, your payments will all automatically come in through PayPal. However, if it is not, the platform itself may "hold" your funds until you choose to withdraw them into your bank account, or elsewhere.

You can learn more about how you will get paid by reading the policies and guidelines on your platform, or on the platform, you use to host your sales. Some people prefer to host sales through Etsy or Shopify while hosting their blogs on something like WordPress or Squarespace. If you choose to do this, you will need to read the guidelines for receiving payments through your e-commerce host to make sure that you are clear on how to receive these payments.

Chapter 15 Other Monetization Methods

Advertising on your Blogs

Blogging and media work for money is the agenda here. You create a mass of audience by giving them information they need, education, entertainment, or a combination of all these items. You lay out your life for them to see so their minds and emotions are refreshed. In turn, the audience you gather behind you can be used to create income or generate money. This process is called monetization and so far, we have talked about affiliate marketing and email marketing and sales. Affiliate marketing and Email Marketing are both great as seen above, but it is not the only monetization process. There are many ways to generate an income using a blog as the anchor. The information below is an overview to the world of Direct Blog monetization.

As a blogger, you have worked hard to build a loyal audience and fanbase for your blog, as well building a readership with thousands of readers daily. For example, your travel blog is having 3000 visitors a day and that pet care blog is generating daily traffic of 5000. These are a good number to start converting to money. How do you do it?

You can place ads directly on your blog. As your visitors read your postings, there can be strategic adverts in the site, usually appearing on the sidebar of the site, but they can pop up over the text. Therefore, be careful about the types of ads you use on your blog, as you do not want to drive readers away. You can either sell that space directly or link your page with Google AdSense that will channel ads to your site. The two styles will be discussed later in depth.

As an authority, you can write recommendations and reviews of products and services and receive money from the mentions (affiliate links). But some useful products may not have affiliate programs or not allow sites like Amazon to make them part of theirs. So, using straight up ads are the only way to integrate those products into your blog. The best products and services to advertise are the ones directly connected or related to your niche. In this case if you are a travel blogger, you can do recommendations of hotels, airlines, tours and travel companies, tourist attractions sites and cities, unique wear and fashion from the different areas you cover. The Pet Care blogger can advertise pet food, pet accessories, adoption, foster, or rescue programs. You are already trustworthy and respected enough to be an authority, so be careful when choosing those products. Below is an overview of the types of ads that are regularly on blogs.

All of the following methods and types of ads have two avenues of achievement. The first and most profitable is to be your own agent and broker by negotiating with companies and other bloggers for advertising on your site. This takes a lot of work up front, but once done, it becomes a very passive way of making money. The second is to partner with either Google AdSense or AdWords (Google, Reddit, and YouTube), Facebook/Instagram, or Twitter for targeted ad placement on your site or Social Media for money or for targeting advertising of your site, blog, products or services to increase your audience and sales. It is definitely a circle of life, so to speak.

Types of Ads and Methods of Using Them

Publishing Contextual Ads

Contextual advertising connotes the word context. Context involves keywords. This is a smart way for a client to pay for a specific targeted audience to get their ads. A blogger is also guaranteed more ad clicks with the right audience landing the related ads. Here, search engines are smart to channel advertisement where the context displayed matches the industry of the product or service. Search engines are also in a position to categorize and reach the intended users of the contextual messages.

The best example for Contextual ads is Google's AdSense. This is how Google knows what traffic they can channel a particular ad for maximum click on the ads. The ads also can be URL specific If you choose to skip AdSense and sell your space directly to companies, they usually have a similar system using search engines to do the same thing.

As a blogger, you are paid by impressions (the number of times and ad is viewed, it is measured by the pause and reading of it. Click through Impressions are the number of times someone clicks on the ad and visit the advertisers page) any additional can go in your blog. The advertiser pays for each Click Through Rate (CTR), and it can be profitable, so consider publishing contextual ads only. However, remember you must not overwhelm your readers with ads, so the make sure all ads are of the most related product or service to your niche or blog.

Using text link ads

As the title suggests, this is an ad placed as text in the normal context of your writing, but then it is highlighted and hyperlinked (very similar to you placing affiliate links yourself). A reader who wishes to click on the ad may either be redirected to a new page with the host advertiser or the blog may redirect him to the advertiser on the same page. For a reader who was no interest in the ad, the redirections may make him lose interest with your blog and you may lose the reader. Many a times, they are too annoyed to return, so make sure to make wise choices or make sure these ads are easy to spot for those who do not wish to click them.

Yes you are selling to people, but you should not make anyone feel sold. That's the name of the game. In-text ads usually have the advertiser pay a blogger pay-per-click. This is the most common, but sometimes a blogger may be paid a flat rate fee for advertising in their blog. It is purely negotiated by you up front with individual companies or outlined in the Terms of Service on Google AdSense.

Placing Impression Ads

Companies can also pay to place impression ads that appear when people are searching a particular niche or pay you for the same status when people search a term on your blog. You can also pay to advertise your blog to others using the same system. Placing ads impressions work with two factors; placements and keywords. You can use either of the two or combine the two to get outstanding refined results. You have the power to decide if you wish your ads to be featured on all selected Display Networks (the sidebar of the Google search page where the ads remain static and never change, since the advertiser has paid to be there whenever the keywords are searched) and you also decide the budget to go into the same, whether you are paying or being paid.

When you use both factors to zero in on your audience, you enjoy having refined audiences who are likely to click on your ads and convert with great sales. You also are in a position to earn more as a blogger if the two factors are applied. Placements make it easy for you to play with your bidding chances for higher wins on your end as an advertiser. Placement can also help you to place bids on the exact URLS of your taste.

In addition, you can pick keywords and direct ads to websites which only focus on the industry you are in. You are better placed when you are in control of who sees your ads. What you pay as an advertiser for clicks will eventually convert to sales or traffic (to draw more paying advertisers) with reasonable rates.

Publishing Sponsored Reviews and Paid Posts

An advertiser may choose to write a very good review on his product or service then approach you to publish it on your blog. Or, they may even pay you as a blogger to write and publish a review on the product on your blog. This is direct advertising and it pays well since there are no intermediaries. However, this is an ethically gray area as you do not want to endorse a product or write essentially an unfounded review on a product or service, you have not used. Proceed with caution and make sure you give the product or service a whirl and be honest in your endorsement.

Advertisers can shy away from doing a direct review of his product and prefer some mentions and endorsement on a post. The post might be talking about touring Mt. Kenya while the blogger chooses to focus also on the accommodation he had at the client's hotel. The blogger ends up selling both Mt. Kenya as a tourist site and the client's hotel as the best choice while at it. Just make sure you have actually stayed at the hotel.

Guest Posts

Guest posts are the shortest route for a blogger to make their brand or blog known to other readers in another influential blog. For beginners and newbies, guest posts will skyrocket you to greatness. Here you tell people, "hey, I have not been around for long, actually I just started blogging, yet I am so resourceful you should check me out". If the guest post is likeable and informative to them, then you will easily win yourself followers. In some cases, you will pay the bigger blogger for the chance to guest write for them and in turn once established smaller bloggers and influencers will pay you to do the same.

Guest posts benefit your blog in three ways:

1. You earn from someone by simply taking the time and writing for your blog.
2. You earn time off your weekly schedules because your loyal readers will find something to read that is informative, while you took some time to rest from your schedule or get ahead on your posts for later.

3. You prove to your readers that you are influential enough to attract guests to your blog. This helps seal your value and makes you a leader in your niche.

Placing your own Ads selling your Products-services

Oh, this is beautiful, and it is my favorite. This is where you reap the fruits of your efforts. Imagine having a blog with a monthly traffic of 2 million readers and going ahead to run a business that will directly benefit your audience! It sounds fun. So sometimes it will become necessary to pay for ads to sell the product or service you offer. Personally, why I choose to endorse this mode of advertising more, is because of the rule of reciprocity. Today if my favorite blogger decides to sell some jewelry or perfumes, I would definitely want to promote them. Even if as a way to say thank you for keeping me on my toes for their next publication.

Loyal readers are more likely to promote your business if they see it outside your blog. This can be either as a legitimate business person, product inventor, or being advertised as an expert. If they see paid promotions from other influencers or ads on Google, then it established your validity a more than a blogger. This will make them feel more at ease in promoting you and they will share your content or product/service. You may be out 200 dollars in paid ads, but you may get 500 dollars in sales and free advertising through shares and shout outs, because of the perception of being legit.

Now what can you sell? I mean the possibilities are limitless, but make sure whatever it is it relates to your niche and blog in a natural and fluid way. If there is not an existing product you can sell, then create your own. The most obvious is putting a very detailed and expanded niche advice or information into an eBook. You are already a writer, so why not write manual or informative book, beyond your blog? Being a published author carries a huge amount of weight, especially if your niche and blog are mainly information that would not easily tie to any other physical product. Your business does not have to involve anything else other than writing or it can be an actual product, service, or gadget. Just find something valuable to sell. You will do well, especially if you have created an audience for yourself already. It is only fair you do yourself some a favor and take advantage of the ready market. Why create influence to help every other person sale their products yet deny yourself the benefits?

Don't be worried about how to get your product out there. In the case of a book you can self-publish through Amazon Kindle or Audible, as well as many other sites. Then you market it to your built-in audience and possibly others. Remember we are going for 500 hundred people giving you 20 bucks a month to reach 10k a month. This is just another way to hit that average. So, no book deal is required. Though that is a possibility, you can write a chapter or two and send (along with complete information on your brand, blog and reach) to an existing publisher. They may have the systems in place for marketing beyond your means, and they may offer you money upfront and a cut of sales to put it out or buy it outright. The possibilities are endless, just make sure you crunch the numbers and do what is most profitable.

In the case of a product or gadget, there are many companies (just Google ghost or 2nd party manufacturing) that will work with you on developing things like skin care, cosmetics, supplements and gadgets to your specifications and produce them under your brand. Just make sure once you know what you want you put together the blueprint or formula and get a patent, so the idea is yours. There are many websites like LegalZoom that can help you file for a government patent if it is needed. There are fees involved, but to start your own business, it is worth it. The same is true of a service. Put together a game plan and perhaps offer it free or discounted to a few people to get good reviews. Then market it to your audience.

Displaying Ads in your Blog's Feed

There are many companies will pay you to channel traffic to their site at a fee. A good example is Google's AdSense. You will need to sign up for an account with them and give your full details including payment ones. On your WordPress website, assuming you are using WordPress, click on the

WordPress widget, then click on appearance, then select widgets, pick custom HTML and drag it to the best location on your site then drop it there. Remember to paste the Google AdSense code. From this point, you will be golden, waiting for advertising money to reflect in your bank account.

With Google AdSense, you do not have to worry about finding individual advertisers yourself. Although you will have to part with half of the ad revenue due to Google AdSense pay model. This is simply because you did not broker your own deal with the advertiser, but Google did. Google acts as a middle man and brings advertisers to your site for a cut of the fee. This brings us to our last option for now. Read on.

Selling Ad Space Directly

You can have such a great blog that advertisers will be either be approaching you directly to feature ads on your site or responding when you reach out to them about a deal. So, you will find yourself booking sales meetings with potential clients to sell them advertising space. Whether you go fetching for them or they come, the bottom line is you have advertising space up for grabs. Here, you make a lot of money and you pocket it all.

Apart from writing great content, selling as space should be another priority. It pays well. Have fun selling it. Just note somewhere, you will have the added job of finding and brokering deals with clients, along with managing and creating for your huge visitor traffic to your blog or site. Let traffic building motivate you to increase the worth of your advertising space. Again, just like other forms of advertising, make sure you are choosing relevant and helpful companies to partner with.

Chapter 16 Income Streams

Once you have successfully created your website, all that is left to do is to start actively monetizing it in as many different ways as possible. It is important to keep your expectations realistic at this point and to remember that just as starting your blog was lots of work, so too will be monetizing it. The end results are well worth it, however, and if you persevere, then passive income awaits.

Additionally, you need to be aware that getting a full-time paycheck from a blog at this point is going to be a full-time job. Each new post that you create takes you one step closer to a passive income stream. However so, slow and steady wins the race. Early on, it is crucial for your blog to have plenty of new content on a regular basis, not just constant advertising. You need to build your readers trust first before you start trying to make money.

Create the right type of content: When it comes to successfully monetizing your blog, the first thing that you are going to need to do is to create the kind of content that is in your niche or sub-niche so that your readers are genuinely interested. If you are already very active in the niche in question, then this should be relatively easy; otherwise, you will want to start by doing research on the most popular blogs on the topic as a way of learning not just what those who are interested in the topic are most passionate about but also how they express themselves, what types of slang and jargon they use, and the types of things that are important to them both personally and in the workplace. Additionally, spending plenty of time on these sites will provide you with the opportunity to look for gaps in their coverage that you will then be able to exploit on your site.

Once you know what type of content that you should be providing, the next thing you need to think about is how you will put a personal spin on it. Regurgitating standard information will get you nowhere, which is why you are going to need to create a niche-specific persona if you aren't naturally a person your niche would turn to for advice. This persona shouldn't be a stereotype but, instead, needs to be someone that a large portion of your audience will relate to. Once your audience can relate to you, you will find that it is much easier to sell them things.

Finally, once you know what you are going to write about and what slant you are going to put on things, all that is left to do is to get writing. Once your site goes live, you are going to want to post multiple pieces of new content every day to ensure that you force people to get in the habit of checking your site regularly, which means you are going to need a log of 50 blog posts or so to ensure that you have time to keep up the flow. While this might seem high, if you post three times a week it will only last you 2 weeks. If that seems like too much writing, you might want to reconsider your choice of passive income.

Start with monetization basics: No matter what platform you use, you will have the ability to sell ad space. Normally you are going to be able to get a few pennies every time that someone clicks on an ad, and the most popular way is to enroll with Google Adsense so that relevant ads are placed without you having to go out and find individual advertisers. Depending on the amount of traffic that your site sees, you could be getting up to $0.50 every time someone clicks on the ad.

Ads are going to be the easiest way for you to make money on your site, but they require lots of page views to be profitable on their own truly. The best way to increase your revenue stream right off of the bat is by joining what is recognized as an affiliate marketing program that is going to allow you to have a more targeted form of advertising. The most common affiliate advertiser is Amazon, and anyone can sign up to be an Amazon affiliate. Once you join, all you need to do is to choose products that your niche is interested in, write positive reviews of the products, and include a special link that will be provided to you to let your readers buy the product if they are so inclined. Each purchase that is made from your link puts money directly into your pocket in an amount that is proportional to the cost of the item in question.

If you plan on going down this route, it is important only to choose products that you have first purchased and can genuinely vouch for. As a blogger, all you have is your name and your reputation, and if you tarnish that reputation by selling cheap products, then you will lose readers faster than you can possibly imagine. Likewise, it is important that these types of product reviews are only one of the types of content that you provide if you want people to stick around in the long term. A ratio of 10 percent advertising-based post is typically considered acceptable by many bloggers.

- Paid Content: If you regularly offer useful information on your blog, then paid content is a good method for you to consider, especially should the information that you are putting out there help your readers make money. To proceed down this path, all you need to do is make a separate members-only section of your site that allows paid access to various types of content.
- eBooks: You can put all of your top tips or put something new altogether in an eBook, and it will be a reader-friendly way to not only get your content offline but also package that content.
- White papers: These are similar to eBooks, but they are going to be smaller and more technically written.
- Phone calls: If you are offering a service, phone calls are a good way to sell that advice; have your readers pay for the phone call and any other consulting you may be offering.

- Miniguides: Short guides can be a helpful series that you can sell to your readers on how they can do things.

- Tutorials: Video tutorials can be comprised of the same material as the guides, and you will have the ability to compile tutorials together on what you are an expert at.

- Podcasts: They may be a rare gift to your readers, and if you have a loyal reader base, they may be willing to pay to be able to hear any additional advice that you have to offer or just to be able to keep up with your blog whenever they are on the go.

- Videos: This is another good addition. Some readers will be willing to pay for it because it makes it easier for them to read your blog without having to stare at your blog and read the words.

Physical products

If you have the ability to create things with your hands, then you may want to sell them on your blog as well! If you have a website where all of the products that you have to offer can be seen, place that on your blog so that people are able to go to your website and see what it is that you have. There are websites such as Etsy that allow for you to sell your products to people without having to be fearful of if you are going to get the money because you are going to get the money before you ever send the product out.

However, with physical product, you are going to want to be careful about what you are putting on your blog. If your product is for those who are 18 years old or older, then you are going to want to hide the link to the website because you do not want anyone who is not supposed to have the product get their hands on it.

Also, keep in mind that what is legal in your state may not be legal in another. So, before you ship any products out, you need to ensure that you are not shipping them to a state where it is illegal to have that product.

Begging

No one likes begging, but no one likes someone who is being sneaky either, so be upfront about wanting to earn money with your blog. But, be polite when you are asking. The people that actually value what you are writing about are going to be more willing to show their support in order to help you keep going and be successful.

- PayPal: It offers a button that you can put on your blog that is going to allow your readers to give you donations.
- Amazon Honor System: This is similar to PayPal's donation button, but it is through Amazon.
- Patreon: With this, you are going to be using a platform that is based on crowd funding. By using Patreon, you

can get donations for your posts on a regular basis or per post if you prefer. Using Patreon, you are going to be able to get monthly donations as well as set a monthly goal.

- Tangible objects: Some readers want to give gifts that they made to their favorite people. For people to be able to do this, set up a PO Box that is dedicated to letters and anything else that people may want to send you.

RSS Ads

For more specialized advertising, RSS is going to allow bloggers to monetize their feeds. But, remember that readers do not want to see their favorite blog overtaken by ads, regular or RSS. So, be sure to limit the amount of RSS ads that are on your blog.

- Pheedo Inc: This RSS platform offers an interactive trigger as well as video options.
- Feedvertising: This is part of text link ads that will be embedded in the RSS feed.
- CrispAds: This platform is going to focus the ad network so that you are able to place the ads into entries that are going to show up on your site as well as the feeds.

- FeedBurner Inc: The ads are going to be embedded in the RSS feed while featuring high-quality advertisers such as Best Buy.
- FeddM8: Your blog is going to be mobile ready while having the relevant mobile advertising embedded.

Chapter 17 Common mistakes

Business blogs are just as capable of, and in many instances more likely prone to, failure as personal blogs. In fact, over ninety percent of business blogs that go live on the internet end up failing. The reasons for the failure are generally the same. However, there are also some things that are specific to business blogs that can lead them to fail as well. Knowing what frequently leads to failure can often help you learn what to avoid and how to ensure you can avoid making common mistakes and therefore, can lead yourself to success in your business blogging.

Lost purpose
If all you are posting to your business blog are repurposed press releases, company news or glorified advertising copies, you are not going to be successful in reaching your customers. Your customers don't care about those things. Your customers want to be educated and informed about what you are selling them and information that relates to that. However, they don't want to be sold your product through your blog. Instead, post things that are going to let your customers know about things without making them feel that your goal is to sell them your product.

Don't believe in the power of blogging

If you begin a blog believing it is going to fail, then you might as well not even begin because it is going to fail. If you believe that you are not going to be successful, you are not going to be putting the work into the blog that it requires to be successful. Tell yourself that you are going to be able to succeed with a business blog and you are much more likely to put forth the effort that is required to be successful. You have already created a business; there is no reason you can't also create a blog.

No goals or strategy

Do you know what you are hoping to accomplish with your business blog or are you creating one because you know it has the potential to benefit your business? If you don't create any real goals for your business blog, it is not going to have a direction to grow in and isn't likely to get off the ground. Just like you needed to set goals for your business to succeed, your blog needs them too. Set goals that pertain to the number of people you want to reach and the time frame you want to reach them in and watch your business blog's success

No patience

If you are expecting your blog to bring in a whole bunch of new customers right away, you aren't going to see that. Having unrealistic expectations is more likely to leave you disappointed in how your blog is performing and, as a result is more likely to cause you to quit when you don't see instant results. Just like it took some time for your business to take off, you need to understand that it is going to take time for your blog to reach people. Instead of giving up after a few short months, commit to a time frame of at least a year before you tell yourself it isn't working and stop using your blog.

Nothing substantial

Just because your topic and title are appealing to the customer, it doesn't mean that your content is going to be automatically great. If your content is lacking substance or is full of errors and is hard to read, you aren't going to be able to maintain any readers. Ensure you are taking the time to edit and proofread what you are posting for its readability. On this note, you don't want to have content that is full of industry specific words and acronyms that your customers aren't going to know, and you also don't want to dumb things down to the point your customers are going to feel that you think they are uneducated.

Aren't giving opinions

Every blogger needs to be opinionated, and this extends to business bloggers. If you are stating facts without giving a true opinion of what you believe, your customers aren't going to be interested in reading what you are writing. For example, if you use a particular type of wood in all of your furniture, they want to know why you think it is the best. They don't only want the statistics about why it is best and the research backing it up;

they want your opinions. Your opinions are what tell people they can trust you.

No updates

Coming up with fresh content for a business blog can be difficult. But if you aren't regularly updating your content, your readers aren't going to be loyal. Instead, they are going to go in search of another blog that is always posting new content. You want to be consistent in adding new blogs, and this is why it is recommended that business blogs keep their posts shorter, as it leaves more room to build off previous posts. Set a goal to post at least two blog posts a week to ensure that you are constantly providing new content, and you keep engaging your followers.

As you can tell, keeping a business blog appealing to your customers isn't the easiest job out there. However, if you use the tips in the previous chapter, and you are aware of the possible places you can fail that we covered in this chapter, you are much more likely to be successful at creating a blog that is beneficial to your business and encourages your customers to be long term followers.

Conclusion

Thank for making it through to the end of this book, I hope it was informative and provided you with all of the tools you need to achieve your goals whatever they may be.

To make passive income with your blog, you can use it as a marketing tool to promote your other passive incomes streams. Offering eBooks and other information products can allow you to make an almost pure profit if you compile the information yourself. You can put together a collection of blog posts you've written and stitched the information together, then add a bit of valuable information that wasn't previously included and publish it as an eBook. It doesn't have to be long, and it will be worthwhile for your customers to purchase because they can access the information in one easy form rather than searching around for it. You can also create manuals or reports if they are relevant to your niche. Digital goods are a great source of passive income because the profit margins are high, but the investment of time and energy can be extensive.

If you don't wish to create your own digital products, you can still profit off of the demand for these goods by selling other companies' products as an affiliate marketer. As mentioned earlier, sharing products or services that are sold by other companies can create passive income by earning you a commission of each sale you create for them. Digital information products generally carry a much higher commission because the profit margins are greater. You can share these with your audience to create an opportunity for them to learn about topics in your niche from an expert source besides yourself.

To increase traffic to your blog and improve your likelihood of affiliate sales, put your blog wherever your target customers traffic frequently, such as Reddit forums, social media hashtags, or Facebook groups within your niche. Share your blog post in these areas, and let your audience come to you. You can also increase traffic by being actively involved in these forums or groups so prospects begin to notice you and gain interest in checking out your site. Other ways to approach affiliate marketing and create passive income are detailed earlier in this book.

As you may have noticed, Amazon is a prime tool (no pun intended) for creating passive income online, and affiliate marketing is no exception. Amazon Associates, the company's affiliate program, allows users to link to products listed on Amazon and earn a commission on sales made through their links. This program also allows affiliates to earn a commission on any other products that are purchased through Amazon after a customer clicks through their links, and continue to profit from any purchases that customer makes for up to 15 days afterward. This is a great affiliate program to gain commissions from, but it is best suited to bloggers who write about shopping, merchandise, or retail products already. Readers of these blogs are already more inclined to make purchases, so the likelihood that they'll purchase through the blog's links is higher than other readers.

You can also monetize your blog using Google AdSense. This entails displaying Google ads on your website, and when a visitor clicks through the ad you get a percentage of the ad costs that the advertised company paid. The ads Google displays on your blog are relevant to your site's content, so they cater to your niche and increase the likelihood that readers will actually click through.

To get started, you'll need a Google account and a blog to host ads on, as well as a phone number and the mailing address associated with your bank account (so you can set up payment). Google will check that your site offers useful, original, and relevant content that brings value to its readers. They also look to see if your site is clear about what you stand for, what topics you post about and what value your content brings to your audience. Your contact information should be readily available in an easily accessible part of your site, the whole site should be mobile friendly, and the site should not have pop-up ads which are a nuisance to users and prevent them from enjoying a pleasant website viewing experience.

Google ads also require that you are upfront about why you collect readers' personal information and what will be done with said information, as well as clearly clarifying which links on your sight are sponsored. Your blog will also have to include a privacy policy that informs viewers when third parties may be using and reading cookies on the users' browsers or collecting information with web beacons. Their ads may also not be displayed on websites that violate copyright laws or link to sites that violate copyright laws. Their list of specifications is long, but it's not unreasonable. A well-made, respectable blog would likely fit these criteria easily.

Your blog is a great way to grow your following and establish yourself as a trusted authority in your field. Once your followings have grown, you can easily begin making passive income off of your site. It will be a key element in maximizing profits in other business ventures, and there is no limit to the amount of money you can make through blogging and your online business. If you wish to take a more active role in making money off your blog, you can even offer one-on-one coaching to your readers so they can get personalized expert advice and answers to their questions when they pay you a fee.